Janet Kingsley

Discover How I Overcame Abuse

&

Believe You Can Too!

A Survivor's Journey

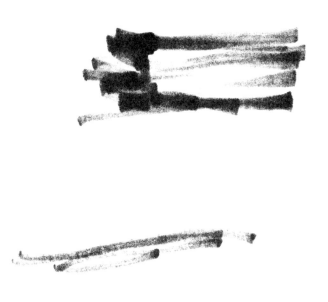

ISBN-10: 1477516107
ISBN-13: 978-1477516102

What others say about this book...

"Janet's book is a great book that teaches us that your history does not have to dictate your future. Regardless of how tough or even abusive it was growing up as a child anyone can turn it around into the life they want. Very inspiring!"

- **Bob Burnham** Author of the # 1 Amazon Best Seller:
101 Reasons Why You Must Write A Book
*How To Make A Six Figure Income By
Writing & Publishing Your Own Book*
www.ExpertAuthorPublishing.com

"In sharing a personal narrative of childhood trauma, Janet Kingsley provides hope for the victim: The myth of isolation can be the greatest obstacle; sharing, the start of the healing process."

-**Dale Hardy**, Education Instructor & Academic Advisor

"Janet's book shares personal experiences that help the reader to understand the world of an abused child, it gives the reader an understanding of the raw emotions that impact their world. For any teenager looking for a way to heal their wounds to be able to move forward, she has included some tools to help them understand and overcome the sabotaging behaviors that the pain of living in a toxic abusive environment can have."

-**Dawn Mathe**, Career Consultant

"Janet's book is a very courageous and positive account from an abuse survivor. It let's all of us know that we are not the only ones and that it is not only possible to heal and move forward but to enjoy an amazing life."

-**M. D. Nielsen**, Abuse Survivor

"As someone who has been through sexual abuse I have read more than a handful of [self help] books, not finding any of them very helpful. However, I felt very connected to this book. It has helped me to understand some of my thoughts and feelings. Making a personal connection is important for any abuse victims or survivors. I feel others would benefit from Janet's book."

-**K. Smith**, Stay at Home Mom

This book is dedicated to every person who has suffered abuse and wants to find an escape from the hampering affects of it. If you feel you are being restricted by boundaries in your life that are holding you back from being who you really are, as well as who you were meant to be...then this book is for you.

"So often in time it happens, we all live our life in chains, and we never even know we have the key."

-The Eagles

TABLE OF CONTENTS

About the Author   1

Acknowledgements   3

Introduction   4

What is E.R.A.S.E.D.?   6

Chapter One – Remember & Acknowledge   8

TAKE THE FIRST STEP
Remember it -Acknowledge it - Own it

SEXUAL ABUSE
By family and others

SHYNESS
Can make life very difficult

ALL ALONE
Separation from others, feeling singled out

WHY ME?
Is it really worth years of wasted time while we
try to figure this out?

Chapter Two – Seeing it & Believing it

52

READING WHAT YOU WROTE
How this helps

WHAT CAN YOU DO WITH WHAT YOU WROTE?
Healthy healing methods I used

UNHAPPY PARENTS
How this affected me

WHEN OUR PARENTS ABUSIVE PASTS ARE PUT ONTO US
Always feeling obligated to understand and justify their actions

BELIEVING IT!
This can be hard to do, but it's very important we do it!

Chapter Three – Take Control & Talk About it

69

MY TEENAGE YEARS
Molded by Abuse

WHEN PARENTS DO NOT COMMUNICATE POSITIVELY
The impact it can have

ENDURING OVERLY STRICT PARENTING
Not being able to express myself

FAMILY SUICIDE – WHEN A PARENT COMMITS SUICIDE
Feelings left to deal with

DISCUSSING PERSONAL MATTERS WITH OTHERS
Time to let it out!

Chapter Four – Research it, Find a Solution   132

WHEN ENOUGH IS ENOUGH!
When we know we deserve better - let the research begin!

MY RESEARCHING STAGE BEGAN HERE
Deciding when the time is right...

GOD DURING MY ROAD TO RECOVERY
With & without him

TIPS ON MAKING FRIENDS WHEN WE NEED THEM
Are there times when you feel you don't have any?

Chapter Five – Take Action & Apply it!   153

CONGRATS, YOU'RE HALF WAY THERE!
Hanging in there while keeping an eye on your prize

CO-DEPENDANCY/ SPOUSAL ABUSE/BEING A
SPOUSE OF A SUBSTANCE ADDICTED PARTNER
Take on their pain not their burden. Do you stop being you?

BREAKING FREE - IT'S TIME FOR ME!
Learning to be strong on our own again can be a great thing!

HOW TO DO SOMETHING NOW & NOT TOMORROW
Tips on taking Action!

Chapter Six – Be Determined   181

WHAT DRIVES YOU CAN GUIDE YOU!
Focusing on YOU!

WANTING TO FIT IN & JUST BE ME
Finding YOU again is possible!

IS IT IMPORTANT TO HAVE GOD IN OUR LIVES?
Dare to believe!

Chapter Seven – Learn from it!   193

CAN OUR ENEMIES BE OUR FRIENDS?
A look into an enlightening response

BEING AN ADULT CHILD OF AN ALCOHOLIC
Talk about exasperating!

WHAT'S MY PURPOSE?
Finding a reason

Chapter Eight – Start to Heal   223

FINALLY, LIGHT AT THE END OF THE TUNNEL
Thanks to a secret I learned!

HELP IS OUT THERE WAITING FOR YOU TO
MAKE YOUR MOVE!
Where you can seek help

MAKING A NEW NORMAL
The new you!

LEARN HOW TO LOVE YOURSELF EVERYDAY
Practical fun methods that work!

Chapter Nine – Inspire Others Using Your   **239**
Experiences & Accomplishments

HOW ARE YOU FEELING?
Seeing your achievement

'RE' WRITING & 'RE' READING YOUR WORK
What the heck! Why would I do that?

HELP OTHERS!
Easy tips to assist you

Chapter Ten – Enjoy Your Freedom Today!   **246**

TAKE A DEEP BREATH YOU DESERVE IT!
Soaking up your accomplishments!

A GREAT SELF ESTEEM BOOSTER
No turning back

WHO DO YOU REALLY WANT TO BECOME?
Be free to grow!

THE UNIVERSE IS YOURS!
You are a gem on this planet!

Conclusion – YOU WILL 'BE HEARD'
CONTACT INFORMATION   **255**

Resources – HELPFUL INFORMATION
AT YOUR FINGERTIPS   **257**

You... are in control of *YOU!*

Remember it ▶ Acknowledge it
▶ See it ▶ Talk it out
▶ Take Control ▶ Research it
▶ Find a solution
▶ Apply it ▶ Be Determined
▶ Learn from it ▶ Start
to Heal ▶ Inspire Others using
your own Experiences
& Accomplishments ▶ Enjoy your
Freedom it's yours!

You CAN...

Reach Your Personal Goal of Well Being!

About the Author...

Janet Kingsley grew up in Port Coquitlam, British Columbia, Canada where she lived together with both birth parents and is the eldest of two siblings. Their family home was in an apartment suite above a busy commercial complex surrounded by gas stations and various businesses. Playing with her two sisters and some friends out in the back alley of the parking lot and hanging around inside the business establishments downstairs was her favorite pastime. Later when Janet was about eleven her parents upgraded to a townhouse where she was happy to finally have a yard to play in.

She attended public school along with her two sisters until grade ten. At the age of sixteen her education was cut short leading her into a few very trying years. Janet found that working helped keep her mind from wondering to places that she was not willing to visit. During her career she discovered many things about herself which she reveals further on in the book. In addition to that, she gained new skills and learned by having commitment she was able to reap the reward of being able to discipline herself to get ahead.

Her great love and zeal for animals led her on an exciting path of learning hands on with them in her mid twenties. Just a few miles from her home was where she became involved in the care and handling of wild and exotic animals that worked in the film and television industry. From bears and wolves to tigers and lions with even a couple of kinkajous in there are great memories she treasures.

Moving forward and being the mother of her own daughter now, Janet has found her other great joy in life. Learning from her past experiences of her own upbringing she raises her daughter with entirely opposite beliefs and actions of how she herself was brought up. It works for her and overall has worked out for the good.

Taking a deeper much closer look into her life reveals one horrible thing after another happening throughout her childhood.

The secret years of sexual abuse she suffered as a young child branched out to many other forms of abuse during her life. She eventually learned that most of the other abuses she endured throughout her life were all derived from one man's personal problems, her father.

Growing up Janet couldn't help but wonder why she had to go through all of what she did. She inside felt she was a good person, therefore there had to be a reason for it all. Now with this book she finally discovers the meaning.

Having uncovered the answer to her question of *why*, her yearning desire has become a vital part of her day. It is now her goal is to enlighten and help others through writing through sharing her delicate stories of abuse to help make that connection. She along with others offer their thoughts, feelings and personal coping methods that helped them carry on in life.

Janet truly believes that she is one of the chosen individuals selected endure and survive these ordeals to be able to help and guide others. It satisfies her to know that from her personal experiences she will be able to help people that have gone through similar realities, people that may not be able to get through it on their own.

Acknowledgments...

From the bottom of my heart to the depth of my soul I am so very grateful to God as well as very thankful for these wonderful people in my life. Without them this book would not be complete. Each one of you is or has been a significant part of my life experience who have all helped me in some way or another along my journey to becoming who I am today.

A big thank you to [My mini-me] **Nikayla Neeson,** my beautiful daughter for just being you and your excitement for me over this book - I love you so much & thank you to your charming bf from Mexico **(R.S)** for his interest in it as well, both of you helped energize me to keep going; Thank you to my hubby **Rob Taylor** for hanging in there while being my sounding board. I appreciate all your help with the ever so grueling task of revising & finalizing this book, it may have brought on a few minor battles but it also brought us closer together. You supported me in every way a wonderful man & spouse could, I love you.

Thank you **Angela Clarke, Anita Moyer, Kristen Abbott, Katrina Sinclair, K. Smith, M. D. Nielsen & Jessa Castro** for your strength & courage which is why you all came into my life for special reasons; Thank you **Carol Pow & G. Klassen** for your support in giving as well as for your unconditional love based friendships; Thank you **Dale Hardy, Dawn Mathe, Coralee Sanderson** & last but not least **Best Seller/Author Bob Burnham** for each of your remarkable expertise, experience & guidance.

It's with much appreciation to you all and a sincere thank you for your time and efforts into assisting me on this book. Your individual and unique contributions are all done with the common goal of helping others in mind. Together we are the definition of success and the purpose of survival.

*I*ntroduction...

It is unfortunate but as a child and throughout many of my adult years I experienced much physical, sexual and mental abuse as countless numbers of other people have in this world. Well there is one thing I know for sure, we are not alone in this. With the help and advice from others combined with certain circumstances that have come my way time and time again, I have grown to be a strong person. Learning to adapt myself to many different situations and different types of people has made my journey much easier on me. I can confidently say today, "I am a survivor".

People I have met along the way have been stunned when they hear me speak of my past. When I hear others say they feel I talk about the abuse in my life as if it was no big deal confirms my accomplishment for me. It's not at all that it wasn't a big deal; it's more of an *'I understand my feelings, my life and I like myself now'* kind of deal. I accept what has happened to me as it was not at all within my control. Continuing to learn from what has happened to me helps me grow as a person. I choose not to take responsibility of others actions.

It feels great when I say, "I am free from the burdens that others tried to bestow on me." Having a burning desire inside of me to share and connect with others is why I find it important to make a connection with you. I enjoy planting the seeds that I feel need to be sowed in order for others to stop feeling the way I did for far too many years.

Wanting to feel free and to gain some control over my feelings is why I decided that the best way for me to get my messages out to others was to write a book. This book is meant to serve as the second step toward healing in your life, the first most important one being acknowledgement of a need for help. When someone desires to follow that need with a want to heal, they in turn will yearn to be free.

I believe you experienced your abuse because your creator knows you are strong enough to handle it. "What doesn't kill us makes us stronger!" I find that statement to be very true. Hang in there with an open mind and allow it to prove it to you. I also believe that negative or traumatic life altering experiences can be turned into positive ones. You and only you can allow that to happen.

It came to a point in my life when something just clicked in my head and I realized that the choice was mine all along. With a different outlook on life and some stern effort the same choice is there for you too. It is a decision that requires strength, courage and determination. It is a choice that only you can make for yourself.

Changing our negative experiences into positive ones can help each one of us as people grow into determined, resilient and knowledgeable individuals. Healings and changes of any type need to be worked through in layers. I would very much like to help you through peeling off your layers one at a time as you aim to reach your desired goal of inner peace in life.

Due to the sensitive nature of this book and it's fact based stories no names in reference to one's personal contribution is written other than my friend, companion or acquaintance in lieu of with the exception of my daughter's name Nikayla.

Let's go behind...

E.R.A.S.E.D= Easy Real Action Spiritual

Exercises *that* Deliver!!!

Erase the chains of abuse that bind you using **EASY** made, **REAL** life, **ACTION** steps with **SPIRITUAL** outlook & hands on **EXERCISES** that **DELIVER**!

"With the power to commit oneself into action it defines the importance of focusing on the end result with help to be set free. Placed conveniently at the end of more than twenty worksheets it will serve as your key reminder that it was you who set out on this path to strive for and reach a point where you can feel free to comfortably say with confidence, I am a survivor."

"Using my will to strengthen yours; from one heart to another."
~Janet Kingsley

YOU'RE _NOT_ ALONE!

You were never alone,

You are never alone

You've always had…

YOU!

"We have to learn to be our own best friends because we fall too easily into the trap of being our own worst enemies"
-Roderick Thorp

Chapter One – Remember & Acknowledge

TAKE THE FIRST STEP
Remember it - Acknowledge it - Own it

Everyone has a story and every story is different. That's why you are unique. You were born for a reason, deep down you know this because you can feel it. You may not understand this because you may believe your purpose was to be picked on or abused for whatever reason, I thought that too. Well, I'm telling you that you were not born for that reason. You want to know why, Right? Of course you do, you're human!

It's our nature to want to know why things are the way they are or happen the way they do. It is also our nature to choose a path of least resistance to get to where we want to be. Give this a thought for a moment. With the large number of people that are on the planet, have you considered how many of them may be out there feeling just like you? Have you put thought into what that number may be? Well let's think about that for a moment.

The current world population is approximately seven billion people. Out of that number globally each month tens of thousands to millions of people are searching their computers for topics on abuse in one form or another. This tells me I'm not alone and neither are you. Looking at these facts of the world this way helps me to keep going on. Keep in mind these figures don't include the number of people globally that have no computer access, nor does it take into account anyone who is not ready to take action to outsource a better way for themselves like you are.

For myself learning this reality helps me acknowledge that I am a great example and mentor for others. Could this be true for yourself as well? Of course it can! By reading this book and taking action to heal yourself, you're already on your way to being stronger and more knowledgeable for someone else who isn't. Not only does that feel good, isn't it also a fantastic reason to exist as a purpose? Everyone has their own purpose designed for them. It's a matter of figuring out which one is yours. It could be a gift from birth that you possess? It most likely is something you are good at that really doesn't take much effort, start with that.

Are you able to talk about what abuse happened to you or is happening to you? Can you talk freely about what you went through with just about anyone? Do you have someone to talk to? Are you going through abuse right now and feel alone with no one to talk to? Maybe you're not sure what to think or feel. If you don't even know who you are anymore I can relate, I felt like that too. Alone and different. I hated feeling that way.

I know those feelings all too well, but ended up dealing with them in my own way for many years as I didn't know what else to do. Sure, I was lucky enough to have friends and family but I didn't feel I had anyone in my life that I felt comfortable enough to talk to or tell everything to. I didn't have anyone there for me that I felt I could trust enough to say hey this is what I'm going through and this is what's happening to me, so instead I held it all inside in fear of being judged.

I knew it wasn't anyone else's fault for me to feel the need to bottle it all up. I judged others as if they were unapproachable. I am referring to when I was being sexually abused as a child, I didn't tell anyone about it because I did not want to get anybody in trouble. I also did not want the already poor image that I had of myself to get any worse.

So there I was bursting at the seams and nowhere to turn to except a fluffy stuffed animal named 'Rocky Raccoon'. Sad but true. Rocky knew my inner most painful feelings and comforted me as best as a stuffed animal could. It wasn't until my teenage years that through therapy I discovered new ways to release my thoughts and feelings. From that day forward my life started to change. I headed into a world unknown to me. I began to go through my own layers of change from the dark side into the bright side.

The first step I took was remembering the acts of abuse I suffered. From that point I then had to own up to it and say, "Ya that did happen to me, yes me." I needed to face it after all it was my reality and no matter how many walls I built or tried to build, it was always there haunting me in the back of my mind. I remember getting the jitters when thinking about my abuse. I felt scared, sad, confused and dirty. I experienced a whole bunch of other mixed up feelings as well that got me to believing I wasn't worth much as a person. Inside I felt I didn't belong anywhere because the powerful voices in my head told me so. All lies.

You may have the same voices in your head too. You know the ones that say "Don't tell anyone," and "I must have done something to deserve it", or "I caused it". Another one of mine was, "I can't play with, hang out or get to close to anyone because I'm not like them. I am different." There are countless other things that your inner voice will come up and attack you with. These words repeat themselves all in perfect timing to destroy our being and cripple our self worth.

That was what it was like for me growing up. Positive thinking was very limited for me as it was covered up by many negative voices in my head for many years. I was led to believe those lies about myself and others. It wasn't until I was in my thirties when I got fed up with hearing them and decided to do something about it. "Enough was enough!" I thought. So as crazy as this might sound [which I know it will], I started fighting back.

Even though these voices were my own, they were still on a mission to tear me down in life. Deep within my gut somewhere in my internal being I knew this was not me. Even though I still felt different from other people inside, I just knew I was not any of those things I was made to believe. I kept thinking," I did not do this and I did not ask for this to be done to me!"

I set out on a mission to learn to take control of my thoughts and feelings. I wanted to take charge of myself using my new found anger of retaliation, the question was how on earth was I going to accomplish that? I found it difficult to even think about taking on another challenge with life being so overwhelming as it was. I honestly wasn't sure if I was mentally strong enough to do it. I listened to my gut feeling and went for it anyhow, head on!

It's funny how things appear out of nowhere right in front of us to help us out once we decide to take charge of ourselves. Going from one psychologist to another I finally ended up with a doctor who connected with me. I guess I let down a wall for a bit for whatever reason as he was able to get his great message through to me.

This advice that he gave me was the best advice I had ever received. I didn't realize then at sixteen years old how much my life was going to change for the better. It changed in such a huge way but not until his message finally clicked with me, I was in my twenties.

I don't think that doctor realized how much he had really helped me. In fact he actually saved my life. His message led me on a great path of healing and bettering my mental well being right down to my heart and soul. I'll go over with you what his message was to me in the next chapter. Until then you may want to review the key points that you feel are of importance to you in this topic and start right now on your road to recovery.

You control what *you* want to hear!

"Change the voices

in your head,

Make them like you instead"

-Pink

SEXUAL ABUSE
By family and others
Why me daddy?

When I was a child my father started touching …I mean fondling…I guess what I'm actually saying is he started sexually molesting me often. I remember feeling confused, scared & uneasy especially having two sisters in the same room at the time. As the years passed I became accustomed to my dad doing these things to me, it was normal for me to do sexual things to him as well. I believe I was about ten when I started accepting it thinking all dads touched and played with their daughters. Having my dad order me not to tell the rest of the family confused me at the time as I didn't really understand why. I figured I was 'special' to him.

I was really shy as a kid, I mean very shy. I was so shy that I couldn't even raise my head in a group setting among friends nor at most of my family gatherings. I remember getting teased alot because I was so standoffish. I remember going to school and analyzing all the children around me without their knowledge. I wanted to see if I could somehow seek out another shy insecure kid just like myself. I found this to be difficult. All the other kids around me appeared to be happy and outgoing, smiling and holding their heads up which made me feel much different from all of them. In those situations I didn't feel very special at all, I felt alone.

This really came into play in school when the local police came for a visit. I believe I was in grade three or four. They held an assembly in the gym to make sure that all the kids were aware of what happens in the real world. One of the topics of discussion was sexual abuse situations. The examples were similar to what I was facing at home. I thought it was weird when the police kept referring to the strangers as 'bad people'. "How can they be 'bad people' unless my dad is one of them?" I remember thinking.

They gave us several examples of situations where 'bad men' in vehicles would hunt children as they still do today. The police emphasized that they would lure kids into bushes with candy as well as pretending to need help to look for their lost puppy or bunny. Then it happened, the heart stopping whopper of reality for me. The police had changed the topic slightly to talk about both bad men and women being family members like mom or dad touching our private areas! I'm pretty sure I stopped breathing at that point.

As their words repeated in slow motion through my head it felt as if the world around me froze and stopped turning for that moment. I remember feeling a huge rush of excitement, fear and disappointment charging at me all at once. I also felt that all eyes were on me so I didn't dare look around. I sat waiting in shock with my head down. I thought the policemen were going to call out my name in front of a couple hundred or more kids to go up front and stand with them. I assumed they knew what I was going through! I was scared to death they were going to tell everyone there , even worse my dad!

The police continued teaching each of us to loudly say, 'NO!' if we found ourselves in one of those types of situations. They had all of us students repeatedly yell it out. Doing this helped me understand what was happening to me at home with my dad was WRONG! It confirmed that I wasn't special after all, I was a VICTIM as the police said.

The shame I felt made me go further into my shell figuring I was too late in saying, "NO!" like I was told to. The fear of not knowing what would happen at that point if I said no to my dad was what kept me from even thinking about trying. I felt that I was the one that let this happen to me all along.

The first time my dad sexually abused me is the time that stands out most vividly for me. While lying on my stomach sleeping in my bed [which was beside the window and parallel along side of my sister's beds] is when it happened. I was awakened by the feeling of pressure on my bed from having someone sit down on it.

I made every effort to pretend I was still sleeping because I was scared. I managed to do a fake toss and turn over toward the window a bit. In the moonlight I could see the silhouette of my dad perched on my bed right behind me. My eyes opened wide in horror as I felt my private parts being rubbed through my panties. He did this for a few minutes. I felt his hand pull the crotch part of my underwear aside, I didn't know what to think or do.

He stopped suddenly when I started to roll over. I guess my instincts kicked in. I wanted him to know I was awake and that I knew what he was doing. I rolled over stretching and yawning with my eyes closed. When I ended up on my back I opened my eyes and saw the large scary and dark figure of my dad sitting on my bed looking directly at me. When he noticed me looking back at him he calmly stood up and said, "Shhh, go back to sleep." I closed my eyes again until he left the room.

I heard his footsteps on the creaky floor in the hallway, I opened my eyes. I laid there thinking about what happened all night. I recall looking over at my two sleeping sisters while staring at the door waiting to see if he was going to come back in, it was a long night. I didn't want to be touched like that and I knew that. I was seven. I felt very uncomfortable and I wasn't sure what he was doing or why he did that to me.

The next morning I heard my mom and my sisters out in the living room. I nervously replayed what happened in the night over and over in my head trying to figure out how I would bring up what happened. I didn't hear my dad so I knew he was still sleeping. I got up and went out to the living room but still ended up waiting a little while longer before asking if I could talk to my mom.

My dad worked shift work so a lot of the times he would sleep in the daytime so I knew I had some time. While my younger sisters were playing and doing their own thing in the front room of our apartment I finally got the courage up and asked my mom if I could talk to her in private in my bedroom.

I sat on my youngest sisters' bed which faced the doorway and our old brown wood closet. Many thoughts raced through my mind while I waited for my mom to come and join me. My heart pounded as I rehearsed in my head what I would say to her. Eventually she walked in and sat down right beside me on the bed. I hummed and hawed and even beat around the bush a wee bit before she urged me to talk. In a low voice but not quite a whisper I said, "Daddy came in here in the dark last night, he sat on my bed and touched my private parts." Even though I wasn't looking right at my mom I could still feel her silence.

After a brief hesitation she asked me if I was sure I saw dad on my bed, suggesting I may have been dreaming because it was dark. Feeling disappointed like she doubted me I told her again that it was dad and explained to her what happened. My mom sat quietly beside me for a couple minutes longer then said, "Let's go talk to your dad." My heart pounded faster than ever, I became very dizzy and lightheaded. I found it hard to breathe in between begging her not to make me go in their room and tell him. I was terrified, he was just down the hall and around the corner!

Rushes of panicky thoughts came flying at me. She took my hand and walked me down the short hall to their bedroom. With the reassurance of her hand holding mine and the quiet tone she used while she told me it was going to be okay, I had felt a sense of calm come across me by the time we reached the bedroom doorway.

Still holding my hand she called out his name, he awoke and sat up. Standing at the foot of the bed she confronted him with this bold statement, "Janet says you were on her bed last night touching her private parts." As strange as it may sound I felt a huge relief and almost a streak of contentment come over me for a brief second. My mom glared directly at my dad waiting for a response. I was so nervous as he looked straight at me with his calm and intimidating smile. It gave me the chills, sweaty palms and all I remember wanting to run out of the room.

His response was shocking, "You were dreaming Janet, I was in bed all night." I was completely stunned to hear him say that while at the same time I noticed my mom who seemed to look satisfied with his answer. However I was not.

Sighing a deep breath and fighting back tears, I remember back to that split second when my lips moved without rehearsal. I heard myself quietly say to him, "No, it was you. "My dad let out a bit of a demeaning chuckle as he told me again that it couldn't have been him. He did his best to try and get me to believe that it was nighttime and dark in the room, therefore telling me I must have seen a shadow of something outside. He also tried to make it clear with me that sometimes people dream weird things that are not true.

He didn't think that statement through clearly as we lived on the second floor and just below my window at the side of our apartment building was a gas station. There were no trees or anything else there that would have casted a man like shadow on my bed. I may have been a child at the time but I knew what was real and what wasn't. Future events proved that. However, being a kid and without saying another word I helplessly gave into his charade.

I lost all my trust in people that day and eventually in my own self. My judgment was altered. I spent the rest of my days second guessing myself. After all if you can't trust your parents who can you trust? I remember feeling such rushes of confusion and frustration that I just couldn't understand. This brought me so much sadness.

As disturbing as this may sound, later in my childhood I began to wonder if I had some type of molesting magnet built into me somewhere. The sexual abuse continued until I was thirteen. During those dreadful years I was not only molested by my dad but I also had encounters with other adult men that I was familiar with in some way or another, never a stranger.

One of the men was a neighbor who lived next door, he tried to fondle me while his sleeping wife was present. One evening while I was babysitting their kids I had fallen asleep on a mattress on their living room floor, it was quite late when the couple came back home. Shortly after they got in I awoke to the television still on, the wife laying on the other side of the mattress asleep and her husband sitting between the two of us propped up against the wall.

The short, dark haired weasel of a man about the age of thirty stroked my leg while he tried to coerce me into going upstairs into his bedroom. Luckily I managed to worm my way away from him to run down the hall and out the front door. I got out and ran next door to my home, yes, home for protection to the man who was doing the same thing to me behind closed doors.

I will never forget the knot I had in my stomach as I paused on our front doorstep for a few minutes before banging on the door. Feeling paranoid I kept checking over my shoulder fearing my neighbor was coming after me. While standing there I wondered how the heck I was going to tell my dad as I was scared to death of what his reaction was going to be. I also wondered what would happen if he did believe me?

Time moved in slow motion as I banged on the door for what seemed like forever. The sound of the metal locks unlatching echoed in the night as the door flung open. I was hoping for my mom to answer the door but she did not. Standing there in the dim lit doorway was my dad, all six foot three of him.

Panicky and feeling more than awkward I told him what the man next door had done to me. I pretty much felt like running in the other direction, I was so nervous. Totally to my surprise, my dad pushed past me and ran next door! I heard the neighbors front door open at the same time my dad yelled inside their house that he was going to call the police. I didn't budge at all, I stayed on our porch frightened, startled and confused.

I couldn't believe what was happening, it felt like I was going crazy! He had me puzzled, it was as if he didn't know himself what he was doing to me? I mean really, by that time it had been about five years that he was molesting me off and on, how could he not know? At the time I wasn't aware that he was going to great lengths to cover it up.

It turned out that my dad did call the police on that neighbor the next day, the man was angry at this and retaliated. He tried scaring me by chasing me around the townhouse circle. He pretended to run me over by driving up close in behind me in his little red car. I believe I was around eleven years old when this was happening. That day was the only time he harassed me.

Once again I told my dad. Shortly after he went over to his place and engaged in a yelling match outside with him. It was all short lived. I am not sure of the technical details that went on between the two of them regarding the police or court but I do have a vague recollection of my dad mentioning something about calling off charges. I was incredibly relieved when the neighbor and his family moved away not long after.

I bravely brought up that incident again to my dad after a few months had passed, in doing so I was left feeling even more confused. I bluntly asked him, "Dad, remember when I told you about the neighbor touching me and you called the police? He replied, "Yes." I then asked, "Why did it make you so mad when you do the same thing?" Looking angry he raised his voice at me and nervously asked, "I am doing what?" Now I was terrified and wondered why I even brought it up. I wanted to back down but couldn't. In a low questionable voice I pretty much whispered back to him, "Touching me too?" After a tormenting long pause my dad simply answered, "He's not family."

I was freaked out by his comment but accepted it and went off to bed. At that moment I realized there was something wrong with my dad, not me. That conversation with him didn't stop him from touching me like I had hoped but the frequency of it eventually grew further apart. Throughout all the pain, anger and frustration that I had to endure I ended up coming out on top becoming wiser, stronger and more courageous as a person.

It all came to a sudden halt was when I was thirteen when my dad came into my bedroom one last time. He sat down beside me on my bed and as usual I didn't make any eye contact with him. I shied away when he asked me to scratch his back as that was his way of letting me know that when it came around to his turn to scratch my back, he would let his hands wander.

I can remember getting angrier and angrier the longer he remained next to me. I repeatedly yelled the word 'No!' in my head several times over. I wanted to make sure that when I said it he would know I meant it! Regardless of any illness that my dad may have had I still felt he had deliberately done those things to me.

It was all very routine for me, I felt like a programmed robot. When his turn came around to scratch my back I held my breath fearing the outcome. I watched his hand wander further down my body when out of nowhere I boldly blurted out, "NO, STOP!" Completely alarmed he quickly backed off. I really didn't expect that, it shocked me. Even though I practiced saying no to him many times there was nothing that could have prepared me for his next response.

I thought I was going to be sick. I felt an urge to apologize for saying no like that to him, it was strange. My powerful moment that I looked forward to for many years turned into a horribly terrifying cold and quiet few minutes. I'll never forget how he stared back at me then put his head down, I thought he was contemplating killing me at any given second. I stared at him with wide eyes as he slowly got off my bed, he made his way over to the chair at my desk and just sat there with his head hung low. I had no idea what to think at that point, I didn't understand what was happening. Inside I was freaking out!

After a long dead silence he lifted his head, fixed his eyes on me and quietly said, "I was wondering how long it would take for you to learn to say no and speak up for yourself." He went on to tell me that he was trying to teach me a lesson and that he was happy I finally learned. I couldn't do anything but just sit there. I could feel my heart pounding but I don't think I was breathing. I was extremely frightened that he was going to tell everyone what I made him do all those years. I believed him, I felt like a fool. I honestly thought I had caused it all, I was disgusted in myself.

He shook his head at me in disappointment and mumbled, "It's about time." I looked back at him feeling nothing but utter humiliation. He got up from the chair and walked out of my room leaving me with a silent, yet excruciatingly painful and haunting memory of a lifetime.

I don't think my dad knew how much of me he had destroyed by telling me that it was my fault for not speaking up sooner. It was a long while before I told anyone, I tried but the words would not leave my lips. I became more withdrawn and very bitter toward others. I contemplated suicide many times feeling like I just wanted to die. What he said to me just kept repeating itself over in my head putting me into a silent depression.

For what confidence I did have in myself, I lost it all at that point. I felt like a loser and thought everyone around me could tell. Even with understanding and forgiveness it still took me a long time let go of the anger. It is very upsetting to know my own parent would do that to me. He manipulated me into thinking I was to blame and that it was my fault for not stopping those things from happening to me. Privately I mentally suffered year after year with nightmares and daydreaming thoughts of, "If I only would have listened to the police at school when I was younger, I could have stopped it sooner." These thoughts distorted how I looked at everything. I lost my sense of right and wrong.

It is difficult for me to relive that memory today while writing this book. My breathing gets heavy and slow, my heart beats faster, my palms get sweaty and I can feel a headache forming. I still burst into tears on occasion as it becomes overwhelming. I think that's okay though, for me it is a great release.

Even though that remembrance is still vividly strong enough to affect me so emotionally today, it doesn't change the fact that I know the blame he put on me was a lie. It had absolutely nothing to do with being my fault whatsoever. I can't change what happened but I can control how I deal with it. It is what it is and I do not allow it to rule my life. His lie was his way of protecting his own self at my expense, hence the reason he confessed to the police later on.

You will read about that particular life changing experience for me in a later chapter. Even though the abuse had stopped I still held it inside me like poison for the next three years, finally an opportunity arose that allowed me to confide in a close friend as well as the proper authorities.

Following my dad's confession before and after his suicide, I attended many therapy sessions with and without him. Being a teenager was hard enough to cope with but then to add this on top was almost unbearable let me tell you. I tried different coping methods and all sorts of band-aids aiming to cover it up and forget about it. I hoped I could make it all go away. It didn't matter how much I drank or how many drugs I had taken a new day still dawned and with each sober morning that came my dad was still dead. His blaming words along with the pictures in my head were there to remind me that no amount of therapy, drugs or alcohol will ever erase the visual or audible memory that I've been left with. So for the most part I just learned to deal with reality by thinking that's just life I guess.

Therapy, confiding in friends and self help books played an important part in my healing over the years. All of it all taught me that what I went through was not my fault. Understanding that my dad was sick and had a severe problem helped take the onus off myself.

One of the several therapists I ended up seeing encouraged me to 'TALK ABOUT IT', regardless of how hard it was to do. He stressed the importance of 'GETTING IT OUT' of me. He told me that if I can't do it by talking about it, then to do it 'ON PAPER'. Of course being a teen I struggled with listening to adults but somehow through our generally one way street conversations I did manage to pick up a couple of things. I heard him say that what I thought other people were thinking about me or noticing of me was usually not their actual opinion at all. I still recall that advice to help me through uncomfortable situations.

I realize I have endured alot and have suffered but I also understand that traumatizing experiences greatly affect our inner being and that they don't just easily go away. I've learned that when we accept it we can deal with it. It is a lifelong healing process and THAT'S OKAY because you and I are here today and we are not alone. I know this because I am fortunate enough to be surrounded by people I love and care about who have also shared their sexual abuse stories with me.

These stories that I share come from both males and females and are not just geared toward one or the other. Many of us are in the same boat, it's just that some people are more willing to let go and share such personal information than others are.

This may be common knowledge to some whereas it may not be to others; being male certainly doesn't disqualify one from this particular type of abuse. I remember back in my twenties a male friend told me he was sexually molested. I was kind of surprised to be honest I had no clue that happened to boys. Now as time goes on of course I have learned that it was of my own ignorance as many males have been molested in some way by another and are no exception.

It seems to me we generally find this out through media via newspaper, televised news reports and talk shows on this subject. In my experiences I find most males are tightly sealed when it comes to communication and it's quite normal for them to hold things inside alot more than most females do. Assuming that is due to beliefs from their family upbringing, social life situations and from not really having the need to share like we females do. Sometimes there are exceptions to that rule.

I have had a couple of males trust me enough to divulge their deepest and utmost darkest secrets to me. One of them whom I most recently chatted with rehashed his story for me to shed some light from a male perspective.

His story dates back to when he was just eight years old. He recalls two incidences with the son of his moms friend. One of them being a time when he went with his mom to her friend's house where they stayed overnight. His mothers' friend had her sixteen year old son living with her at the time. The son came into the living room where he was asleep on their couch. He remembers being woken up by this teen boy who was reaching in and under his pajama bottoms. In confusion of what to do, he pretended to be asleep. The teen boy forced his uninvited contact on him and performed oral sex on him. No longer pretending to be asleep he sat up in terror and tired to stop him by pleading no repeatedly. This didn't work at all, so he thought of a quick escape and said he had to go to the bathroom.

The teen let him go to the washroom, twice actually, but both times he came back to find him waiting for him. On the final return from the bathroom when the teen made physical contact with him again he finally told him to stop and leave him alone or he would tell his mom. The boy finally left the room and left him alone, for the time being.

The other confrontation he had with the son of his mom's friend was when he was hanging out in the basement of his own home when they had come over for a visit. The sixteen year old boy approached him again making him feel extremely uneasy, he tried to verbally coerce him into exposing for him what was under the shorts he was wearing. Suddenly someone turned a light switch on at the top of the stairs turning on the light to the basement, it was his older brother. The teen boy saw this and was startled enough that he stopped perusing him any further. He [the young boy] took the opportunity to get away and out of the house rushing past his brother along the way.

That day was the last time any of them visited each other's homes. To this day he is not sure why that was really. He does remember his mom mentioning another visit at her friend's house, however when she brought it up he boldly responded with a no and flatly told her that he will not go there again. His mom's intuition may have told her that something was dreadfully wrong because the visits came to a halt.

Regrettably a female friend of mine has a similar story. This took place while her mom was at work on a graveyard shift. Her mom's boyfriend leaped on that opportunity taking advantage of her when she was a young girl in grade three.

It was about three o'clock in the morning when he woke her up. He lured her by allowing her to watch her favorite cartoon movie in his and her moms' bedroom. She was told not to wake up her cousin who was present at the time. She watched the movie like a good girl while the animal awaited the right time to pounce on his young prey. About fifteen minutes into the movie he made his moves. She remembers him sexually touching her inappropriately and forcing her to do the same to him. She told me he ended up raping her that night.

That horribly violating sexual assault changed her life forever. That was just one of her many stories she divulged to me, others included her being raped as she got older. She had been violated by other members of her family as well, a next door neighbor like I had even another of her mom's boyfriends. It happened so often that she felt it was all she knew.

When she got older and into her teen years she found herself having sex with strangers for money, clothes and other things that she wanted. It wasn't until her late teens when something triggered her into thinking about her own well being. I don't think she even knows what prompted her to do so, regardless she came to realize that something bad could happen to her if she continued carrying on that way. She decided to challenge herself to seek out other means of survival by focusing on finding skills that she had already possessed and new ones that she could learn.

Along her new chosen path she eventually learned to value herself and better her ways. She never ended up telling anyone about the molesting or being raped until early high school. Sometimes when you're scared and feel alone you just don't know who you can tell. Today she is a brave and wise young lady who looks back on her past knowing that all her experiences have made her stronger.

Another dear friend of mine lived through the experience of sexual abuse from the young age of five years old. Not only was she abused by a couple of people that were supposed to be taking care of her but when she was nine her mother's six foot one and two hundred pound common-law husband sexually assaulted her. She didn't tell her mom anything about her step dad abusing her until she was fourteen years old.

When she finally did tell her mom he was also present in the room, they both made it out like she had made it all up. Being intimidated by her spouse and under his control her mom went along with it siding against her own daughter. Later on that same afternoon when her step dad wasn't around her mom took her aside and told her that she did in fact believe her but in the same breath still blamed her for wearing sexy pajamas around him in the first place.

Without doubt those were shocking and hurtful words coming from her own mother. My friend told me how harshly demeaning and contradicting it was to her considering that it was her mom who gave her those pajamas in the first place. Her stepdad had all the control over everything and everyone in their home. He not only sexually abused her but also physically abused her and her mother. He beat her mom all the time, breaking bones and all. She was in a life threatening and dangerous no win situation.

Her story is not new, she is not alone. Many people reading this will resonate with her. She too is a survivor. Over a span of five to six years my friend endured countless times when he would enter her room while she was sleeping. Being suddenly awakened by his presence always startled her with such fear that she could hardly breathe.

Her stepfather even went as far as involving her childhood friend. The monster would read his porn magazines downstairs then go up stairs butt naked and disgustingly prance into her bedroom to where she and her friend were having a sleepover. Other confrontations involved giving them each piggy back rides while going as far as to slipping his fingers under their clothing.

A lock was eventually put on her door. It not only frightened her but also devastated her when her mom chose to stay with him. Much abuse continued to carry on in that home, yet she knows she stands a stronger woman today because of it. As a child and well into her teenage years she suffered horrible amounts of physical abuse by this same man.

One violent recollection she has is at fourteen years old when she tried to defend her mom against her stepfather. She yelled at her stepfather who was beating her mother up. She remembers yelling out, "You won't be happy until you kill us!" He turned around toward her and swiftly kicked her. He kicked her in her upper thigh with everything he had and sent her flying across the room! She couldn't move on that one leg for a couple of weeks as it was badly blackened with an enormous bruise.

His kick actually pushed her hip out of alignment in the fall she took. She was thankful she was able to see a chiropractor for he told her if she hadn't she would now have been lame in the one leg and restricted to a wheel chair. He is unaware of how severe his kick really was as she had not seen him or had any contact with him since that incident. If she had she knows he would not have cared.

She feared verbally telling on her moms' boyfriend so she tried another way of notifying people without using words. She made every effort to grasp the attention of others by wearing shorts often exposing her massive bruise. She was desperately seeking an opportunity to tell all, waiting for the right time when someone would see the bruise and ask her what had happened. She felt more comfortable having someone else initiate that sensitive conversation.

That moment she waited for came, someone finally inquired

about her bruise on her leg. She had every intention on telling the truth but lost her courage. Instead, she led the person to believe she had fallen down the stairs. Imagine how she must have felt about doing that. Back at home her mom blamed it on her again by telling her it was her own fault for trying to stand up to him.

That terrible time in her life lasted until she was fifteen. My friend finally got up the courage and told her aunt. From there her aunt suggested that she write down all the events that have taken place involving her step dad because she may need to defend herself against him one day. She did just that but felt she was betrayed and misled by her own aunt in the end by having her writings taken to the authorities. Even though my friend knew it was for her own safety and well being she and her brother were removed from their home.

My friend made a comment that I personally can relate to, she stated she always felt 'older' than her friends. 'Older' meaning more experienced which had her feeling like the odd one out. We may have been more life experienced than other kids our age but we were a lot less confident and far less trusting of other people than they were.

Through our eyes as children we figured that everyone around us was 'good'. No words can really express how shocking and beyond disheartening it was finding out the way we did, that 'good' didn't mean all people and that included our parents. It's especially hard when the people that you love, the ones that bring you up and whom you are suppose to naturally trust in life, ruin that trust for you before you yourself even understand the meaning of the word.

Here is your opportunity now to "Get It Out"!!!

If you are persistent in improving your well being one day all the pieces will fall together just like a puzzle. This will happen but you need to truly believe that abuse by others is not your fault. You may need to adjust how you accept things that happen to you. Never allow another person to steal your inner joy away from you, it's yours you own it. It is normal to feel like there is no escape. Sometimes we get overwhelmed, our minds shut down and all we need is someone to show us the way. There are many times in life when we rely on others to guide us, this is one of those times.

It is natural to feel guilty or less than competent, I did. It is okay to take help when it's offered, that is why it exists in the first place. Whomever offers to help you has most likely gotten on the right path because they accepted help somewhere along the way themselves. Start today by making a decision to move forward. Finally, put yourself ahead by making that first step and begin getting rid of the bad in your life by only allowing the good in. That is the choice I made.

It doesn't matter how old you are, the abuse may be in your past or you may be still living with or suffering some form of abuse today. As I learned through my therapy sessions it is healthy to express our inner thoughts and troubles through talking. We need to do that. If talking about your personal self is difficult for you then consider getting your words out on paper. I found that putting my thoughts on paper was just as therapeutic and eventually led me into talking about it. When you hold your troubles inside they tend to become toxic like poison which acts like acid eating at your very soul. That is the beginning of a path to self destruction.

It always helps to know someone that can relate to you, hear and understand your hearts cries. When we are restricted from communicating our thoughts in a healthy normal manner, our minds will still somehow manage to find a harmful path to get the information out. This kind of information will sometimes come out through negative physical expression which may show clues to others that something is wrong. Some people will pick up on these and some won't. Not a good situation to be in at all. Some examples of negative expression I have seen and experienced are excessive drug and alcohol abuse, cutting oneself, violence, isolation and suicide.

Bring yourself back to remembering your past. Recall any situations where you have felt violated, confused, angry, shut out or threatened. Now consider what brought you to this point in life today? Why are you reading this book? What is it that you feel you need to get out and say, deal with or handle differently? What do you think you need to get rid of inside yourself to be emotionally free?

I am here to help you express yourself and find methods you may not have been aware of before. I want to help you take control of your inner being but you are the one that has final say of what action you will need to take in your life.

You will find that this next page is one of many to come. I designed an exercise page to help guide you through the chapter topics. These exercise sheets will encourage and support you while you write out your own stories and how they make you feel. It will be helpful to write out what you are hanging onto in life from your past for example the things that angered you, upset you and even traumatized you. These exercise sheets can be used as guidelines to start your own agendas, record the stages that you are at and as your resource pages overall.

You are the only one that is going to read them if that's what you choose. What a great personal and very private way to initiate your first steps into healing your emotional well being. Congratulations!

EXERCISE SHEET: Use separate sheets of paper or a journal style book. It helps to record the applicable chapter names along with the relevant page numbers from this book on each of your writings for easy reference later.

Record your story: How you relate, situations, agendas, notes, thoughts & anything else related to this chapter. Use paragraph writing, point form or whatever you're comfortable with. Think back & take a deep breath! Now take some time to read over what you wrote.

_____

_____

_____

_____

_____

_____

_____

_____

_____

_____

_____

_____

_____

_____

_____

_____

_____

_____

_____

_____

_____

_____

_____

E.R.A.S.E.D. = Easy Real Action Spiritual Exercises Deliver:
Erase the chains of abuse that bind you using EASY made, REAL life, ACTION steps with SPIRITUAL outlook & hands on EXERCISES that DELIVER!

Early on in my life I made these decisions that I feel saved my life:

"I refuse to allow others to decide for me what I will think. I refuse to allow others to bring me down on their negative journey. I will be empathetic toward them but I will not let their unhealthy personal issues affect me. I am going to make my journey the way I want it to be. I will be the one to decide how I will feel inside."

SHYNESS
Can make life very difficult

As mentioned previously in the first topic I used to be a very shy person. I believe you can be shy by nature but I also know you can be made shy by abuse from others. Shyness can come from shame and the fear of being judged. I have always had the fear of being judged by others negatively. I did not know how to respond to defend myself, I found it easier to hide my head or hang my head low in hopes no one would notice me.

I spent the majority of my adulthood struggling to make eye contact with others, fearing that when I did they would be able to see inside to my soul. Back then I didn't want anyone to see that deep into me because I feared they would come to know all of my shame, secrets and insecurities that I carried. In school I rarely raised my hand in class not even to ask to go to the washroom.

As a young adult I remember not being able to walk up to a dinner buffet to get my own plate of food as I thought people were staring at me, reading me or judging me. I had zero self esteem. That wasn't the real me and I knew it. I allowed other peoples negative actions to change me. I did not want to draw any kind of attention to myself, good nor bad. It felt as if I wore my guilt and shame on my forehead most days for all to see.

I eventually learned that what I thought people were seeing and thinking about me wasn't any different than I was of them. Regardless if they were bad or good thoughts, if mine were not affecting them in any way then why should I allow theirs to affect me. In those situations the other people I am referring to were strangers whom didn't even know me, so really it wasn't at all as dramatic as I thought it to be. I wish I knew to look at it that way long ago. Thoughts and opinions of others have no real affect on us like I had always felt it did. In fact most strangers keep what they are thinking to themselves. People tend to only see your cover, your outer shell or makeup and not the real you.

What we fear others are thinking about us is usually a lot worse than what they are actually thinking, if they are even thinking about us at all. Look at yourself and how you perceive others. When you see another person that you don't know, you may notice something that catches your eye, you may gather a thought but it's not really a big deal is it? When I was walking with my head down that was actually drawing more attention to myself than I had realized. Reading books, listening to others and observing people interacting with each other is how I learned this.

I watched strangers interact with each other in restaurants, passing each other in malls and other places where it would be easy to judge or make mental thoughts and comment on each other. For me I found this to be very effective therapy. Doing this periodically over years I learned that those people weren't making judging each other a priority like I always thought people did. I could tell by their facial expressions that there is no way that they knew what the other person was thinking or even what their secrets were.

What a great relief that was for me, I don't know why I thought that way I just did. The worry of what others thought prevented me from doing things I really wanted to do. Anytime I wanted to do something where others were involved I would somehow come up with every excuse in the book why I shouldn't, this usually ended up convincing me out of the idea altogether.

Thinking the way I did was very unfair to me. At some point I guess I settled on living a life affected by another person's abuse even well after the abuse had stopped and the abuser was gone. We have suffered enough but somehow we are still the ones that end up being punished when it should really be them, this giving us more reason to make it a choice on how we let things affect us.

I finally felt some confidence and started putting it into practice by taking baby steps. In realizing that I am a regular person like everyone else I didn't need to hide anymore. You don't need to either. People will only know what you choose to tell them. Why should we be ashamed when we did nothing wrong? Sexual abusers look for shy people as they know these people are the least likely to talk and that that was me. The abuser should be ashamed not you or I.

Over the years I have been learning to love myself, I do not walk with my head down anymore and I hope that you won't either.

EXERCISE SHEET: Use separate sheets of paper or a journal style book. It helps to record the applicable chapter names along with the relevant page numbers from this book on each of your writings for easy reference later.

Record your story: How you relate, situations, agendas, notes, thoughts & anything else related to this chapter. Use paragraph writing, point form or whatever you're comfortable with. Think back & take a deep breath! Now take some time to read over what you wrote.

_____

_____

_____

_____

_____

_____

_____

_____

_____

_____

_____

_____

_____

_____

_____

_____

_____

_____

_____

_____

E.R.A.S.E.D. = Easy Real Action Spiritual Exercises Deliver:
Erase the chains of abuse that bind you using EASY made, REAL life, ACTION steps with SPIRITUAL outlook & hands on EXERCISES that DELIVER!

ALL ALONE
Separation from others, feeling singled out

As I write this I feel alone in the moment. Not alone in a bad way, alone in a good way. It has taken me my entire life to turn those what I call 'bad' alone feelings that I once had into 'good' feelings I now have when I'm alone. I enjoy being alone now, it's nice being separated from others from time to time. It is good for the soul. As I reflect on these feelings it brings me back to a time in my life when being alone was very traumatic for me. From early childhood to early adulthood I hated being alone. Sounds kind of the opposite of what a shy kid would say but I didn't know how to be alone. I didn't like mc and being alone wasn't what I wanted at the time, unlike now I welcome it.

I hated myself and did not enjoy my own company at all. Mainly because others led me to believe I had no sense of worth and that I mattered as much as the dirt on the bottom of a shoe. I used to feel like I wasn't good enough or smart enough to even bother putting my opinion in. I was so shy that I mumbled. It was hard for me to get my point across or even to have someone understand what I was saying. I still feel like that on occasion, it's like an old habit that's hard to break. I was ignored a lot and told to shut up by classmates as well as some teachers in those early elementary school grades. I guess they found my mumbling annoying. One would think I would welcome being alone rather than be involved in that kind of environment but in my case that wasn't so.

I had learned to really despise people and to hate myself enough that I had no confidence to be alone. When I was alone I would think about my life, dwelling on what others had said about me or what I thought they were thinking about me. When I would do that to myself I would end up wallowing in depression and my thoughts would knot up my stomach and eat at me like acid. I may not have shown it on the outside much but on the inside I felt I always had to struggle to function properly in public, fighting and suffering through anxiety attacks that those thoughts brought on. When I was with other people I never had to worry, I did just fine because the focus wasn't all on me. I spent most of my time focusing on all the bad things that happened to me instead of the good things I wanted to have happen. I tormented myself all the time with poor me, it *only* happens to me and more than ever *why me?*

Those questions were my primary thoughts, very poisonous thoughts. I was unable at the time to see any of the good things that ever happened to me. I realize now that putting all my thought into how bad everything was only brought more bad things my way. I believe in the law of attraction, and I see now how it was definitely working in me. I hated most people because of a small few that had affected my life so badly. I sadly valued their opinion enough to let them take over my life. It was easier for me to just label everybody bad and stay away.

I did not feel any joy at all which is why when I was out and about all I noticed was everyone else's happiness, it stood out like a sore thumb. I hated seeing other people happy. I mean if I wasn't happy, then I wanted nothing to do with those people that were. So they too were quickly added to my hate list. There were many times when I felt unloved and alone. This may sound pretty simple but I reached a point one day when I couldn't stand feeling that way any longer. I got sick of being on the brink of sink or swim all the time. Thankfully all that changed. I'm not exactly sure what it was really but something just opened up or clicked inside of me and I chose to follow it.

After suffering through my dad's suicide and pulling myself up again from that, I knew that sinking wasn't an option for me. I also knew in my own heart that I was a loving, caring person and the way I was living my life didn't fit with that. I remember thinking about *why me* in a different light and wanting to find the answer. It was at that point that I recall feeling overwhelmed by the amount of years in my life I may have left to live. I thought, "Wow, what if I live to be eighty? I better figure out how to make all those years to come easier on myself."

Through reading and research I finally found myself. I was definitely taking the wrong approach to life back then. With the knowledge that I now have I would have watched those 'happy' people that I was referring to a bit closer. I may have been more curious as to *why* they were so happy. Could it have been the 'law of attraction' at work? This I know now would have brought more happiness in my life. A whole new outlook and approach to life. Unfortunately, being a victim of abuse back then made it hard for me to see beyond my own pain to even notice anyone else's feelings. I am ever so grateful that changed.

I turned down parties, many parties and other social events for fear that they didn't really want me there. I remember thinking I was only invited because they were just being nice. Yes it's true, I thought that way. It is seldom that these thoughts still attack me but the difference now is, I do all I can to change them before they have a chance to influence me.

I know those same thoughts have happened to other people where they just brushed them off, but when it happened to me I turned it into a life time experience. I allowed myself to miss out on alot all because I cared too much about and assumed what others were thinking.

Actually, I did this ofton over many different situations. I was very insecure and had zero self esteem. I also acquired a bad hateful attitude which only ended up getting me in a lot of trouble by attracting me to hanging out with the wrong sort of people. Others considered the people I chose to hang out with to be a bad group of people that were going nowhere with their lives, being young I thought they were pretty cool people.

All that did for me though was bring a lot worse into my life and I definitely didn't need any more of that. Some people are able to sort that out whereas some of us don't know how to. You may want to try picturing how you want your life to be. It may take a while but stick to it and you will see that things will eventually start to change around you. Be patient and be positive.

Over the years I made another commitment to myself to talk to as many people as I could about my past and how my childhood was. The more I talked the more I would find people in the same situations with the same pasts. Again the law of attraction at work, surprising isn't it. I also had found out the hard way how not acknowledging or accepting my awful past can do amazing harm to one's health. It led to depression and sickness that I learned all too well how to cover up.

Always remember that no matter what you experience there are others who experience the same if not worse. You are not alone. I started to feel more comfortable finding more people like me that shared my same experiences of one kind or another. It is such a great healing step to talk with other people that know exactly what you're talking about.

I found connections with people at work, in help groups and videos, in talk shows, books and in friends. I was definitely tired of feeling alone and really found it quite exhausting to hate people. It took up a lot of my energy to do so. I was determined to start finding my joy and what made me tick. "I am a human being just like everyone else, why should I miss out?" I thought.

I started off by simply writing a list of things that interested me. My list contained things I liked such as hobbies, movies, music, animals, camping, scents and scenery. I wrote down everything I could think of that made me smile. I read this list often then I started planning in my head time to do some of them.

Over the years I got into the routine of regularly doing those things on that list. It opened my eyes to what I liked and to what brought me pleasure. I needed that. To get me through each day I made it a daily practice to remember those pleasurable feelings that came along with all the things that brought me that joy. It very much helped me learn to enjoy my own company.

I refuse to stay focused on miserable feelings, I don't want to miss out on all the greatness that life has for us out there. Even if you don't feel like smiling, find a way and just smile! It takes a bit of work but is worth it. It's free to use and free to give, it can go a long way. It can change how you feel inside, how others view you and most importantly how you view others and everything else around you too.

Create your own list of your interests, hobbies, sights, sounds, scents and even tastes. Read your list and see how it makes you feel, preserve that feeling for as long as you can. Try doing the things you have listed often to bring out the 'good' feelings that *you* want, when *you* want.

"If I get it all down on

Paper, it's no longer

Inside of me,

Threatening the life they

Belong to."

-Anna Nalick

EXERCISE SHEET: Use separate sheets of paper or a journal style book. It helps to record the applicable chapter names along with the relevant page numbers from this book on each of your writings for easy reference later.

Record your story: How you relate, situations, agendas, notes, thoughts & anything else related to this chapter. Use paragraph writing, point form or whatever you're comfortable with. Think back & take a deep breath! Now take some time to read over what you wrote.

_____
_____
_____
_____
_____
_____
_____
_____
_____
_____
_____
_____
_____
_____
_____
_____
_____
_____
_____
_____

E.R.A.S.E.D. = Easy Real Action Spiritual Exercises Deliver:
Erase the chains of abuse that bind you using EASY made, REAL life, ACTION steps with SPIRITUAL outlook & hands on EXERCISES that DELIVER!

WHY ME?
Is it really worth years of wasted time
while we try to figure this out?

Focusing a bit more on the *why* of things? Why does this stuff always happen to me? What did I do to deserve this? I'm a good person but bad things always happen to me? I didn't ask for this? Maybe if I did that differently? Why doesn't that person or those people ever have anything bad happen to them? There are many different questions that run through our minds when we have something awful happen to us or when we are put in any type of unpleasant situation.

I think every person at one time or another in their life has fallen into the trap of dwelling on things they've gone through. We cannot control the actions of others, we may try to but most often don't find success in that. We can try and defend ourselves against the actions of others but that is not always possible either. Once a circumstance has taken place it is done and over with and the best you can do for yourself is to deal with it by learning from it then do your best to move on. It's all up to you.

Easier said than done I know. In some cases we can prevent or avoid circumstances before they occur but not all of them as some things I believe are meant to happen. We need to have the experience to enable us to grow.

Unpleasant things that do happen to us do not just happen to only us. As much as we may be made to feel or how much we may think it does, it doesn't. Nobody is born asking to be abused and as horrible as it is, it does happen. Pondering the question *why me* is natural. It's okay to ask that question but don't allow yourself to carry it on to the point where you are repeatedly questioning yourself over long periods of time. I did just that. After working through it I found in most of my situations that it wasn't just me as I thought, but rather a matter of time and place as well factoring into those situations that also made the difference.

Dwelling on the reason why things happened to you in the past only prolongs your agony and blocks your visions for your future. Your feelings need to be dealt with as they are a part of you yes, but also keep in mind that there is more to you than just feelings.

Why is it that some people seem to have a squeaky clean life with no problems? I believed that for a very long time, how about you? If you are one of the many that have then those people did a great job of getting others to believe that. Granted I'm sure there are a few people with close to perfect upbringings and lives but I have yet to meet one.

I do not believe that one can grow without having any adverse experiences to learn from. Life is full of difficult and undesirable situations and would it make sense to have no reason in behind them? For me it's simple, it's all been designed this way.

You may wish to try viewing your life as an adventure and look forward to what is going to happen next. I do. Of course I did not always see life this way which is reflected in my stories but as I said in the last topic I wasn't prepared to bail out, I was in it for the long haul. During those dark and desperate times in my life when I didn't love or even like myself, I somehow managed to learn that it's best to find a reason to be. Mentally I had hit rock bottom and had to find a reason to keep going.

At that point it didn't matter to me whether my reason to be was for a family member, a friend, a co-worker, a support worker or the neighbor across the way because what did matter to me was my will to be here. What should matter to you is...YOU.

As I mentioned before I reached a point where I figured I should find a way to make the most out of the rest of my time I have here on earth. I needed to figure something out that wouldn't leave me feeling like crap every moment of my days.

Everyone is a unique individual with their own blueprint. We each have our own road map to follow in life which leads us into various interests, beliefs and values. Different things happen to different people to help each person figure out what their own plan really is.

When in a gloomy and uncertain state of mind it is very difficult to see how much there really is in life to explore. If and when we do choose to seek out life, we can find that there are many things out there that are customized for each one of us. It's all there for you and me. We have our pick of different activities, different types and flavors of food and a wide variety of sounds and styles of music. These can open up a large array of places for us to visit, sights to see as well as a ton of people we can meet along the way. We waste so much of our precious time dwelling on the question *why* that we end up missing out on all of life's treasures.

Seeing life from this perspective makes things much clearer for me, so clear that it helped changed my whole outlook into bringing better things into my adventure I can call my own. Being able to step back and look at the bigger picture helps me in a great way to look at things that happen to me as learning lessons.

Give it a try. Think back and take a look at some of your own not so encouraging or 'not so good' memories that you may have that do hold some kind of personal significance for you. It may be difficult at first but don't give up trying, you may have to ponder the idea awhile. There are things that happen to us and stuff we go through in life that may not make sense at the time. Some of those things stand out in our minds for a reason wouldn't you say?

If you can recall a situation or two analyze them further. What were the factors that were involved leading up to those events? Write them down. What was else was happening around you or to you at that same time? Again, write it down. What happened shortly after or even a long while after that have an obvious similarity that could help you link them together? Read what you have written. Can you see that these not so favored events in your life could be pieces of a puzzle being put together?

I wrote down two or three events in my life that I found rewarding in some way or another. I then went back a few more years and wrote down events and other happenings that I felt stood out in a negative way or out of my comfort zone. I took some time and put some thought into it then connected the dots. When I did this it was as if a light bulb lit up in my head. I thought, "Wow now that makes sense now!" Doing this helped give me some insight into answering my question as to why. It cleared up my confusion and satisfied me. It's a pretty cool feeling when you can figure yourself out.

It may be helpful to look back on the pieces of your life like an unsorted puzzle. It may be complex or not depending how deep you feel you need to dig according to what you want answered. Let me give you an example to help you with this process.

Being molested was horrible, degrading and invading but I chose not to let it ruin my life. I never asked for it to happen and I am glad it's over. Back then I felt there had to be a reason to be put through all that and if there wasn't one I was going to find one. I did not believe it just happened because it happened and that was that.

Well it turned out that I did find my reason I was looking for after all and that was to help other people. I took that answer and turned it into a purpose. To make sense of why such a thing would happen to me more than once and by more than one person, I wrote down when each event took place and with whom they took place with. In doing that I was also awakened to how much I had really endured as a child.

I thought about all the times I had come across other people who had told me their own stories of sexual abuse. I encountered more people struggling with the affects of it than there were people that had healed or were healing from it. I would hear them speak in regards to their feelings about it and what havoc it still played in their life. I had a hard time relating to the distress that it caused or was still causing them. Even though I went through similar ordeals oddly enough I felt like an outsider as I listened to them. Some of the problems these people were still struggling with because of it all truly blew me away at the time. I couldn't understand why the heck they would let this happen to them.

Thinking about these people triggered me to write down another significant time in my life. This was a time when I had gone along to counseling to support my spouse that I had at the time with his drug and alcohol abuse. I ended up seeking separate counseling due to the fact that my involvement in that relationship was that he would regularly mistreat me. I was moved away from him and placed into codependency counseling on my own. It makes sense to counsel each individual separately on healing before they can learn to be in a healthy relationship together.

Besides opening my eyes and counseling my own self right out of that relationship something else happened that assisted in that process. My counselor managed to manipulate his words while he was questioning me and ended up digging deep enough that he pulled out my sexual abuse experiences. We were supposed to be discussing my spouse and his drug and alcohol dependencies, so I thought. Once I realized where he was headed I questioned it, "Hey, wait a minute, how...did...ah, it doesn't matter." From then forward our sessions went from being somewhat about codependent relationships to not even being about my current relationship at hand, it was strictly all about me.

When chatting with me during our few sessions he told me that he was astonished at how well I had healed. Once again I felt like an outsider. I was confused as to why others seemed to think it was such a big ordeal for it was over and done with in my mind. I didn't feel that is was too difficult to overcome. I apologize if that sounded a bit arrogant, by all means I don't mean it to be. According to my therapist being able to freely talk about my past abuse to others along with what he said were positive responses to his questions, wasn't at all what he was used to hearing in his everyday sessions.

Now getting to what I wrote down regarding the importance of that memory. My therapist asked me to be a guest speaker at one of his female sexual abuse group sessions, he said he felt the majority of the women were still struggling to overcome. My heart pounded with anxiety as he spoke. Yes I had come along way at that point by learning to speak to strangers within small groups of people here and there, however publicly speaking in front of a larger group of strangers was not my thing.

To be honest I felt a bit embarrassed by the praise he gave me as I felt he was overly congratulatory about it. It is through others that I realize how much of an accomplishment it really was for me and how different we all are.

I completely felt caught off guard with no experience with doing that sort of thing. I worried about how I really would come across to the group of women, I knew I would want to let them know I was on their team. Though feeling like an outsider even with my counselor's reassurance, I wasn't sure if I could relate to them in such a manner that would give those people really what they needed. He may have considered me to be ready for that but I didn't see it at all. It wasn't my time to explore that path that's all.

As I wrote out the things that were note worthy for me from our sessions together, I looked back at that particular moment as a chance for opportunity. Perhaps I missed the boat? I don't know. Over time I did learn from that experience, it was one of the dots I needed to connect which helped me find my reason that I went looking for. These experiences directly led me to wanting to help educate those who may not be aware of how to help themselves heal on their own.

This method opened my eyes. I looked at everything I had written down, connected the dots and clearly saw that one thing led to another. I'm sure you've heard people say, "Well if it weren't for this I wouldn't have that, or if I didn't do that then I wouldn't have been able to be this." I look at my life stages in comparison to a course curriculum, I must complete specific prerequisites before registering in the next level. It's that simple.

Looking at the sexual abuse I endured in my life, I choose to believe that this happened to me because a higher being knew that I would in some weird way be able to handle it. In helping others by informing them and setting a positive example to follow I offer to share the tools that I used so they too can open up and talk about it. This is the area a lot of people struggle with when it comes to abuse. Some people bottle these things up their whole lives not realizing what harm it does or who is out there that will help them. I fully understand how scary that is.

I have met a few people along the road that have told me their story finishing it with, "By the way I have never told anyone other than you." Even though I resonate and empathize with them I still can't believe how some people can hold inside such negative things for most of their lives. They touch my heart.

I look at this as a blessing of signals and signs to let me know I'm on the right track simply because I was able to get the ball rolling for someone else. It touches me to know that these people warmed up to me in seeing no threat feeling comfortable enough to divulge their information to me. Each time someone confides in me I feel weight lifting off my shoulders.

As saddening and disappointing it is to hear someone else say they've endured similar and sometimes even worse abuse, on my part it feels like a job well done to me in a really strange way. I love it when people talk to me about it because I know firsthand how healing that is.

It is very touching to be involved in the encouragement and initiation when someone is willing enough to divulge their story. I find it gratifying to share a person's feelings of relief and freedom before and after the moments it takes for them to say the words. Every bit helps and even if it is not the first time they have told someone, the time they take to tell it again is another step closer to personal healing freedom. I would not be the strong person I am today if I didn't have anything happen in my life to compare my weakness or strength to. I know now that I can overcome anything and pick myself up again no matter what I go through.

This also brings me to another time where connecting the dots in my life make sense now. Once I clued in to this I learned that I would not be writing this book at all if it weren't for a specific job I held in my past. In that position I was required to write up various things like staff performance appraisals, letters and contributions to our newsletter. I was a high school drop out with no writing skills or experience, thankfully that job filled in for that.

Of course sporadically reading some self help books helped contribute as well. I found myself buying and borrowing those type of books often enough that it became a habit. Goes to say how many issues I had really and I consider myself pretty normal!

I do owe the enhancement of my writing skills and passion for it now to when I went back to school a couple years ago to graduate as an adult. Great instruction from influential teachers helped me to achieve high marks. Seriously who would have 'thunk' it? Sorry I couldn't help myself, I still love that word!

Writing what seemed to be endless essays and receiving great marks is what gave me the confidence into moving forward with my writings of my biography. The writing opportunities that I really dreaded have now turned into something I fully enjoy! It's crazy how English was my least favorite subject in school but has now led me into successfully finishing this book. Ironic. Never being really keen on reading books and always avoiding it as much as I could, I find it funny now that I'm writing one! It is enlightening for me to be able to connect the dots for it gives me reasons as to why some of the things in my life happen.

Do you see the preparation work that has gone into me? The same prep work is going into you as well just in different ways to suit you and your blueprint. All your prerequisites you go through in life when you are on the right track are designed in accordance with the end result of your personal roadmap. So you choose wrong turns, that's okay you'll eventually be nudged and in some cases forced back on the right path. Some sort of mild to extreme event will occur in your life to guide you back there again, just keep following your gut instinct.

I do believe it all depends on if you take note of these nudges when they are happening and if you put effort into seeing why they are coming about. Once you know the why let it drive you, sit back and relax as it guides you. You can choose to see the negative or the positive side of things, that option is there for you. All I can say is take your time and think about your life's patterns to get the most out of your days.

When you encounter a situation that you don't want to be in, relax and take a deep breath then step back and think about it by examining the situation. Ask yourself these questions, "Self, how am I going to handle this? Is there something good that can come out of this?" Affirm it with, "I am going to be ok, yes I am!" Sounds funny but it keeps you responsive in a proactive manner. It will help you control your emotions giving you a better handle of the situation. It also prepares you for coping with it in a more positive light. Each time something undesirable comes my way I almost feel ready for it like I was waiting for it to happen. I just deal with it, learn from it and move onto the next one when it arises. What other 'good' choice do I have?

Try and see each affair regardless of how bad it is or may become as something you are to learn about yourself. I believe when things happen to us they are for us to learn something about ourselves. First I learned I was much stronger than I thought I was, secondly I learned that is it okay to ask for help and thirdly I learned that there is a lot more to life than what I was limiting myself to. I apply this same thinking to when people come into my life that I do not get along with. I believe we are meant to see something about ourselves that normally on our own we wouldn't be able to.

To help you make sense of this imagine for whatever reason a new person comes into your life, short term or long term doesn't matter. Let's just say that all you notice is everything they do that angers or annoys you, okay. Now you have a choice to make don't you? You can keep getting angry and irritated or you can try to ignore that person and see past their behavior.

Another way I like to look at this is to consider that people who we let get under our skin come into our lives perhaps from their own purpose in life to point something out to us. This could be anything really but what comes to my mind is when I was growing up, I didn't spend enough time in acceptance and forgiveness. We are taught to accept others for who they are but what we also consider to be 'normal' behavior may not necessarily be the other persons perception of it as everyone is different. Letting others get to me can still be a trying thing for me so to get past it I make an effort to remember that if all else fails, forgive!

What have you missed out on while letting your mind run wild with the question, "why you"? Better yet, what could you have been doing instead of dwelling on this question? It is perfectly okay to ask yourself these questions but don't spend too much time on it. Some people dwell on that question their entire lives to the point those questions control how they live their lives. Life is controlled by time. We age and we age fast with no real power over slowing it down. Sure there are ways to cover it up but you can't stop the clock. I am also guilty of spending too much time on one issue and I am grateful for these reminders when I get them.

We were meant to move ahead and keep going! I have naively made a lot of wrong decisions about how I was going to feel and what I was going to think during my times of abuse, loss and other turmoil in my life. I lost mass amounts of time in my past but I don't stop putting in the effort. I try to do what it takes to ensure my time is quality time in my life, for me and for others. Time is something we cannot get back once it is lost no matter what we do.

You need to start today and now, this minute and this very moment. It already took a few seconds of your life away just reading these words. Consider how it makes you feel when you are trying to figure out the question 'why me?' Do you feel good? I don't assume you do as I never did. It's a horribly depressing feeling, wouldn't you much rather like to hang on to and dwell on a good feeling? Remember that. Remembering those feelings brought me to writing down ten things in life that made me feel good, ten things that made me feel happy. I kept this list with me and would read it when I was feeling down, glimpsing at it for more than a few days. CREATE YOUR OWN LIST ON THE NEXT EXERCISE SHEET.

This may sound cheesy but it worked for me. I would read my list and pick one thing to focus on for me to do. I know it's hard to get your butt up and going when you're feeling down but it is something you must do. For example I would force myself to sing a song or dance which helped change my mood. Trust me it took more than a few tries struggling with the difficulty of doing this but it works.

Whatever it takes it is extremely important to change your mood and when you don't you can lead yourself on a downward spiral of undeserved self torture. You waste more of your time. I lived that vicious cycle and each time I would give up and give in. It wasn't long before I would be thinking things like, "Wow where did this past month go?" It can really affect other people around you too and can create a domino effect. What good is that doing? Just remember to keep moving and keep learning!

Think of all the things you can accomplish with all the lost time that can be prevented. You could put that time into figuring out your life's path by linking the puzzle pieces together to better your situation. Your thoughts are crucial to your well being. What thoughts were you having when you were brought to reading this book? It takes time to figure things out about ourselves and we need all the time we can possibly get our hands on nowadays, right? Right.

We waste a lot of precious moments wondering why all these bad things keep happening to us or have happened to us, leaving little room for any good things to happen to us. I learned the hard way like most others, I hope it will be easier now for you.

"When you change the way

you look at things,

the things you look at change"

-Wayne Dyer

EXERCISE SHEET: Use separate sheets of paper or a journal style book. It helps to record the applicable chapter names along with the relevant page numbers from this book on each of your writings for easy reference later.

Record your story: How you relate, situations, agendas, notes, thoughts & anything else related to this chapter. Use paragraph writing, point form or whatever you're comfortable with. Think back & take a deep breath! Now take some time to read over what you wrote.

_____

_____

_____

_____

_____

_____

_____

_____

_____

_____

_____

_____

_____

_____

_____

_____

_____

_____

_____

_____

_____

_____

_____

_____

E.R.A.S.E.D. = Easy Real Action Spiritual Exercises Deliver:
Erase the chains of abuse that bind you using EASY made, REAL life, ACTION steps with SPIRITUAL outlook & hands on EXERCISES that DELIVER!

Chapter Two - Seeing it & Believing it

READING WHAT YOU WROTE
How this helps

You now have had the opportunity to jot down some notes, write down paragraphs or stories of how you personally relate in some way to each of the specified topics in chapter one. It is time to move forward but first you need to **STOP** here and go back to chapter one and read your notes, preferably out loud to yourself.

Didn't I say move forward? Don't worry you are, you may just not see it like that right now. I ask you to read your notes aloud because it allows you to **HEAR** what you've said as if someone else is reading it to you. Your brain will make better sense of what you wrote. You don't need to edit anything unless you wish to. Once you have read each page you have written I recommend reading the pages one more time out loud. After you have read your pages of writings a second time around continue on reading this book, you will be given further instructions as to how this is helping you.

Okay, you're on the right track! Have you read what you wrote twice over? If not I really suggest you do before going any further. I thought I'd throw that in here one more time, not so much to annoy you but to ensure the importance of not missing any steps is understood. If you have read what you have previously written over a couple times then congratulations! You have now taken an important second step and **heard** what **you** have to say. When I do this step I feel silly but it is a good release of psychological pressure at the same time. I also feel empowered by my own words. How did it make you feel when you read your story? Even if it is in point form it is still your story.

Maybe you are at a point where you are not ready to divulge sensitive or personal things to your own self yet? It will come when you let it. Following these guidelines will help ease you into that. You could still be in the remembering and acknowledging stage of what you've been through, I don't know? Only you know that answer. Whichever stage you are in is okay, there is no rush.

Set your own deadline and take your time because your comfort level is important.

These are steps for you to use now and in your future. Feel free to read the first chapter as many times as you need to until you feel ready to move on. Read the whole book in its entirety like I do then go back to chapter one and start again. Be more thorough the next time around by 'doing' the exercises outlined in each step. Do whatever you are comfortable with and whichever will help you retain the information.

You are getting closer to finding out how reading what you write helps you but first I need you to do one more step. This will help your brain understand the key points of what you need to express in your writing. I love brightening things with color so I choose to use highlighters that are pink, purple or yellow to emphasize key points. You can also use a different color pen to circle or underline groups of words in this step that is up to you.

In this step you will need to read your material a third time, yes a third time. Only this time you are not going to read aloud unless you want to. I need you to go through and highlight, underline or circle anything you feel that is significant. Make bold anything of meaning and of importance to you like your thoughts and how you felt for example. You may choose to highlight something that really angers or upsets you. In addition to this you may want to highlight some specific places, events or even people in the occurrences.

There is no limit on how much you can highlight or bold, the more you do the better. Don't forget to proofread what you've highlighted. Whoops! I guess that could be considered the fourth time. On the bright side you may get sick of it but at least it will stick. Some people feel the abuse or tragic events they've lived through stick so much that they can't get it to stop replaying in their head. Other people know what has happened to them but are in denial of it because it is hard to deal with, they just can't wrap their head around it. Sometimes when it's in our mind it doesn't mean we can clearly see it.

I know you are still wondering what the purpose of doing all this is and how it is going to help you, let me share that with you now. Reading your words out loud benefits you by allowing you to be more thorough which helps you focus better because it makes you to read slower. Thoughts usually go racing through our head. Reading out loud forces you to pronounce each word out instead of seeing a quick picture of it. Reading out loud also allows you to spend more time reviewing every word, sentence or each line you have written more clearly.

Making it stick is important in accepting it. This way you will be confirming to yourself, "Yes this happened to me." Reading out loud helped it sink in for me which helped me deal and allowed me to let go. When you read out loud you hear how your own words and phrasings sound. It is most likely how it would sound to others. I've also recently learned that standing while studying helps retain information in the brain. Try it while going through this handbook, it may aid you in the future when you are ready and able to freely discuss your past with others.

If talking about your past with other people sounds frightening trust me I know! Don't worry no one will be forcing you to do that unless you are willing. I was eventually brought to that point in my life. I will tell you how I did it later on. I will give you some helpful tips that I used that were given to me.

WHAT CAN YOU DO WITH WHAT YOU WROTE?
Healthy healing methods I used

That was a lot of work that you did in chapter one. Feel good that you took the time and initiative to write down your thoughts, memories and feelings. Assuming you have repeatedly read your own writings hopefully you are getting closer to the stage of accepting what happened to you if you are not already there. That is the time when you will be able to deal with it, whatever it may be.

It's time to explore your options now. So, what can you do with everything you have written down so far on the exercise sheets? For organizational purposes and easy referencing keep those sheets together in this book and copy what you have written on them on separate sheets of paper. Write each story or page of notes on its own sheet of paper and keep in mind you may be writing a lot. Remember **getting it out** is the key!

I know you're thinking here we go again! Please try not to get discouraged from the repetition of this exercise as it will lead you into more hands on active ones. It will help your mind release unhealthy information and make room for you to learn to be at peace with your memories. Ideally you want to be in a place where you feel at ease. Get the harmful memories that are in your head in a place where you can be in control of them so the toxic memories will no longer be controlling you. That is where you want to be. You will notice the phrase 'getting it out' is repeated throughout this book many times as it is my desired healing proverb. It is the notion behind this book and is exactly what you are doing. In the end you will be getting out the bad and replacing it with some good things to help you heal.

The best thing about rewriting your exercise sheets is you get to revise them. Doing this gives you the opportunity to add more information, you can add an entirely new situation or a story that you feel you still need to recover from. I found that writing things out on paper was a much safer way to express my anger, hurt and pain. When you are writing something that really upsets or angers you, try writing it in bold black or red felt letters.

I just want to touch briefly on an upcoming chapter. During my older childhood days and up to and even far beyond my dad's suicide I occasionally wrote my feelings of anger down on paper. I know if I didn't do this, I'm pretty sure I would have exploded. I remember writing my thoughts and feelings down expressing my hatred and pain. I wrote hard on the paper with big felt pens. I would also cover my paper in evil sketches and doodles, but hey I was a kid right.

Reading them made me cry. In a weird way I guess I looked forward to it because it released a lot of my pressure. After I finished crying I would take the paper and crumple it up into little paper balls then throw them in a dresser drawer. When I got around to it I shredded them into tiny pieces and flushed them for fear of someone finding them. Although I wouldn't recommend this to others now of course that we have means of shredding and recycling.

My point in all that is to show an effective way of getting rid of your *garbage*. Carrying around bad thoughts of abuse or any negativity is *garbage* and will not benefit you in any way. At the time I didn't realize that what I was actually doing was saving my life. I can only imagine what my life would be like now if I were to have bottled it all up all those years. All along I was pulling out unwanted harmful feelings and thoughts from inside my head and throwing them away so to speak. Crying is such a great form of release. Don't you usually feel better afterward? I do. I would say it was every few months I did this method without even realizing it was a method! By doing so throughout my teen years I was able to accomplish two healthy healing releases all in one shot!

After my father had died I was left hanging with a lot of unsaid things which is usually how it ends up it seems. I was sixteen and due to the circumstances at that time surrounding the situation I was left behind with a lot of unanswered questions. Now that my dad was gone how was I going to discuss those with him? Well I figured what better way to get them to him but through the mail!

Yes, that's right you read that correctly. I was uneducated in any religious beliefs but one thing I did hear people say is that when you die you go to heaven. So that is exactly where I mailed my letters to, heaven. I stuffed my letters into envelopes and addressed them to 'Dad, Heaven'. I didn't see the point in adding postage so I never did. Into the big metal mailbox on the street corner they went. I kept this a secret for many years as I thought people would think I was crazy.

I did this quite often as it allowed me to un-bottle the things I needed to and at the same time it brought me closer to my dad. It helped me gradually deal with the reality of having him cut off from my life so suddenly. Writing and mailing my questions to my dad in heaven along with my thoughts and feelings I was having, eventually helped lead me into talking about it all. I don't want you to rush into it as that can be a giant leap out of our comfort zone for many. It does take time to learn how to do it for those who find that difficult. Hang in there it will come and the 'right' ear will be waiting for you.

Mailing your questions or expressions can be done for anyone in your life that has passed on. When I would close the door to the mailbox hopper I would feel a rush of peace go through me. I would feel weight lifted off my shoulders. As for mailing letters to heaven you can label the envelope and mail them to anywhere you like. Keep in mind if you put your name or address on the envelope or even inside the envelope it may find its way back to you! I did not have any returned to me so I choose to believe they reached my intended destination.

Father's day, his birthday and any other yearly occasions or holidays that arrived where I felt alone and separated is when I found myself in stores buying cards for my dad. I'd write them out just like the letters. I would also add how much I missed him. Yes after all he put me through I missed him. I continued mailing the cards into my twenties until I felt it was time to stop. I had reached a point where I felt my unanswered questions didn't matter as much anymore. I felt a satisfying distance between me and my traumas. I remember getting a tingly feeling rush all over me when I confidently entered my first stage of peacefulness within myself.

In this next topic I am going to share with you some more of my realities of growing up. This part of my life had a huge affect on me but fortunately my parents lives share only a portion of mine. Our lives are made up of chapters just like you see in a book, one section leads to the next. I have learned to close one chapter to open new ones. This doesn't mean you are not going to feel any hurt or pain from earlier chapters in your life when you take the time to remember them, it means your hurt and pain will be more manageable. You will have a better handle on how long you choose to feel that way.

There is always something that you can do to move on and not dwell. If you're a dweller get out of that rut as it is unhealthy. Dwellers are very clever people, they concoct many believable excuses so don't get caught up in that rut. Let it go. Take action, get the toxins out of you and continue moving onward.

UNHAPPY PARENTS
How this affected me

I grew up in a strict toxic environment. It was for the most part a controlled, unhappy and unloving household. My dad was a control freak who loved to raise his deep bellowing monotone voice. When he wasn't yelling it still came across that way to me. My dad worked and my mother stayed home with us kids. Sad but most of my memories to do with my parents together are horrible ones. Dad dictated to mom every move she made right down to when she smiled and didn't smile. My dad ordered my mom around telling her to get him this and get him that.

Dinner was served on the table precisely at five o'clock pm. My poor mother was so stressed out by my father's demands she quite often burned dinner rushing to meet that deadline to save

read to me by her after that.

My dad yelled at my mom all the time. He yelled enough times that when I think back it still echoes in my head. My dad repeatedly called her called her the 'R-word' and the 'M' word' in place of mentally challenged or special need. Back then the 'R' word wasn't as banned as it is now. He constantly threatened to divorce her in front of us kids. He would take me out to walk endlessly around the mall and tell me it was a way for him to get away from my mom. He repeatedly asked me who I would want to live with. I hated it. They had very deep marital issues my mom should thank her lucky stars that she was set free from that but I don't think she sees it the way I do. Her actions have shown otherwise.

My mom carried a clipboard around that had my name along with my sisters names at the top of nicely penned in columns. The clipboard was used to make notes when we misbehaved. Give me a break! I hated that thing! I don't think I need to say whose idea was behind that hey. This way my dad didn't have to talk much to my mom, he could just read it and punish us according to her point form notes.

I know my dad coerced her into ranking our bedrooms on the clipboard weekly too. It was loads of fun in our house. We were timed and recorded on how long we spent in the bathtub. I mean seriously, writing down that I wouldn't get out of the bathtub when ordered to, Get real! What kid jumps out when they are asked to? My daughter never did. This would be the after dinner bath times and nothing to do with us needing to rush out the door. We were always hurried. I look back and laugh at all the wasted energy and time that was put into that clipboard! It was all about control.

I was scared to breath in our house with fear that I was using too much air or not enough who knows! Thank God I've always had a sense of humor it greatly helped me keep my sanity.

Having to ask to go into the fridge or cupboard before getting a drink or a snack even in my teen years wasn't as punishable as the rest of the rules. When I broke those rules I would generally just get yelled at and reminded to ask first. If it were my dad that caught me though, when he felt like it he would make me wait a certain amount of time before making me ask again to re-enter the fridge or cupboard with permission. I remember having to ask my dad even as a teen at fifteen for permission to use the bathroom. Sounds funny now I know, wasn't funny at all living it. And yes, we had to raise our hands to get my dad's attention before we told we could speak."Yes, Janet?" He would reply as if he didn't know what jumping around and holding my crotch meant!

My dad would slack off sometimes but it wouldn't take him long to remember he had to keep us in line. My mom followed the majority of his rules. I know she did her best in relaxing on a few of them while he was at work. It all depended on her mood; she was pretty easy to read. When I reached the age of thirteen I could start to see that she didn't agree with his rules and that she was just enforcing them out of fear of my father. He never wanted her opinion on anything so she didn't have a say. I spent a lot of time wondering if the reason she rarely talked to us kids was because we were a part of him and a part of the whole negative picture that she so obviously hated.

For me it was understandable but hard to swallow. I remember hiding in my room many times when my dad would lose his temper. I recall one frightening night back when I was really young, while we were driving in the family car my parents got into a fight or an argument. My mom demanded my dad to let her out of the car so he did. I was shocked that she actually got out! It was dark and rainy and we were quite far from home. I remember him yelling at her as she was slamming the door behind her. I was scared and worried she wasn't going to come back.

She left us kids in the back seat. We were stuck having to ride with my dad and listen to him go on and on about how bad of a person he thought she was and how everything was her fault. He scared me, I knew it wasn't true. I felt sorry for her but I was also angry that she up and left us. Thank goodness she came back after all. From what I remember she made her own way home as dad wouldn't have left us kids alone and I don't remember going back for her. I have a faint recollection of her coming in the door late on that rainy night.

I shamefully remember using all my dad's accusations and other insults against my mom as ammo in retaliation when I wouldn't get my own way back when I was a teen. I learned it was okay. I carried that behavior of mine throughout my life with boyfriends. One day I looked in a mirror and realized that I didn't like being this way at all. As an adult I didn't figure out why I was behaving that way until I started reflecting on my past. All of a sudden it clicked, "I've turned into my dad!" I thought.

I try to remember that each circumstance I am in is just the situation at that particular moment in time and that things change beyond our control. It's a matter of waiting it out and using patience to the best of your ability. That may take all the strength you have within you. Things do change stay positive. I have always held onto hope and I believe it is very important to do so!

I went into my room alone one day and wrote down as many of the good and bad things I could come up with about my mom and dad. Well you know which one outweighed the other. I then wrote down all the ways I would like to treat other people down one column and how I want to be treated down the column next to it. I started slowly putting those actions and words into place. I still to this day struggle with it but I continue to practice it the best I can.

EXERCISE SHEET: Use separate sheets of paper or a journal style book. It helps to record the applicable chapter names along with the relevant page numbers from this book on each of your writings for easy reference later.

Record your story: How you relate, situations, agendas, notes, thoughts & anything else related to this chapter. Use paragraph writing, point form or whatever you're comfortable with. Think back & take a deep breath! Now take some time to read over what you wrote.

_____

_____

_____

_____

_____

_____

_____

_____

_____

_____

_____

_____

_____

_____

_____

_____

_____

_____

_____

E.R.A.S.E.D. = Easy Real Action Spiritual Exercises Deliver:
Erase the chains of abuse that bind you using EASY made, REAL life, ACTION steps with SPIRITUAL outlook & hands on EXERCISES that DELIVER!

WHEN OUR PARENTS ABUSIVE PASTS
ARE PUT ONTO US
Always feeling obligated to understand and justify their actions

My dad was adopted at birth and very bitter about it. He had told me a few times that he was physically abused by his adopted father. I remember him telling me a story about when his father had asked him which music record was his favorite, my dad showed him which one it was and when he did his dad grabbed it and broke it up into small pieces. My dad told me how much he hated him for that. Understandably he never let go of that abusive moment. Every time I would hear the song "White Christmas" my dad would say something about that story. I was told this story over and over throughout my childhood. Each time it would remind me that I should feel lucky that he wasn't doing that to my stuff. My dad trained us kids never to let anyone know he was adopted because it embarrassed him. That story is the only one I was told or remember which validated his bitterness.

On top of being bitter my dad was also extremely atheist. He would not allow us to mention God or even the word bible in our house. My dad viewed the world with very negative eyes. He tried hard to get me to agree with his opinions and ideas by brainwashing rubbish into me. I do remember thinking a lot like him for years until I came to realize there are always two sides of every story. I was under the impression all families were like this. I felt he tried to poison my mind. He had deep issues. He made me so miserable and negative that it took almost my lifetime to change that.

One of my reasons for changing the way I think is because I questioned why I was put on this earth? It didn't make sense to me to think I was brought into life to be miserable when I felt just the opposite. As a child I played happily alone with my imaginary friend, it was a joyful escape that I wish I could have felt all of the time. It was with determination that I brought that same feeling I had in fantasy to my reality, it may be over thirty years later but I did it! I feel free and joyful.

I wish I knew back then what I know now that's for sure. I chose this style of book as a way to share information from my memories to help another. I relive my life whether I want to or not by doing this, if I can benefit a reader in any way then it is well worth it for me. It gives me great happiness to know my purpose is something so loving and caring. It's a blessing that these stories along with tidbits of advice from my life's book will help other people speed up their healing process. Hopefully it will happen in a shorter period of time than mine took.

I guess I should get back to my past. I tend to get off track when I have so much in my head to share. Forgive me. Well now you know my dad's character let me tell you a bit about my mother.

My mom was the second eldest of six kids. She quit school in a very early grade . Unhappy with her life growing up for many different reasons, she carried around a lot of bitterness and hatred. Wanting to get away from it all she ended up abandoning her family late in her teens for very personal reasons of her own. She moved to the other side of the country where my dad was from, married him and had us kids with the hope of a brighter future. It wasn't long before she came to know that this change in her life was really just the beginning of a new chapter of much more unhappiness to come.

It was hard growing up around my mom. She did not show affection or closeness or even force a smile to resemble one. That was understandable as it was obvious she felt beaten down. Sometime we let others problems become our own when we are conditioned to have certain beliefs or are unaware of a way out. It affected her whole outlook on life. My mom and I clash most times, our two worlds collide. It's difficult when one can see the bright or positive side of things and the other person can't.

My mom may have had a chance to change her life and her actions if only she knew to focus on how she wanted to be treated. Instead of dwelling on how she was being treated many things may have been different for her and our family. That, I honestly believe is the key to a healthy life ahead with or without abuse put on us. Easier said than done, oh I know!

I love this positive affirmation, "I only think good thoughts, speak good things and I try to see the good in everyone and in everything." Say this enough and you begin to brainwash yourself in a good way! Give it a shot. Eventually you will be able to only think and speak good thoughts for the most part. When you are in the company of another person behaving or speaking negatively you will be able to brush it off easier. Parents are extremely influential on children and if yours or any person in your life is anything like mine you will need this coat of amour!

I try my best everyday not to let other people's emotions or words affect my mood which in turn helps block out the negative. I make every conscious effort to flip my mood around as quickly as I can regardless of how bad the situation may be. I affirm this regularly, "I am a great person and I am going to be happy even when they are not!" It works for me, I hope it works for you.

EXERCISE SHEET: Use separate sheets of paper or a journal style book. It helps to record the applicable chapter names along with the relevant page numbers from this book on each of your writings for easy reference later.

Record your story: How you relate, situations, agendas, notes, thoughts & anything else related to this chapter. Use paragraph writing, point form or whatever you're comfortable with. Think back & take a deep breath! Now take some time to read over what you wrote.

_____

_____

_____

_____

_____

_____

_____

_____

_____

_____

_____

_____

_____

_____

_____

_____

_____

_____

_____

_____

_____

E.R.A.S.E.D. = Easy Real Action Spiritual Exercises Deliver:
Erase the chains of abuse that bind you using EASY made, REAL life, ACTION steps with SPIRITUAL outlook & hands on EXERCISES that DELIVER!

BELIEVING IT
Hard to do but very important we do it!

Believe! You are now at the point where you are able to start remembering and acknowledging different types of abuse you endured. You also have some new tips to help you with that stage in your life. I laid it out in step form to make it easier for you to follow and to be able to open up and relate to the content of this handbook. I have given you simplified steps to help get you on your way.

It would be a good idea to get a lined notebook of some sort to provide as your journal while you are going through each chapter. The first part of your notebook pages can be used to write out everything you can possibly remember. Think back to things that have happened to you in a negative or harmful way from your early childhood through to now.

It may be best to get a notebook with loose leaf or tear away pages so you can mail your expressions or crumple them up and throw them away as I discussed earlier. This practice may take you some time depending on your life's history and how much you remember or are willing to deal with at this time. My thoughts on that are get as much out as possible no matter how awkward it may be and feel to you. Your objective is to be successful in reaching your personal goal.

I mean a few things behind saying 'Believing it'. You must *believe* you have made the right decision in wanting change to your life. You must *believe* what you write on your exercise sheets to be factual that it did happen to you. You must *believe* you deserve to heal and *believe* you can be in control of your own joy and inner peace. You must also *believe* that you are worth it. Say out loud, "I am worth it!" Finally you must *believe* you can reach your goal. Say out loud, "I will reach my goal!" I *believe* you can!

Chapter Three –Take Control &Talk
About it

MY TEENAGE YEARS
Molded by Abuse

Yes it's true. I was an unruly and rebellious teenager, common story of a lot of kids in their adolescence years. Now as an adult looking back on my life I can clearly see what I was trying to accomplish during those years. Reflecting back on my youth from when I was about fourteen to seventeen years old it seemed as if those years really dragged on. I spent that time trying to figure out who I was as an individual. Sound familiar? I changed my personality, my lingo and style from week to week all with a goal of proving my independence. I wanted to get noticed and to feel special again. I went looking in all the wrong places.

In a way I guess I was wanting to get caught up on all the years I had lost spent in my shy shell. I did get noticed but not at all how I wanted to. I broke out of my shell at little too abruptly and tried being as social as I knew how. When I was fourteen a friend and I started hanging out with older guys...I mean men. They worked on the local amusement rides whenever they came to town. We had a blast with them off and on for many years. Most of them were great people to party with until it all came to an end when I was date raped by one of them shortly after I turned sixteen.

The fun was over. This gave me another reason to hate men even more than I already had. My friend and I stopped going to the fairs. I was used to being let down in that way, I expected it. Being resilient to it I brushed the severity of it off as just a bad experience. After all I had agreed to date him is what I thought. In fact that was something like our fourth date or time we hung out together. That was the night I learned that *no* meant *yes* to some guys.

Even though I pretty much brushed it off, I still went into a short lived gloominess that I managed to hide from others. I was used to keeping things to myself. I didn't feel worthy enough to think somebody else would have really cared. My worse fear was having it blamed on me. It was my sixteenth year and from that moment it was only a few weeks later that my history with my dad would be exposed to everyone. Once again, you will read about that further on in the book.

Deep down I was upset and angry to have been violated like that. I was mad at myself as I felt responsible and guilty for drinking alcohol with a twenty year old that I hardly knew. I know that is no excuse for his actions, I wish I knew that at the time. He had no right to take away something that I valued one day to be special. The fact is it happened and as disappointing as it was, I made my own justifications of it and moved on.

Over time I did end up confiding in a few people and was taken off guard by their understanding and empathy. That is something I would have never expected from anyone in a million years. One of my friends was upset that I didn't report it to the police. I understand why but I told her I wanted to forget about it so that it would go away. I eventually buried it but my friends words still ate at me because I knew she was right. There are some things people shouldn't get away with and if I could go back in time of course I would do the right thing.

For the next while I did my best to ensure I was always in the presence of friends from then on to avoid similar situations. My frequent method of transportation was hitchhiking. The majority of the time I had a friend or two with me as hitchhiking terrified me but of course I was too cool to show it. After all it was free, fast and convenient way to get around from city to city, so foolishly I risked my life. Being picked up by random strangers along the way I ended up in a few scary vehicles with some pretty shady people.

I think back to that now and wonder what the heck I was doing? Especially being a female with the kind of past I had you would think I'd be forewarned? Not the case. I get freaked out now thinking about some of my rides where I had held the door release handle just in case. There were a few times where I was so scared I just pointed out a random home and told the driver it was where I lived, I was dropped off on unfamiliar streets often. I still can't believe I put myself in those situations and lived to tell about them. I guess I figured I was invincible like teens do at that age. Crazy! I thank my lucky stars that I'm still here to talk about it.

I grew up in a small town outside the big city of Vancouver. I wasn't too familiar with the city layout much but that didn't stop me from hanging out downtown on the streets at night when I was fourteen and fifteen years old. I would be with a girlfriend of mine so it was okay, so I thought. My girlfriend and I would meet strangers from time to time and sometimes end up at parties where we knew absolutely nobody. Going to parties where we didn't know anyone really wasn't a big deal to me. I mean, "What's the worst that could happen?" I remember thinking.

Well I was wrong. On our way home from the big city one night we ended up at a house party. We were kind of leery to go in as it sounded pretty rowdy but we entered the house anyways. There were a couple people we thought we recognized but other than that we really didn't know anybody. It looked like everyone at the party was well over twenty five possibly into their mid thirties. Sitting on the couch drinking the beer they gave us we could hear a group of males hollering from upstairs over top of the loud music.

I was accustomed to my girlfriends' promiscuous ways so it really didn't faze me too much to watch her disappear up the stairs with a couple guys. I don't think my friend was prepared for what was happening up there. From downstairs where I was I could over hear conversations between some of the other people at the party. I heard them talk about a group of guys upstairs that were 'gang banging' some girls.

Their discussions very much corresponded with all the yelling and screaming that I could hear coming from up there, which scared me. It didn't seem as if anyone else was too concerned with it though, so I tried to ignore it by minding my own business.

I wondered around the house a bit and found a way out to the back porch through the kitchen. I perched myself on a ledge of the deck. It wasn't too long before a drunk and obnoxious man in his thirties came to sit with me. He was loud and pushy. My mind was on my friend as I was eager to be on our way. Each time he tried grabbing my hand I would pull it back and shy away. I was so nervous. Feeling awkward I pulled away every time he made a pass yet I didn't move away from him. I wanted to move, I really did. I beat myself up for many years afterward for not having enough courage do so.

I lived with a lot of shame for so long over my reactions. I couldn't get these questions out of my head, "Why wouldn't I just remove myself? What's wrong with me?" I had real difficulties turning men down when they made passes at me even in dangerous situations. Periodically this happened until I was well into my thirties!.

He became annoyed with me. He forcibly grabbed my hand and yanked it over to his crotch where he made me rub him for his pleasure. He wouldn't let go. I swore at him and tried forcing my hand out of his clutches! He laughed and slurred some words at me along these lines, "Oh, come on what's your problem your friend likes it." I wanted to puke. I had to get out of that house! I was terrified and didn't know where my friend was or what she was doing. I was panicking trying to figure out how I was going to get away from him and every thought I had more than frightened me.

I managed to get away finally when all of a sudden through the doorway I could see my friend running like mad out the front door! The creep next to me noticed her escaping. He startled me when he yelled something out and took off running into to the house after her. That was my get away opportunity. I ran down the steps of the back porch to the dark alley way, scared shitless that someone would follow me I just kept running. Looking over my shoulder behind me every few seconds it didn't appear as if there was anyone chasing me. I was somewhat familiar with my surroundings but still felt alot of fear as I wondered around alone out there that late at night, I wasn't as brave as I thought I was after all.

I wasn't sure if I would see my friend again that night or not, but I did. We ran into each other on a nearby street. She was also cold and visibly shaken. She talked a mile a minute about what the men were trying to do to her. She fought her way out and managed to get away after a long battle. I was so happy to see her yet so mad at her too. I felt at the time it was all her fault for going upstairs with those awful guys in the first place. I didn't want to leave the party without her so I too was trapped. Later I realized it wasn't really all her fault as we both had no business being there in the first place. We were just asking for trouble and that is exactly what we got.

Being that we were pretty far away from home with no money

we did what we had always done and hitchhiked back. So once again we made that stupid move. All the way home I kept thinking about how my dad was going to kill me if he finds any of this out. We had our driver drop us off far enough away from home so not to get caught in a strange car.

Back in the eighties kids didn't have cell phones and any contact with their parents was very limited, this made it pretty easy to make up stories of why you were late. Our lie about how we lost our money, missed the bus and had to walk home pulled it off for us once again.

As I write this book I have only recently told one woman about how I would freeze in the presence of a man making unwelcomed moves on me and how I reacted feeling to ashamed to share it with anyone. I always felt alone on this until I spoke with a friend not all that long ago about her sexual abuse experiences, I was surprised to hear that many of her reactions to men were similar to mine.

While conversing through email back and forth she opened up and told me her own story. Still feeling ashamed of myself I didn't pipe up right away and tell her that I could relate to her. I waited and read her message as she typed out all she had to say first. I spent the whole time debating telling her or not which made me feel like a pretty crappy friend. I mean why wouldn't I want to share my experience with her to let her know she is not alone. Debating that made me feel even guiltier than I already had.

I'm glad my heart ended up getting the best of me. With a sick knot feeling in my stomach I braced myself as I told her that I used to react the same way. I spent years feeling that something was very wrong with me because I knew my reactions were not proper. She agreed saying she felt the same as I did.

It was nice to finally talk to someone about it. She brought it up at that time because in just this past little while she had to go through it again with a man she knew in a restaurant and at the bus stop later on. Her reaction to his passes really upset her. Unlike normal men and women where light flirtation is acceptable, he was not one of them. We like to call these guys 'dangerous' or 'predators'. They deliberately go past the point of a little natural flirtation until it becomes inappropriately intense and unacceptable flirting. We pick up on the negative vibes from them and freeze!

We talked about it and tried to make sense of it by coming up with different justifications for our actions. One thing my friend and I have in common is that we were both sexually abused when we were younger. We feel that because we were abused in such a way we learned not to speak up for ourselves. We had troubles seeing the point of no return, meaning we would end up waiting too long to the point the guy would be thinking it was okay. When we allowed it to get that far we had to struggle our way out. We were always afraid and powerless. It's like the silent scream, you're so afraid you can't cry out.

I've watched other females stand up for themselves against men making them back off right away! I personally could not do that at all untll I had played over in my head several times how I was going to do it and what I was going to say. Once I got the courage up, out of nowhere and with bad timing I would blurt something out. This would bring everything that was happening to a sudden halt sending mixed messages to the guy who would often get nasty and retaliate in anger. Another mental obstacle for the both of us was that we didn't want to be perceived by the guy as 'not nice'. Therefore it would take us awhile to get up the guts to do anything about it, even though we would be in a state of panic the whole time.

Many times I remember thinking, "Oh my God, I did it again." Feeling responsible for leading them on is where the shame kicked in. Hopefully this was the last time she has to struggle with this knowing now she has my support. I myself put an end to it about ten years ago, I got angry enough at myself and risking feeling like a fool inside I spoke up sooner than I normally would have and it worked. If I were to be in that kind of situation now I know I would still feel extremely awkward and uncomfortable but I'm confident I would speak up to save making things worse. If it is uninvited and against your will get it over with right away, there's really no point in waiting it out.

There were many times through my ignorance and stupidity that I found myself in a spot where I did not think I was going be okay. I did dangerous things like jumping into the back of trucks with strangers. One night these guys drove us up a mountain four wheeling and also took us into the bushed area under the main city bridge to party with them. Once again we were in our young teenage years while they were at least a few years older maybe into their twenties.

We hung out with these guys drinking their beer under the dark starlit sky until we were no longer feeling comfortable and felt we had enough party time. When we asked to be taken home because it was getting late we were both surprised when one of them yelled no at us.

That threw us for a loop! We hadn't planned on that happening so once again I put myself in a position where I didn't know what to do. We didn't know if they were going to sexually assault us or what they had in mind. Fear and panic set in. My girlfriend and I chatted a bit and figured the only thing we could do was to nervously wait it out we didn't have much other choice. We pretended to join in on their fun so not to cause a big scene. We were hoping the guys wouldn't get too carried away with their drinking for we knew we were going to be driving back with them.

After quite some time the group of them decided they had enough and it was time to go. They caused no harm to us, we were very fortunate since on the way back we held our breaths and prayed to make it home alive. Stupid.

Our parents were pretty easy to read, we had them totally figured out. We were rarely caught on anything. The feelings of fear I went through didn't stop me at all so I kept doing things like this over and over until it was no longer exciting to me. Looking back on the things I have done I can't help but be grateful that the novelty wore off when it did as I may not be here today if it didn't.

When I look back at my mischievous ways it was all just meant to have fun and to do what I wanted. That was to be cool and get some attention. In fact what it turned out to be was my selfish need to satisfy my own wants without caring about me or the affects that it may have on others in my life.

As a mother of a beautiful teenage daughter now, I can only imagine what my families concerns would have been if they knew how I conducted myself. They would have been devastated to find out the worst had happened to me. That never occurred to me at the time I guess because I was young. I found it hard to believe that my dad cared about what happened to me anyways, my actions showed that. Why would I care about myself when I felt that no one else did is pretty much what I had in my head at that time.

How could I believe my parent could even really care about me when he was abusing me? Coming from teenage eyes or not my dad was overboard strict as well. It didn't end with the sexual abuse he also dished out quite a bit of mental abuse on top of it all. The lengths of my punishments were unrealistic as they weren't suitable for my 'bad' behavior. Grounding me to my room for weeks on end to a couple months at a time for talking back, not doing homework on time or not eating all of my dinner and such just angered me more. What was I to learn from that? Chatting one on one was not his style.

I didn't see his logic at all especially when I was caught drunk around fourteen years old, dad grounded me for one week and let me off early because he thought my night I spent puking was punishment enough. I tried asking him why he was so harsh with the 'small things' and not so harsh when it came to the 'bigger things' but he felt my questioning was out of line so I never did get an answer.

I just couldn't understand my dad. Taking this memory for example, frequently he would find not so pleasant articles in the newspaper then make me read them. That's all fine and dandy except for the fact they were all stories of violence and sexual assault against females. He would point them out, even cut them out and tell me to read them in hopes to prevent me from falling into the same traps as those women. It was as if he had never done anything like that to me, like I wouldn't take notice. I didn't get that? A very strange way for someone to show they care.

Growing up I saw it all as attacks against me. It wasn't until I was older when I learned through the knowledge of others that it was all his problem and not me at all. Learning and believing this set me on my path to valuing my own well being for a change.

I was cultured into not having respect for family in general by my dad's own experiences and beliefs of it. To me family means that each member has an important role where their thoughts and opinions are valued, not one person ruling the roost. Recalling his behavior and words in reference to any of our family gatherings over the years certainly showed me that family was not of much importance. It just taught me to have little respect for mine or anyone else's for that matter.

As I brought up earlier, one major issue my dad had that really bothered him was that he was adopted. He talked about it so negatively so often that it showed how much he really resented it. Sadly I grew up hearing about my extended family being referred to as our 'Fake Family'. Whenever I mentioned anything at all to do with any one of them he would be sure to remind me that they were not related through blood. This always left me confused as I was too young to understand how he felt at the time.

There was this one time I was about ten or eleven years old, I was visiting my grandparents at their home when I was out of line for whatever reason and my nana tried to discipline me. In a mouthy rebellious tone I yelled back at her telling her that she couldn't tell me what to do because she was a fake adopted grandma and not a real one.

What a shocker it was for me to watch her burst out in tears! I honestly expected her to back off agreeing with me, if I wasn't confused before that I sure was then. I stood there with my mouth hanging open wondering what the heck she was crying about. I even remember thinking, "wow, maybe she didn't know?" I didn't know how to feel. I felt bad for upsetting her but at the same time I was also very mad feeling like I was forced to do it. I read this now shaking my head, it makes me want to cry just thinking about it. She wanted to know where I got that information from so I told her that dad [her son] told me so. I was embarrassed. I remember feeling a horrible resentment toward my dad at that moment for causing it.

My respect for family only got worse from that point and I am far from proud of it. Due to my shame of it I actually considered not putting this following story in here. However, I am human and we all make mistakes that can't be changed. This is not to say we can't do our best to prevent them from happening again, so here goes.

Further into my teen years I proved I had little or no respect for adults or family, I was a horrible nasty teenager. At home I was not only very abusive verbally but sometimes physically to my mom. While dad was at work I walked all over her and told her off. I suppose I lost respect for her years ago as a child. When I expected her to protect and defend me she didn't do her best in my opinion and I managed to subconsciously carry a grudge. I don't believe in blaming someone else for our own actions but sadly I do feel that was the root of it all. After many discussions in counseling and soul searching, that was one of the things that kept resurfacing. I've learned to accept the fact she told me once that she did not know that the abuse was happening and I've left it at that because she may have very well believed my dad.

I remember a couple of times when my mom tried to stop me from leaving the house while I was grounded while my dad was at work, normally she would just let me leave to save a fight but these times she tried to enforce my grounding herself. Out of nowhere she told me I couldn't go out and argued with me about it. I couldn't help but think, "How dare she!" I lost control of my temper and hauled off and hit her with and without an objects.

At the time I justified my disgusting, atrocious poor behavior by thinking, "Well, I learned from the best having a wooden spoon broken across my face and being slammed up against a wall in front of my best friend taught me well." After I hit my mom I felt bad but not for long. I quickly turned it into feelings of control and justified it as her punishment. My mom was abused by my father and was completely under his control in every way. I know I lashed out at her over things that were irrelevant to the current situation but sadly that's the way it usually goes.

I know it was absolutely horrible what I did, but I did it. I have thought about it but have never dwelled on it nor brought it to the surface until now. My relationship with my mom was never a close one like a mother with her daughter should be. Living in the same house together was in more of a roommate type of setting. We don't talk about family matters especially ones in the past, which is the way it has always been with her. Thus why writing this out is a great exercise for me as well.

I know I am truly sorry and I know she is too and that is what matters to me. Personally in this type of situation I can only ask for forgiveness from God and find the same within myself now. I have accepted what happened and have moved on and have let go. I can only hope and pray my mom does the same one day. My mom hangs onto the not so good things she has done as well as the terrible things others have done to her in the past. It saddens me. Watching and listening to her I know it is her past troubles that still haunt her.

Life contains many chapters and it is totally your choice to decide which ones to keep open or not. Personally I'd much rather choose the chapters that bring on good feelings than bad, wouldn't you? Everyone handles life differently that is true, but what is also true is that a lot of people let excuses rule their life because it's easier. That's human nature. I have always been a very determined person when I set my mind to doing something, I do it. This makes it very difficult for me to watch other people give in to the chains that bind them.

Our family troubles have rarely if at all ever been talked about amongst ourselves. We seem to just brush everything to do with our feelings or thoughts pertaining to our family matters under the rug. I find it to be an awkward situation, it's like no one has taught us how to show ourselves to each other. A lot of blame, anger and bitterness over the years has shut us up I guess. It was even harder when I shared a house with my mom, for many years I watched her as she drank herself into a wobbly mess every night because of the demons she chooses not to let go of.

All the hate I carried during my childhood years didn't help me much through school at all either. It didn't matter how hard the teachers tried, I didn't care what they had to say. Regardless of the importance of what they wanted to get across to me, in my mind adults were adults and I had no respect for any of them. I felt at the time they were cruel people making my life miserable. My mind wondered so much while I was in class that it left school entirely, I just didn't care less.

More adults just trying to control me, was the only way I could see it. I could not see any benefit other than an easy way to make friends and mingle. My mind was so preoccupied that I had difficulty finding any particular school subject of interest tome no matter how hard I tried. I figured with the life I was living there was absolutely nothing in school worth listening to that would help me through these times. I couldn't figure out why they would force me to sit down and read through a social studies book or dissect a sheep's eyeball? I had so many more questions about life going on that would actually have made a difference to me. "How boring, who needs math?" I thought.

Well, I became an adult and as luck would have it I found myself working in the financial industry for over twenty years! For the most part I really enjoyed that job, it had many ongoing changes keeping it fresh. I like to learn something new each day, it helps to keep us young and our brains active as we grow older. One thing I did learn from working there was that math which I truly despised definitely came in handy! As for dissecting sheep's eyeballs that's another story.

In high school my grades were average for the most part. At home my grades were rewarded with money. If I received low grades I was punished by being grounded for extensively long periods. I did not find that motivating or supportive at all. I quit school at sixteen years old in grade ten immediately after my dad died. He was the one who enforced us kids to go to school so as soon as he was gone, so was I.

Being a high school dropout who ended up with such a great career I frequently wondered if I 'fluked' out or if was I being guided by God? Whichever it may be I was fortunate to have had met great people that were willing to give me the chance. That doesn't always happen for everyone and I am ever so thankful. I was given a job to do with a lot of skill learning opportunities and I know that without this I may have led a very different and difficult adult life.

I was tremendously lucky when I landed that job in the finance world at age twenty as it helped carry me through the next couple decades. It wasn't until recently in the past couple of years a new door opened for me. When another company that I was working for shut down, shortly afterward I found myself enrolled back in school at the age of forty two! I graduated with honors at the age of forty three. It amazed me when I saw my report cards and my grade twelve transcript reflecting straight A's.

Twenty seven years later shows it's never too late. If I could do it all over again I would have stuck it out through high school the first chance I had. It may have opened even better doors of opportunity for me where I could have landed a lifelong career at doing something I had a passion for. My suggestion from my experiences is no matter how hard it is to get through school just do it. Put your mind into the short time it really takes during your life to complete it. Once it's done, it's done.

The reality is that the first initial excitement of it when I quit school as a teen lasted maybe a few weeks. It didn't take long before I was alone and bored! All my friends were still in school so it didn't turn out to be as cool as I thought or hoped it would be. One reason I left was because I felt I had no other choice. My dad was no longer in my life enforcing the importance of going to school making it difficult for me to keep at it. I had other reasons for quitting as well but I will talk about that in the next chapter. There really is no excuse I guess but it is my reality. The shame I felt for being a school dropout and the lifelong career possibilities I may have missed out on I'm sure was alot harder to deal with than getting through each grade at the time when I should have.

EXERCISE SHEET: Use separate sheets of paper or a journal style book. It helps to record the applicable chapter names along with the relevant page numbers from this book on each of your writings for easy reference later.

Record your story: How you relate, situations, agendas, notes, thoughts & anything else related to this chapter. Use paragraph writing, point form or whatever you're comfortable with. Think back & take a deep breath! Now take some time to read over what you wrote.

_____

_____

_____

_____

_____

_____

_____

_____

_____

_____

_____

_____

_____

_____

_____

_____

_____

_____

_____

_____

_____

E.R.A.S.E.D. = Easy Real Action Spiritual Exercises Deliver:
Erase the chains of abuse that bind you using EASY made, REAL life, ACTION steps with SPIRITUAL outlook & hands on EXERCISES that DELIVER!

WHEN PARENTS DON'T COMMUNICATE POSITIVELY
The impact it can have

It breaks my heart to know that I am not alone on this topic. It saddens me to know that many children have to live through a lot of negative communication daily in their home life. It's difficult for the kids not to pick up the same traits especially when it is coming from their parents. Monkey see, monkey do is what often happens. It is very overwhelming for kids especially that they do not comprehend it.

Children are very in tune with their surrounding environments they don't need to see things happen because they can feel it or sense it in some way. As an adult caught up in someone else's negative vibes can be easier to justify your feelings of what is happening, how can a child do that when they don't understand what is going on? I hardly find that fair seeing that it can do a lot of mental damage on kids as well.

Parents or guardians are not always aware of how negatively powerful their verbal or non verbal expressions are. From my past experiences of being surrounded by non verbal silence everyday generating from both my parents was just as bad. These unconstructive communications are forced upon children as they have no control over it. Anyone that is exposed to the tensions coming from people fighting or ignoring each other is difficult to be around, now imagine how a child feels when it's happening.

This negative atmosphere greatly contributes in the 'shaping' or 'molding' of the child as they grow. Children are not developed enough to *choose* how they will feel and sadly in some cases they learn to cope by building thick and invisible walls to protect them. I built walls. My walls were so thick at one point I feared I was going to be lost behind them forever.

I grew up with parents who were extremely cold to each other, no show of 'normal' love or affection at all. This left me feeling uneasy and unsecure when I was in the same room as them. Even when all five of us in the family would be sitting together in the same room for long periods of time, it would be quiet. Much tension was always felt. It would get so quiet for so long that when someone did speak it would startle me. My mom didn't speak much and I knew she was always mad at dad. Not the best impression to give your child.

As a parent myself I guess I can't be too judgmental for I am guilty of falling in that trap from time to time. It is so easy to do in the heat of the moment when we are consumed by ourselves and not focused on our children. I feel it has similar adverse affects on children no different than verbal communication has on them through yelling, screaming and profanity. Having one parent yell at the other one while the other parent sits alone cringing with no verbal retaliation is not a two way street. Usually communication has more than one participant doesn't it?

Body language and physical gestures are another part of non verbal communication. I don't know if my parents realized that their bad vibes were so noticeably strong that they could be felt down the hall and into the next room over! I quiver when I think about how I felt when I was in the same room as them, I was used to clenching my fists and holding my breath around my mom and dad. I would stare at them cockeyed wondering what was going on in their heads, never knowing when something may boil over is a very stressful feeling.

My dad was always mad at my mom and my mom in turn was always mad at my dad. It came across to me throughout my young years that they hated each other, I know hate is a strong word to use but it fits. Granted, my father had personal issues with his own mental health which I know my mother tolerated. She really didn't have much independence in her life to do otherwise. From my understanding of the past or that generation at that time, our household wasn't the only one that was ran like that.

When I talk about communicating positively I am not just referring to orally talking. Too many relationships are comfortable where some folks actually become a part of the furniture. These couples lack outward expression of affection portraying no sense of partnership or even companionship. How are children suppose to learn about love or expressing their thoughts and feelings in their own future? My parents were in this boat too. They were two people who were extremely unloving, unfriendly, negative, non-conversational and non-partner like to each other.

Family time in the living room for the most part was nothing less than ice cold. With dad in his favorite green velvety chair and mom in her favorite matching chair my two sisters and I would sit upright, neat and tidy just a few feet away. As normal routine would have it we would all be seated quietly gazing at the shows dad wanted to watch on the television. Not mom though, she was too busy with 'zoning out' of her over controlled environment by keeping busy with jig-saw puzzles.

My dad would force us to sit perfectly centered in the middle of each of the cushions on the adjacent sofa or chesterfield as it was called. We were made to wear only clean pajamas and no day clothes on this piece of new furniture. Dad definitely feared we may dirty the newly bought gold-brownish colored sofa, the one with the Wild West wagon and country scene imprinted in the material.

Every now and then I would forget mom was even in the room as she was so quiet. I was aware that she knew it was best not to talk for when she did my dad often took what she said the wrong way. He would start a fight with her until she would cry. I would then nervously watch as she walked out of the room crying on her way up the stairs to go to bed. Then his fun with me would start if the night was right for him.

Dinnertime was not much different in our house than the evening time really, it was just as horrible but more vocal. I love having dinner with my daughter Nikayla when I can, it brings us closer together. It gives me pure joy to watch her in excitement as she tells me some of her daily adventures, I get to find out what is going on in her life and most importantly it shows her how much I care about her and her life. I guess everyone is different and my dad proved that.

Growing up family dinnertime was regulated with a lot of rules. As I mentioned earlier dinner would typically be served right at five o'clock p.m. when my dad got home from work which I guess was pretty normal standards for most families back then. After my dad and both my younger sisters and I were seated, mom would then be okayed join us.

During this time my dad would hold boring discussions with us regarding whatever hot topic he had read in the newspaper or saw on a news broadcast on the television. The topics usually had something to do with missing kids or women or violence against them in one way or another as I said before. A long and tiresome lecture would follow in between his bites of food.

I remember only being allowed to answer him or even talk at all when he allowed. I do remember his most popular constant reminders, "Slow down you're not going to the races!" or "You talked with your mouth full your grounded for a week!" He would stick to his guns on those decisions there were no threats, he wasn't much for joking.

That of course was a bit different than how he would talk to my mom. This was more of how he would speak to her, "What did you do all day sit on your butt do puzzles and drink coffee while I worked for twelve hours?" and "Get me another plate of food please." Then he would complain if the meal was cold or burned. I always chuckled to myself when I heard my dad trying to come across as polite, talk about mixed messages.

So there you have it, a regular Tuesday night at the Kingsley's dinner table with no positive chatter whatsoever. This kind of thing happened daily and when added to the ice cold silence in our living room during the evenings, I could never tell when it was okay or safe to talk to anyone.

Being a sexually abused and extremely shy kid this negative non-communication really did a number on me. It hid who I really was, I wasn't allowed to be me. Before others imposed their problems on me I believe I was an extroverted, happy, caring and fun loving girl.

A few years after my father died back in the mid eighties so did my teenage incoherent party years. I hid behind fantasy, I allowed it to take over my reality. As I entered my twenties reality started creeping its way back into my life as my fantasyland seemed to slip further away and for me that was a good thing. Holding down a full-time job, maintaining a spousal relationship and having the responsibilities of living out on my own made me see a different realism for myself.

With that it became apparent to me that I had to at some point also face the facts of who I was inside. Being clean from constant mind altering drug use certainly did help me to face random life issues that would come up more easily. I was forced to take a look at myself whether I wanted to or not. Of course I tried fighting these as they arose out of my control by ignoring them, only to find out that they just kept coming back until I dealt with them one by one.

Some things are easier to deal with than others depending on how much work needs to be done to get you started on the path that was designed for you. In my case it was a healing path. Some of those issues that came up for me were to some people everyday life occurrences, nevertheless they were certainly immense tribulations for me to deal with. Dealing with them is what gave me my life back, it all depends on how you view matters I guess.

I wasn't always the most pleasant person to be around and I caused quite a few needless conflicts by judging people, being rude or disrespectful and speaking up a little too truthfully without considering the other persons feelings. A couple examples are disputes in or out of work with people and various family problems that would arise, I could no longer blame other people by lashing out then brush them off and carry on my merry way. I had to deal with the stuff. Yes, stuff, my stuff. Getting off my high horse and humbling myself helped me do this.

It was around that time that I began to really become self aware of the affects of being brought up in such a poorly communicative family household. Without the courage of drugs or alcohol I was afraid to express my thoughts, feelings or speak loud enough for others to hear me. I consciously did not realize what was happening then but I look back now and see how I was not allowed to express myself, I had no good examples to mock either. There was a point in my life when I looked at the issues that kept arising as a burden on me. I gradually felt overwhelmed by having to deal with life's issues sober.

From feeling and thinking this way I drastically reverted back into my early years down the wrong path again. Repeating my childhood behavior, I was trapped finding it difficult to function properly in public once again. I began shying away from others and I was terrified to speak my mind or join in a conversation socially within a group of people. It didn't make a difference if I knew them or not, I felt defeated.

If I wanted to say something I mentally had to go through hell. My palms would get clammy and my heart would beat faster. I literally had to repeat the sentence in my head quite a few times to ensure its accuracy before I would get the urge to spit it out. When I finally did speak up I found out that each time to my dismay, the group of people I was talking amongst could barely hear me. They made obvious remarks such as, "What? Speak up!" or "Did you say something?" This happened to me all the time, it drove me crazy!

I found this to be a real challenge when I got hired into a position as a customer service representative. I worked in a place of business where I had to speak to the clientele through a thick glass barrier. It was extremely difficult for the customers to hear me back then which is far from good customer service. "Of all things that could happen, it has to happen to me" I thought.

This was one of the issues I talked about a few paragraphs back. It was an opportunity for a great learning experience. I saw it as do or die. I had to take a look at myself and my weakness to learn to overcome it if I wanted to keep my job. Since I felt that I didn't really have much of a choice I ended up pushing all my uncomfortable feelings and fears aside. I had to make a habit out of practicing to talk louder.

Along with patient customers and the help of the company putting me into scenarios like meetings and internal courses I became pretty good at it over time as with anything else. I became too good at it that I had to learn to tone it down a bit as it came across like I was yelling at the customers! Eventually I found a comfortable tone that the customers, the company and I deemed appropriate. This took me a couple years to perfect.

That was an example of one of my demons I was forced into facing. It's funny how life works. In all honesty as silly as it may sound I felt assured behind my wall of glass, without it being there that was a different story. Out from behind my glass wall of courage I was not so loud. I still had to battle with those high anxiety situations where I would go into public and have store clerks, waiters and waitresses to list a few, not hear me when I spoke. I had to endure over and over those same awful dreaded responses that I hated so much being fired at me.

The responses I received from people again drove me crazy! Always feeling humiliated and embarrassed because I felt like everyone around the store, restaurant or wherever I may have been at the time could also hear them. It was like reliving the feelings of having all eyes on me again just like in my elementary school gymnasium that one day long ago.

I guess it was over a couple years that I became frustrated with my insecurity and with the discomfort of not being heard. I grew angry with myself for falling back into the way I was as a child. During a period of approximately the next ten years I reached a turning point in my life, it had angered me so much that I finally decided to take it upon myself and do something about it.

During that trying time I had the help of a couple great friends who supported me. From then on I picked up the habit of reading random self help books with topics that I could relate to. It's a shame that it was so long ago that I am unable to share with you today what their titles were or even their authors names. I was focused on myself for once so the messages in the books were what was truly of value to me, not the author or its title.

I would pick these up at new and used book stores, being that I wasn't much a fan of reading skimming through the books and getting what I needed from them was what I did. I'd then throw them out or put them in storage because I didn't want others finding out I had problems, I feared they would pass judgment on me because I was psychoanalyzing myself.

That was how I spent the majority of my life thinking. I know many people have heard that they should do things out of their comfort zone or have been encouraged in some way or another to do so. One of those books I quickly sifted through mentioned the importance of this as well. At the time the thought of doing that put me into an anxiety attack, "Why the heck would I bother doing that?" I thought. After reading it over a few times I grew more concerned with the idea that I may have to suffer with this issue of mine for the rest of my life, which could end up being a very long time.

I put my foot down and decided to go for it and give it a try. I was willing to pay whatever cost to myself as I knew it couldn't possibly make matters worse for me. I have learned that doing things out of our comfort zones does help one grow, it doesn't necessarily add negatively to existing anxiety but rather helps turn that anxiety into excitement!

I wish I had this knowledge back then I may have given it a shot alot earlier. I started by taking baby steps just like I did at work but without my glass protection. I forced myself to stand tall and not shy away. I pushed myself into speaking whenever I was given an opportunity, I took initiative and bravely jumped into conversations with the same tone I learned through my job.

Well it gave me what I wanted, I was definitely heard! In the heat of the excitement of my new approach to communicating, I have to admit there were quite a few not so small bumps along the way. Every so often I would loudly blurt out things that were inappropriate for the conversation at hand. This of course added to my initial embarrassment which made me feel at times that I was fighting a losing battle. Some people would still be annoyed with me while others would react with laughter like I made a joke. Either way what mattered to me at that point was that I was finally heard!

After years of practice of building my confidence I was then presented with a whole new self inspection challenge, that was learning to laugh at myself. If I wanted to continue to engage in conversations where people could actually hear me, it meant having to get used to my bloopers being pointed out. It was a matter of taking that first plunge.

Even today I still catch myself periodically falling in to that same old trap of clamming up and that's perfectly okay. I now have the ability and the knowhow to escape it. I'm all good, I overcame and I am a survivor!

EXERCISE SHEET: Use separate sheets of paper or a journal style book. It helps to record the applicable chapter names along with the relevant page numbers from this book on each of your writings for easy reference later.

Record your story: How you relate, situations, agendas, notes, thoughts & anything else related to this chapter. Use paragraph writing, point form or whatever you're comfortable with. Think back & take a deep breath! Now take some time to read over what you wrote.

_____

_____

_____

_____

_____

_____

_____

_____

_____

_____

_____

_____

_____

_____

_____

_____

_____

_____

_____

_____

E.R.A.S.E.D. = Easy Real Action Spiritual Exercises Deliver:
Erase the chains of abuse that bind you using EASY made, REAL life, ACTION steps with SPIRITUAL outlook & hands on EXERCISES that DELIVER!

ENDURING OVERLY STRICT PARENTING
Not being able to express myself

Why is it that human beings do not like feeling restrained in any way? I think the answer is a pretty simple, we are beings that are naturally expressive in many different ways. Whether we want it to happen or not our brains are always growing, learning and changing as well as our bodies and mouths which follow right along with it. You are a thinking being with your very own unique mind, it takes in or imports information then quickly studies it to decide if it gets used at that time or if it gets stored away for a later date.

Your mind also gives out or exports information just as fast as it takes it in. So, if you decide to let out information it usually comes out in some kind oral form. The information held in your mind exports its way out by giving your opinion on something or giving some sort of direction or instruction to someone. Your information must come out somehow giving consideration to the amount of knowledge our brains soak up from everything we hear, see, feel, taste and smell. I mean really, have you ever thought about how much information we really take in everyday? Eventually it all has to come out of us whether we volunteer it or not, if it doesn't come out verbally it is usually let out in a bodily or emotional gesture even both sometimes as you will see.

It's hard enough being a kid growing up with reasonable rules and guidelines to follow but to have to grow up with one parent whom was already by nature is a controlling individual is hard. My dad set the rules of the house with no input from my other parent whatsoever. The result was being ruled over by 'out of this world' predetermined punishments. My dad pretty much had a particular penalty that coincided with each and every rule with absolutely no bending of them. I can tell you it was unexplainably hard, mind bending and downright suffocating to live that way.

How are children expected to express themselves as God and nature had intended if this is what they are subject to? Can you relate to that? You may or may not have had the same upbringing as I, but you might have a similar experience even as an adult at some point in your life. A time where you felt smothered for example in your job or in your relationships? It is really no different, just different circumstances.

We all need to express our thoughts and opinions through voice and physical action and should be able to when and how we want. As long as it is done with consideration and in respect of others it can be a very good tool to use to get our message across clearly to attract the empathy, understanding or action we want to get in return. I grew up being prohibited from talking or expressing myself in any negative way. I wasn't allowed to show even reasonable signs of anger at all without being stopped right away. This internally shut me down quite quickly. That is when the turmoil from within me started to brew and it eventually boiled over.

I quite often expressed myself in unhealthy manners. Extreme emotional and physical outbursts along with harmful internal thoughts I created caused destructive psychological disorders in me. I know this contributed to leading me into some substance abuse.

From early on in my life right through until my dad died I was never allowed to voice my opinion, share my thoughts or views on anything in our household. As I mentioned earlier throughout my childhood and through my teen years it was expected of us kids to raise our hands to ask dad for permission to go to the bathroom. Mom was not like that at all; with her we felt we had some freedom.

At one time it was also expected of everyone in our family to use one or two square sheets of toilet paper at the maximum for each bathroom use. When my dad remembered to uphold his rule he would monitor this by how many rolls were used in a week. If more than the allowed amount was being *wasted*, we all would have to endure the 'how expensive' and the 'fairness' to each other lectures until dad was satisfied that his rules would be obeyed from then on.

On the topic of discipline, I recall being punished for walking in the house and stepping off the two by three foot mat at the door way. When I did this I accidentally landed my shoed foot on the clean linoleum tiled floor. Normally this would get my dad yelling at me all except for this one time, I entered the house with a girlfriend and my dad happened to be standing right there. He grabbed me and threw my back up against the hall wall telling me at the top of his lungs that he had enough of me not remembering his rule. I was quite used to my dad overreacting this way with certain things it was normal to me until I saw the look on my friends face, I knew then that it wasn't normal at all. Needless to say that she made her visits to my house less frequent. How humiliating is that in front of your best friend? There are some things you just don't forget.

His other forms of disciplinary action were to have us kids sit in the hall or atop the stairs on the landing half way up facing a blinding painted white wall. I sat there for a long time sometimes, however long a time my dad thought I deserved. It was during my child to early teen years when he regulated the time in fifteen minute to half hour intervals, this depended on the behavior that called for it. Sitting there bored and bugged eyed from being forced to look directly at the wall for long periods of time was excruciating!

I was not allowed to say a peep or be caught with my eyes closed without having more increments of time added to my initial amount being served. I spent most of my wall facing time forcing my eyes to stay open, holding my breath, tensing up my muscles and praying that nothing would come out of my mouth that would incriminate me more! (Fearing my dad usually prevented that). I can tell you that being a teen with an attitude made it hard to just sit there and take it without budging or trying to say something here and there. It was common to be facing the wall for more than a couple hours at a time.

Another example of an extreme punishment enforced regularly in our home from a young age was to belt us kids with the strap. I'll never forget the many times I had bent over the end of my parents' bed after misbehaving or breaking a rule. This went on well into my teen years. An evil cold silence would fill the air as I lined up along side of my sisters. Turning around and putting the palms of my hands on the mattress while waiting to hear the dreaded, "Pull down your pants and underwear" was terrifying!

The silence didn't last long as the sounds of dads' footsteps and the brushing sound of his pant legs together took over. As he paced slowly back and forth behind me, I could hear the echoing clanking sound of the metal buckle at the end of his belt hitting the palm of his hand. This would go on sometimes for a few minutes, it was pure torture. These times were very agonizing.

Even though I knew if I looked back at my dad to see where the strap was I would get more coming to me than what I was already in for but sometimes I couldn't help myself. So of course bare butt and all I kept turning around periodically to glance at him until I was caught, then I would get yelled at and reminded that I just earned myself one more!

I could sense the satisfaction he felt when he delivered those surprise attacks. Each time was petrifying just blindly waiting to feel the sting from the cold metal on his black and brown leather belts, the ones he used to hold his dress pants up with.

My dad applied the same principles to strapping as he did with facing the wall. How many times he would hit us with the strap depended on how severe he thought the punishment should be. Everything in our house had to be regulated.

There did come a time in my mid teens when he actually listened to me. I told him I was too old to be strapped or spanked especially with my pants down! Surprisingly he agreed with me, huh? He stopped strapping me with my pants down, but kept strapping when he felt the need to. It made no sense I was a teenager? I do remember occasionally getting away with putting books in my pants, and other times not. Those times of course resulted in a harder hit.

There was one situation where my sisters and I were lined up awaiting the frightening surprise of being hit with the strap, my youngest sister reached back and grabbed dads pinky finger and bent it backward. I believe she either broke it or sprained it, I'm not sure. When he yelled from the pain of it and ordered us out of the room, we all went running! Strapping sessions were pretty much short lived after that. I'm not sure what went through his head at that moment except that maybe it was a wakeup call of some sort.

As I entered my older teen years the strap and facing the wall was replaced with full 'groundings'. Sounds pretty normal I guess. Some of those times I was 'grounded' were reasonable lengths of time while a couple of them as I mentioned before were maxed out to a couple months. I had two entire summers where I sat on my bed with nothing to do unless my dad made an exception.

It was hard to learn from my punishments and to correct my behavior while my brain was turning to mush from just looking at the walls in my room! The times where I did get to go out was only because the whole family was going out. If they were going grocery shopping for example my dad would drag me along with them since I wasn't trusted to stay home alone.

My idea in sharing these stories with you is to give examples of how I was not able to express myself while I was growing up. It wasn't often when I would be asked how my day was or how things were going with me. Today, I do my best to make that an important part of each day with my own daughter learning from that example.

Right after I share this next experience with you I have listed the methods that I used to escape that mind trap. Remember when I talked about releasing our inner information of thoughts and feelings and that they must come out of us in some way or another? Well, here is another one of those ways where they found their way out of me.

Being a sexually abused child who was unable to tell anyone about my fears and pains I had to find other ways to express it. Without the understanding of what I was really doing at that time, I subconsciously expressed myself by cutting or slicing parts of my body occasionally. Sadly I cut up my forearms with razor blades from various objects. I would lightly engrave in words and make slice marks in front of my friends even in public places such as in restaurants, I tried to come across as it was a cool thing to do but really a lot of it was for attention. I guess deep down I wanted someone to care enough to dig into me and discover my hurt, then help me. I see this now.

I was a 'cutter' as they call it. Off and on and for a year or so whenever I felt the urge to do it I would. I don't even know what my triggers were. My cutting was not an everyday thing nor did I make the incisions deep enough that it would have been all that obvious to other people outside my small group of friends. I didn't feel it was too much of a problem at the time.

My friends would squeal, get all squeamish then lecture me at the sight of it. On one occasion while at home I deliberately sliced through the top of my thumbnail, I did it so deeply and so many times that the bleeding cuts scarred leaving bumps. My nail is ruined today, it's embedded with such unsightly grooves and ridges that I have a hard time keeping it half decent looking. It left me a permanent reminder scar of my emotional pain.

I know of some people who really slice up their arms and legs to the point blood pours out of them. I am aware that there are extremely severe cases where children of different ages are cutting, I have been told that the severity of it is dependent on how deep the trauma is. Cutting one's own body is very serious, it's dangerous and there are professional experienced people out there ready to help someone defeat it.

I wasn't sure why I was cutting or even put much thought into it until some years later during a therapy session. When I learned where it came from it gave me reason as to why I was doing it which made it easier for me to cure. I felt ashamed of myself for quite a long time until I understood that most people have some mental health issue to deal with in some form or another, most importantly I didn't feel alone.

As I mentioned earlier cutting is very dangerous and needs to stop. Thankfully for me it was straightforward for when it was pointed out to me why I was cutting I don't know how but I just stopped. I was lucky, it could have turned out much worse.

Speaking of mental health issues, at a really young age in my life maybe from about the age of eight until I was about eleven years old I frighteningly recall having the same weird repetitive nightmare. Nothing in the dream ever seemed to change. I don't remember seeing walls, windows or doors but I knew I was inside a room. Don't laugh, but each time I had this dream there was only me, the floor and a gray or brownish roll of carpet! Have you seen those huge twelve foot long rolls that they sell in flooring stores? Yep, that would be the one!

The same roll of carpet would chase me by unrolling itself on the wood floor, it wouldn't stop coming after me! Each time I knew it wanted to get me as it had caught me many times before. I could only run away from it a few feet at a time as it approached closer to me. No different really than in other dreams where the chase is on. I ran for my life on the spot for the most part while feeling like something just kept pushing me backward. I couldn't move forward no matter how hard I tried. I hated that!

When the carpet finally reached me I would trip or fall then get sucked inside it! I said don't laugh right, keep that in mind. I tumbled in the dark while it rolled back up. Losing air and not being able to move my arms I would wiggle and try to kick my feet but it would only get tighter and darker in there. I felt fully panic stricken not being able to do a thing about it!

That was the point when I would wake up screaming or crying gasping for air. Ruling many of my nights it just never seemed to end. I still remember waking up all of a sudden with my heart pounding just like it was yesterday. It was exhausting thinking, "No, not again!" I usually laid there for a long time trying to figure it out. It was so traumatic to be awakened by the same horrible suffocating dream over and over again. I was so scared to go to sleep I would lay awake for hours until I exhausted myself.

I remember telling my dad once or twice about my reoccurring nightmare, he just told me to face my fear. Wholly crap! He told me to try and stay asleep for as long as I could to just see where the carpet was leading me. He said that would tell me why it keeps chasing me. He did his best to reassure me that it was only my imagination and that the carpet cannot hurt me. I thought he nuts! From then on I tried my best to wake up the split second I would see the carpet, with no success of course.

Again, later in my teen years it was in the therapy sessions that I had the chance to talk about that nightmare where I learned the possible meaning behind it's torment. It still creeps me out when I think about it now. The reoccurring nightmare stopped in my pre-teen year, I am not certain if these two had a direct connection but it wasn't long after that I started cutting myself. It seems to me that I subconsciously may have replaced one for the other, my brain tried to seek out a more effective way of crying out for help. The carpet nightmare represented the feelings of being controlled and smothered and that is exactly what kind of childhood I was living. That made complete sense to me and in discovering it I felt a lifelong burden lifted off my shoulders!

That entire time my mind was trying to deal with what I was physically experiencing in my outside world. I was too young to interpret it let alone do much about it even if I had managed to. I cannot stress enough that if you need therapy go get it. If you want the help then the doors to it will open for you, look for the opportunities. Thank God for my counseling as it helped validate for me that it wasn't my fault which set me further ahead on my path of healing to be mentally free. Always remember one thing leads to another.

I had to learn to be self expressive in more positive ways. So how exactly did I do that while overcoming such a restricted life growing up? I could have just chosen to live with all the negative expressions but then that wouldn't have allowed me to be myself because of my dad and other people. I wanted to be me and in focusing on that desire I came to realize I had to learn to close yet another chapter in my life but in a healthier way. I wanted to find another way that would benefit me and at the same time help me to express myself and move on and that is what I did.

I have listed the methods that I used to gradually get myself back to being me. It was no easy road. It brought a lot of tears, anger and frustration among other emotions of feeling beat and alone. I didn't know that there were other people out there in this world like me who felt the same way that I did or had the same obstacles to overcome. When I finally discovered there were others like myself I started to feel 'normal'.

I do have to say that finding the right counseling for yourself can be the best kick start to finding your own daily personal methods of release that work for you. I have listed seven of the ones I have used and sometimes still bring into play today to get out any 'bad' energy. Doing these when I need to helps me think clearly and keeps me sane. Each of them gets me to EXPRESS MYSELF IN A HEALTHY WAY NOW THAT I CAN!

RELEASE YOUR ENERGIES

LISTEN TO MUSIC Everyone likes music, I don't know anyone who doesn't. One of the things I have always enjoyed doing is listening to loud music. I love to physically feel the beat from the bass. I love hearing the boom-boom! In saying that I am guilty myself for having the volume up to an unhealthy decibel for my eardrums, not saying I am encouraging that for you. Regardless of my age now I still listen to music at a rather high volume, I get to sing out loud to my favorite songs and release some powerful emotions along the way!

I enjoy a variety of different music but do favor metal and hard rock to help me release anger or frustration. Yep I'm a die hard. This is not pleasing to everyone I know but it really helps me get whatever I need to get out of me, out! Pretty much any music with a good pounding beat and some great meaningful lyrics does the trick for me. You can act out the angry faces and all! Sounds silly but it has always worked for me. If you are not comfortable with that type of music pick a genre that is hard rock, rap or something with a good beat that you can literally bang out your emotions with. This suggestion also works for emotions of sadness, hurt and pain. Ballads are great in which crying through emotional lyrical songs helps you keep in touch with reality and get bottled up feelings out of you. I know most people naturally use music as their personal choice of release but reminders don't hurt.

EXERCISE I love to get on my exercise bike and pedal like mad! Stomping down hard on my stepping and climbing stair machine gives the same effect. It feels so good. I would like to do it more often than I do really but not being an exercise buff means I have to push myself into it like a lot of other people I know. I try to be as regular with it as I am able forcing myself to do it because I know how much of an excellent release of energy it is It helps me feel better especially when I find myself angry or stressed out. Adding music of course helps out greatly by making it fun. Do it now, stomp your feet!

When I am done with my routine I do a bit of stretching and I of course drink a bottle of water during and after. I walk away feeling revived and less stressed. If I was angry over something at all to begin with I find it much easier to handle afterward. It gives me a clearer mind to think through it. Physical activity along with nice deep breaths in through the nose and out through the mouth have such positive effects on the mind and body. I believe it flushes out all my negative energy and gives me a fresh start.

OTHER PHYSICAL BODY ACTION This is a unique way to release some bad energy you never thought was in you. You will also release good energies too! You may find it quite beneficial for you to check out and research a healing method called **EFT** which stands for "*Emotional Freedom Technique*." This method involves the tapping of one's fingers on certain points of the human body. It helps to freely flow natural energies and move the blood flow at a healthy unobstructed pace through our system.

This is fairly new to me but not a new study. I will personally be looking into this further to better my own self healing process. From what I do know and have seen it is very exciting. So far I have heard only great things about it. At this time I am not educated enough on it or experienced with it to be able to give a more detailed opinion. I just thought it may be another idea I could put out there for someone to investigate it for themselves.

Try it and form your own opinion of it. At the end of this handbook you will have an opportunity to share your opinion with me, I would love to hear about it.

BE A COMEDIAN I went through a crazy phase of healing in my late twenties to early thirties when I took on the role of playing a comedian. I found jokes to write down then pulled them out and told them to just about anyone when the timing was right. The best outcome of course is when you tell a joke and people laugh, often this will get you laughing right along with them. Laughing is an extremely healthy way to vent your emotions, it releases a lot of tension and negativity.

Try it out for yourself! I know it sounds silly and may be awkward at first especially if you are not naturally comical but practice makes perfect! If you want something you've never had, you need to do something you've never done. Makes sense to me. This method helped me out so much, let it benefit you too. Laughter as we all know is the best medicine. You can find jokes and riddles online or buy them from stores or borrow from the library to get you started.

READ A BOOK Reading a novel about a story that you can emotionally relate to for example love stories, war stories or something on families or about animals can get you emotionally involved. This is ideal for you will feel empowered, encouraged, motivated and you may cry or laugh. Either one of those will give you the opportunity to express yourself while offering a healthy temporary relief from your reality. I love it! I feel revived after reading a book, and this is coming from someone who spent most of her life hating reading. I trained myself and you can too. If you can read this handbook you can read any book. If it is not already in your daily or weekly agenda make it happen, you may discover a new joy for yourself.

WRITE A BOOK If you want to really have a go at expressing yourself start writing a book. I made the decision to write a book a few years ago, it helps me let out my thoughts and feelings that I still have bottled up. Circumstances, environmental settings, personal beliefs and trust issues make us apprehensive in how much information or emotion we divulge verbally even to family and friends. We tend to put limits on ourselves when we are not in the right setting. When we are overwhelmed with our own personal information it is difficult to organize our thoughts then deliver them sufficiently. I find writing is an easier more indirect approach that achieves what I desire to do.

You can write your own biography or diary type journal to get your story out to others. Write a book and keep it for yourself if you wish too. When you read your own writings in your book you can actually start to work through closing those chapters so to speak in your life. This handbook is my own biography with a different layout. It is very helpful to me to do this for you and at the same time it helps me to continue healing along the way. If you choose to write a book it will be helpful to you and for you as well. You may even find some fun in writing a book about yourself as you control what you say, how you say it and how you want it to look. You can be serious, funny or even a bit sarcastic if you like. You can add a little zing to your book with colored paper, inks or illustrations. Spicing up your book in a wacky sense is much like spicing up your life at the same time! Give it a try and you will see what I mean.

WRITE A POEM I awoke one day thinking, "I'm going to write a poem!" Actually, that thought pre-ceded a time back when I used to go to church. I attended a sermon and the next morning I jumped up from being asleep and said out loud, "I have to write a book!" I ended up doing both. I was dreaming the night before about my dad and how sad I was that he wasn't around anymore. All my other feelings surrounding that time of sorrow triggered spontaneous poem writing. I wrote this poem around the age of twenty and I am so glad that I did, it helped me feel a great sense of release and acceptance.

I recommend writing a poem as you can personalize it however you wish. Try not to put much thought process into what you're going to write, just start writing. Your feelings will be fluently doing the writing for you, not your mind. Your grammar editing can be done afterward. This way you will get out more of what you really want to say rather than if you think about it first. If you think too much about what your writing you will be picking and choosing and that is not the idea of this exercise. Let it roll. Your poem is an avenue for you to express your thoughts and feelings. It's a personal way for you to feel some satisfaction and relief, instead of holding things inside of you.

Give it a try, you may surprise yourself and want to write more than one. You may even write enough where you can put them in your own album of thoughts and memories. When you're feeling down they will be there for you to browse through and remind you of how good it felt when you got the chance to finally let it out. Bear in mind that you and only you will be reading them and the poems will not only be precious but a healthy keepsake for you also. You have the choice to share them with others or hide them away until you feel comfortable enough to do that, when you are ready to do so you may end up helping someone else without even realizing it.

There you have it, my seven suggestions to you that can be implemented right away if you so choose. You may have already done them or be doing a couple of them already, go ahead and try another one or do your own thing. You may even like to join a class doing what you enjoy or a walking group. It doesn't really matter what you do as long as it is therapeutically helping you and is good for your soul.

Add these suggestions to the other tips given in the previous chapters. Make them a part of your daily routine. You will then be creating a new road map for yourself! This roadmap is your map to success and all you have to do is your best to stay on track. Just follow the path that you will have written down for yourself, it is your very own action plan. It is important to design your own plan of action that you can feel comfortable with. Do your best to follow it as it is now time to think of yourself and start putting **you** first.

A lot of people set out on the road of life blind everyday with no sense of direction, that is not you anymore! You have your sense of direction right in front of you in your hands. Keep up the good work!

EXERCISE SHEET: Use separate sheets of paper or a journal style book. It helps to record the applicable chapter names along with the relevant page numbers from this book on each of your writings for easy reference later.

Record your story: How you relate, situations, agendas, notes, thoughts & anything else related to this chapter. Use paragraph writing, point form or whatever you're comfortable with. Think back & take a deep breath! Now take some time to read over what you wrote.

_____

_____

_____

_____

_____

_____

_____

_____

_____

_____

_____

_____

_____

_____

_____

_____

_____

_____

_____

_____

_____

E.R.A.S.E.D. = Easy Real Action Spiritual Exercises Deliver:
Erase the chains of abuse that bind you using EASY made, REAL life, ACTION steps with SPIRITUAL outlook & hands on EXERCISES that DELIVER!

FAMILY SUICIDE - WHEN A PARENT COMMITS SUICIDE
Feelings left to deal with

My heart goes out to anyone who has endured the suffering of losing a family member or anybody close to them to suicide. It's hard enough as it is when someone we love passes on without being left with so many unanswered questions as to why added to our grief. A lot of times the people surrounding that individual are not aware of how much distress their loved one is really in. Even if they are aware like I was, still it is not easy to believe or fathom that the person would take their own life.

When there are obvious signs, hints or even bold threats being sent out by the suicidal individual who is contemplating the fatal decision, I think it's natural to turn a blind eye to it when we don't intend to. From my personal experience these signs were difficult to interpret if my dad was bluffing or not. Turned out he wasn't bluffing.

The very moment when I was told my dad had died I couldn't process the thought, it was inconceivable to me. It felt as if I was slammed hard against a brick wall and had both my stomach and my heart ripped right out of me. I really didn't think I could carry on.

Being left with the overwhelming feelings of anger, guilt and helplessness created a lot of confusion for me making it difficult to work through all the sorrow and betrayal I experienced at that time. Not being able to handle all those feelings and strong mixed emotions that were happening all at once was very shocking but I did manage to get past it all.

It's unfortunate that we as people have to go through these nasty feelings of emotions, being human we are made to feel. Fortunately though, being human also means we have the capability to eventually sort through these types of feelings when they are being slammed at us. It makes a huge difference when we have some support, agree?

Of course we do not see this at that time when it's happening and it is a tremendous challenge but it can be done. It was hard breaking through each emotion as they barreled at me. It took a very long time to overcome them because I had to sift through so many befuddled thoughts that I had layering over those feelings. My mind raced a mile a minute, the process was long and drawn out.

Eventually time had passed and my pain subdued, I reached the turning point where I needed to make sense of all that had happened to me. I was in my twenties when I started randomly writing out the different feelings I had felt on that alarming and dreadful day, the day I was told my father had committed suicide. Writing out the emotions that I experienced made it easier for me to sort through each of them one by one. Being able to see them right in front of me like that made it very clear to me that I was hanging onto some pretty ugly feelings.

Many times over the years I remember asking myself this very question, "Why is it that I am left feeling these horrible feelings when I did nothing wrong?" One day out of nowhere a light bulb lit up over my head and the answer clearly came to me. "My dad is dead!" Well that I already knew but what really had suddenly occurred to me was that he should have been the one feeling these ugly feelings and not I! "He was the one who caused them all, so why I am I taking the blame and feeling shame?" I thought.

How we feel doesn't affect the deceased person at all, not one bit. The same applies to when we allow someone to hurt or anger us, how do you think they are feeling? I decided that my dad had enough going in his favor while he was here with us and it was time I had my turn.

I was allowing those feelings to torture me and ruin my life while my dad wasn't even in the picture anymore. I took a look at my life and where I was headed and how I had been feeling inside all along, I couldn't help but wonder what the point of it all was. I felt disappointed in myself for allowing him to continue to control me. That angered me as I knew I was no longer under his control. It enraged me so much that it sent me on a new path of determination instead of destruction.

At that very instant I didn't feel any sorrow for the loss of losing my dad like I had every day before. It was tricky. No matter how much I hated him for what he did to me or how he raised me, he was my dad and I loved him as I do now. That realism back then also had me feeling guilty for loving him. I gave up on feeling guilty when I learned there is no shame in loving your parents unconditionally. I had no control over his actions, I just innocently waited and hoped he would change. My father was a person who definitely had his own personal issues and demons to deal with just like the rest of us. I know that is doesn't excuse his actions but if there was one thing I learned from it all, I did learn forgiveness.

The memory of that tragic day plays very clear in my mind, it is the most vivid memory of them all. It happened when I was in grade ten and sixteen years old. Often while in class the office would call my name over the announcement speaker to go down and see the school counselor, each time I heard my name it seemed to echo through the halls. Most times they just wanted to give me a reminder for my outside appointments that I had with my family case worker or my psychologist during school hours. I attended counseling sessions for a few months with and without my father.

On this particular day my sister who attended the same high school as I did was also called down by the office at the same time. With no explanation given we were told by the school staff to go home. On our short walk to our house together we ran into one of our friends, she went to a different school but lived in the same townhouses we did. This friend of ours told us that she had seen a couple police cars outside our home unit earlier that morning. Nervously arriving on our front doorstep we paused and looked at each other, I can't describe what I was feeling exactly but I am thankful she was with me.

We tried predicting the reasons why we were called home to prepare ourselves for what we would encounter on the other side of the front door. We figured dad may have committed suicide or was taken away to jail, thinking there was no way he would kill himself we assumed the latter. I know for me this was one of the longest moments of my life. I surely did not want to go inside but I knew I had to. I sensed a new reality that laid waiting on the other side of the door for me. Tense yet curious and having no choice we turned the knob, opened the door and stepped in. I imagine that it wouldn't have felt much different than walking into a gas chamber in the dark.

Once inside our house I could hear mom sobbing, the air felt thick as I stood at the front door looking down the hallway that led into our living room. Feeling uneasy my sister and I made our way down the hall. We walked slowly to the front room where we kneeled down on the shaggy yellow carpet in front of the coffee table. I was completely taken aback seeing a neighbor of ours [whom my parents didn't know all that well], sitting on the edge of 'moms' green chair.

My mom was sitting on the sofa against the far wall, she was bent over crying with her face down in the palm of her hands. My youngest sister sat quietly alongside of her. Finally, after a brief silence our neighbor spoke. Her words hit me so hard it felt like I collided with a semi truck. "Your dad has gone to heaven girls." She said sympathetically.

As those words echoed in my head it felt like my blood rushed right out of my body. My heart collapsed and dropped to the floor. I remember how the room suddenly fell very dark and gloomy, nothing I ever experienced before. While crying myself I looked over at my mom watching her as her cries grew louder. My next younger sister whom I walked home with, was heavily crying while my youngest sister for reasons of her own, remained laying down on the couch wide eyed and emotionless.

It was confusing being torn between feeling a strange sense of celebration while at the same time experiencing vast emotions of loss. That day changed my life forever, I was petrified with worry of how I was going to live from then on. Who was going to tell me how to? My mom was there but she was not my guider. A voice played over in my head, "Well Janet, this is what you wanted." Feeling guilty as all hell I knew that it was true, a part of me did. I felt freed but bound by chains at the same time.

I'm sure I went into some state of mental shock. The words, 'Your dad has gone to heaven' continued to pound between my ears. I felt an instant hatred toward our neighbor. "Who is she to tell us that? She's not family, she is mom's coffee buddy and we barely know her!" I remember thinking.

After time went by I looked at it from my dad's point of view and I understood why he took his own life. He was ordered by a judge to move out of our family home and went through public court proceedings for sexual abuse. The pressure and shame of it all was followed by a very visible depression for many months which then led him to his final day.

Besides raising a family of five on one income dad was more of a window shopper than a spender and limited what he bought for us. This is why us family members and even some of our friends found it odd that the last few weeks to a few days prior to his death he started showering us in gifts. It was strange behavior for him, very strange. He bought my sisters and I things like leather jackets and leather purses that we could only dream of having back then, he never would have given them to us prior to his depression.

My dad seemed to become somebody else. During this really uncomfortably puzzling time he freaked us all out by sitting each one of us kids down along with our mother for a talk. Dad looked directly at us straight faced and bluntly said, "When you girls look at the stars in the sky at night, remember me." He then made us promise that we would. I just stared back at him trying to make sense of what he asked of us. Knowing he was nearing another court date I remember how uneasy his statement made me feel. I was too scared to ask what that had to do with going to jail? What a thing to put your own children through. I was living a nightmare always feeling stressed about what would happen next.

My sister and I privately discussed it upstairs in our bedrooms, we really didn't know what to make of it. We agreed to confront dad together by asking him if he planned on killing himself as that seemed to be the only thing that made sense at the time.

When we stirred up the courage we went downstairs and sat on the hall steps. Looking through the railing down onto the living room we could see dad sitting in his favorite green chair watching television. "Dad, are you going to kill yourself?" we bluntly asked. Quickly sitting forward dad loudly and angrily said that he wasn't, he asked us where we would come up with such a thing and told us we were not allowed to talk like that in his house again!

Well that answer was good enough for me. I backed off giving him the benefit of the doubt since I wasn't so sure if I would have believed him anyways if he would have answered yes. It was a week or so later when I realized that our own father had lied to us when we were told he had committed suicide. The question *why* my dad committed suicide shortly after he told me, his daughter, that he wasn't going to utterly haunted me for many years that followed.

I know it was a cry for help the day dad sat us all down in the living room and asked us to think of him whenever we looked up at the stars at night. He wanted to reveal a part of him to us so we would know what was going on in his head. I had a hard time dealing with the fact that the part of him that didn't want us all to know had won. Not being able to help or solve this for my dad bothered me for many years after his death. I beat myself up for not *'getting his message'*. I felt helpless and completely clueless, that was real tough to get over.

My dad took my mom shopping with him to purchase different apparatuses in which one or two of those items were used to kill himself. Other items that were found in the hatchback of his car were presumed for backup in case his first choice didn't pan out, he then had other options. When mom questioned him about his purchases for them he just fed her believable lies about his intent for their uses.

In the afternoon prior to his death my dad ran into my friend and I on a street near our home. My girlfriend and I were standing on a curb at the vehicle yield way waiting for the streetlight to change so we could cross. My dad approached us looking very sad and noticeably distraught, I remember how embarrassed and uneasy I felt being that we were out in public.

He had a short chat with my girlfriend and I. He asked her to take care of me and then told me how much he loved me and gave us both hugs. He walked away and left us crying at the stop light, I think the light had probably turned green to go a number of times without our realizing it. Meeting my dad on the street that day was just hours before his death. He died around midnight, that was the last time I ever saw him.

I sensed something out of the ordinary was up with my dad but I didn't fully understand. Even being a kid I struggled for years with the guilt that my gut seemed to know yet I did nothing about it. Still crying we just stood there staring at him for what felt like forever while we watched him walk away. This memory for me is the most painful still to this day. As my dad got further away from me he continuously turned around to wave back at us with every few steps he took. I only managed to wave back at him a couple of times as I was too upset. My dad held his hand up in the air waving it side to side as he became smaller and smaller, then he was gone.

At that moment when I could no longer see him I hopelessly fell to my knees sensing something bad was going to happen. As I mentally and physically broke down on the hard cold pavement in broad daylight passerby's simply continued on their way driving past me. I cried for a long time right there on the spot while my girlfriend did her best to try and console me. I will never forget the tremendous amount of pain that went through my heart during those last moments I shared with my dad. I knew my life was going to change forever. I was terrified.

That painful day stayed with me throughout all my days and my dreams at night for many years. It still fills my eyes with tears and my heart cries with sorrow now. I miss him. The amount of suffering I endured because of my dad's choice to commit suicide was nearly unbearable. If I didn't have sleepless nights they were nights that were full of nightmares.

After my dad's death our grandfather ordered my sister and I to clean out his closet and remove his personal belongings from his home. I'm pretty sure he could have found someone else to do this. Begging and pleading with him not to do it didn't work. I was hurt and angry that my feelings didn't matter at all to him and that everything I had suffered was rubbed right in my face. Maybe he thought it was a good way for us to let go, somehow I doubt that. He has since passed on himself so I will never know.

I didn't want to go into my dad's home, I didn't want to make it any more real than it already was for me but I didn't have a choice. Being forced to do this made me very bitter for years. It also hurt to know it was all just brushed off after my dad was gone.

As my sister and I stepped in and entered dad's suite I saw his shirts and pants set out for work, it felt as if I walked into his cold dark grave. We have never talked about this stuff with each other but I've always wondered how my sister felt about this and how it may have affected her, not sure if I will ever know.

While sifting through dad's personal things my sister and I found an entire case of codeine pill bottles. It was strangely odd since dad never liked taking pills and rarely did even if his doctor ordered him too. I've always wondered if the pharmacy staff or the cashier questioned him at all or did my dad collect and store each of the individual bottles. We assumed that the large amounts of codeine pills were also an alternative way to help end his life if 'plan A' didn't work along with the other items found in his hatchback. Being in my dad's home made me feel like my guts were being ripped out. It was hard enough carrying around my burden of guilt but to add this day of grief on top of the great hole that I was left with in my life, undoubtedly led to more of my emotional and mental difficulties. It was unreal, I was a teenager I already had enough to deal with.

When I was between the ages of eight to ten years old I remember sitting on my bed at night while my sisters were sleeping, I would often clutch my teddy bear, toy or Christmas snow globe at Christmas time and rock back n' forth then cry while pretending my father had died. Sounds nuts I know! I kept rocking back n' forth trying so hard to feel what it would really feel like if he died. I did this for so long that I would tire myself out then fall asleep. If I wasn't dreaming about carpets chasing me I was dreaming about a life without dad. It got easier yes, but even today my heart feels distraught every time I think back to those nights in my bed.

My father was the one who held up the structure in our home and enforced the importance of going to school, when he was no longer around to do this I saw it as an opportunity to do what I wanted for a change. I quickly became an incredibly unstructured teen and dropped out of school. My leaving partially had to do with some rumors that were spreading about my dad and I that were not true. "Psst! Look, there's that girl who was raped by her dad." I couldn't stand hearing these whispers among a few other ones in the school halls so I decided it would be best if I left. Over the next few years that came I made an effort to try and complete my grade ten more than a couple times. The collapse of structure and lack of discipline in my home greatly contributed to leaving me unsuccessful.

My dad committing suicide when I was in my teen years was just the start of a whole new parade of torturous events. Some family members threw accusations at me, I'm sure it was just out of the anger and loss that they were feeling but even so it was a nasty thing to do me. The only thing I was guilty of was getting the ball rolling by running away to a friend's house.

While I was at my friends place my mom called their house for me a few times and each time she did I refused to come home. My parents gave up after a few days and called the police. By doing so it triggered my dad into confessing for some reason on his own accord to the authorities, other than that I would never have breathed a word. I still don't fully understand why he would do that but he did and I'm grateful. The facts surrounding our unique case are not only documented in the archives of that police detachment and in the courthouse records but they are also forever imprinted in my mind.

I remember how upsetting it was for me to read my dad's pocket-sized confession, both his verbal and written testimonials were shorter in length than the details of my accusations. At first I was quite shocked, I think my mouth must have hit the floor. I couldn't believe it! The first thought that ran through my mind was, "Why bother writing anything if you're not going to tell the full story?" I couldn't figure out why my dad would go this far to betray me, it made absolutely no sense.

After many frustrating and agonizing hours of questioning both my dad and I, the police officers finally reached a decision. The report from the psychologist/psychiatrist he saw combined with our statements and the thorough interrogation by the police concluded that my accusations were true in nature. Well I knew that! At the time I didn't understand why in the world they would even doubt me, I was completely disturbed by that. It angered me but I know they must do what they must do.

As weird as this may sound, the authorities together with my dad and I thoroughly discussed these issues during the few joint therapy sessions we had together. I still have no idea why in this world they would put me or him in that situation, it was obviously very awkward for both of us.

The reports stated that my dad had a memory block disorder preventing him from recalling certain details. The police along with the counselors that my dad spoke with told me that my dad agreed that all accusations against him were true and that he could remember the situations just not the fine details.

I know I am not responsible for anything that happened to my dad but at the time sitting in that police station with him, my father, I cannot tell you how badly it tore me up inside to pin him to the wall. He occasionally reassured me by nodding and giving me his okay to keep talking every so often during the torturous weeks that followed. It killed me to do it but I knew I had to.

I don't know for the life of me where any member of my family would get such a notion to even consider going against me at that most desperate time of need in my life. I have forgiven but it is very hard to forget. I have to be honest over the years that followed it did bother me to wonder if maybe they were mad at me for opening my mouth at all? Some memories are like tattoos, we can cover them up but they are still under there. I found it extremely hurtful and disturbing. I guess people react differently and don't think as clearly as they normally would while suffering their own loss as they are in such pain themselves. I understand that but still I felt very alone.

It was bad enough that I had my dad betray me, but not having one family member on my side for even that short time was incomprehensible to me. Even though it hurt me deeper than I think any of them realized I don't find it appropriate to point blame at them. I knew right away they were not fully informed of the truth and that they were reacting out of hurt and I just happened to be at the centre of it all.

It took me a long time to get over that. I do believe it was a reflex reaction initiated out of hurt and feelings of loss. A couple of them did apologize sometime afterward so I did what comes naturally to me and I forgave them. I didn't let them know how badly it affected me I just kept that to myself. Over the past years I have told a few close friends but that's about it.

I do not think I would have made it through without the help of a psychologist and various counselors. It took me quite awhile to find one I could connect with actually. Each one I came across pretty much gave their suggestions and recommendations but also included their opinion which I did not care to hear. I felt I was being chucked around from one to another which was a complete waste of my valuable teenage time!

I finally met one doctor who was a psychologist as well as a pediatrician that seemed to click with me for some reason. He was acceptable to me. I figured it was safe to trust him enough to open up to him. Just like my sessions with the others I didn't really say a whole lot. He needed to prove his credibility with me not the other way around. After a couple months of seeing this one doctor I'd say I relaxed a bit. I engaged in conversation when I thought it was worthy of my time. I liked him because he did not give his opinion, he was patient and his body language showed me that he understood where I was coming from. He allowed me to be me. I could swear and as a mouthy teen I thought that was awesome! I know, shame on me!

He was okay in my books, the others were confrontational and they kept reminding me of the rules of the office. Reminding *me*, of all people? Wow I thought, what a joke! Me, really? A teenager whose dad had just off'd himself, who was controlled and abused most of her life and who also just up and quit school a week or so before. Give me a break!

You get the picture it was all about me now, and that's exactly what I wanted. This new doctor opened my eyes with one simple instruction that proved to me he cared about me and my well being. He leaned toward me with empathy in his face and said, "Janet, the best thing to do for yourself is to talk, talk and talk. Don't hold back talk to whomever and whenever to get it out of your head and don't concern yourself with being judged." I immediately thought, "Wow okay, easier said than done!"

I knew that he was on to something but I also wondered if he realized how shy I was deep down. I mentioned that to him in case he may have had a better idea for me which of course he did. An alternative way to speaking about my traumas for the time being was to write down all my thoughts.

This was an ideal approach for me that I could handle to get myself started on my healing journey. Writing and talking it out are the main themes and purpose behind this book in hopes you too will benefit. There is a mixture of steps and suggestions I have input throughout the entire handbook for you. Both tactics offer different ways they can be approached. I hope you will find them helpful.

This handbook was designed to encourage the reader to work thoroughly through it at their own pace. At times a reader may be involved in a particular chapter for quite some time before moving forward and that's okay! This depends on where they are in their life and what they feel they need to focus on. As private and as personal your venture is, having a friends support does play a crucial role in ones healing journey.

Knowing someone is there for you on your side can be helpful in many ways, in a virtual sort of way I am that friend that you can lean on when you need support. I would love to hear a bit of your story that brought you here and of your progress.

As I have mentioned you will find the information on how to contact me for strategy or feedback purposes in the conclusion of this handbook. You may find yourself revisiting certain chapters, this could make you feel an alone silence or at a lull during some point so buckle up! No one said it would be easy. To save you from feeling unsupported and to keep that assurance of comfort there for you, I have put my friendly support reminder randomly throughout the book a few times. I want you to always know that there is someone there for you if you need as I know this book will typically be read through alone.

I started my therapy in my late fifteenth year. Once I received that brilliant life-saving and life changing message to talk and get it out, I stopped my therapy sessions before I turned seventeen. Of course I know that isn't the case for everyone, we go as long as we need to or should. Many years after I had stopped going the ugly side of the world presented itself to me again. I couldn't believe my ears. It was in 1993-1994 while I was at work when I overheard the news announcement that said the name of the doctor that I had seen. That very psychologist I grew to trust was due for a hearing in court. This definitely grabbed my attention. The radio announced that he was to attend court on accusations of inappropriate conduct with his child patients. I'm not sure how it ended up but that was all I needed to hear.

I burst into tears, I was distraught from the shock of feeling betrayed once again. I could not help but think that it just never ends."I told that man everything and in detail!" I just stared at the floor, I was totally taken off guard, just when you think you've seen and heard it all. A sick thought entered my mind, "Was he getting aroused those times when I shared my experiences with him?" Horrible thoughts like that raced through my head. I am trying to put into words how I felt but what stands out at that moment in time for me is feeling very alone and used in every way possible. I was so saddened when I learned that news that I had a flash feeling of giving up, giving up on me.

When I look back on my life I sometimes chuckle to myself and shake my head wondering why all that bad crap didn't do me in for good? Why wasn't I sent over the edge or deep end? Well, the idea that maybe I'm crazy occurred to me, crazy people think everything is alright I'm sure. I sometimes feel as if the tragedies in my life never really bothered me like they should have. That thought has made me feel far from normal.

I've also pondered the idea that maybe I am an exception to the rule of the norm. Just maybe I am the 'strong' one or the 'chosen' one who knows? Regardless of how I look at it the fact is I have physically and mentally experienced all that and in my heart I know it was for a reason.

One thing I did learn from my psychology appointments was that I needed to deal with the fact that I forgave my dad for what he did to me, yet he still chose to commit suicide. I couldn't grasp the reality that my forgiveness wasn't enough. I remember giving him a key chain with my name on it and a note taped to the back. My message to him read, "Dad, it's okay I love you." I remember it made him smile. I gave this to him a day or two after I forgave him because he still looked so sad.

The coroner told me that the keychain was found clenched in my dad's hand along with a small picture of me. That for me confirmed that my dad meant his apologies which gave me some relief. I felt the presence of his love for me through that. I still have the keychain. I may never completely come to grips with it and that's okay. Some painful memories just don't fade, that's life. I learned to cope with it so it didn't rule my life and I know it would have if I let it. My dad's problems were much more serious than I could have ever helped him with. I forgave him but he couldn't forgive himself. I get it.

I desperately needed to bring my stories to the surface if I wanted to overcome any of it. I struggled with many of them but dealt with them as they came one at a time. Here's another memory I was challenged with as I started my healing journey. This one often bothered me as it played through my mind.

Prior to that grim day when my dad met my girlfriend and I on the street corner to speak his wishes and say his goodbyes to me, he had also paid me a visit in a local restaurant nearby. I was hanging out having coffee with some of my other friends when he walked in and toward our table. To my knowledge I don't believe my dad has ever been in there before this. I was shocked and being with my friends I wasn't at all thrilled to see him there.

With his head lowered he approached our table and crouched down beside me. Without any consideration of humiliating me he took my hand and held it in his. With my face red from the heat of embarrassment and my heart pounding I tried not to make eye contact with him. My dad then looked straight into my eyes and sadly yet quietly mumbled, "Will you please forgive me?" I quickly replied that I already had. I reminded him I forgave him when he asked me to in our living room at home. My friends at the table that weren't aware of what was going on in my life now were.

My dad accepted my response. He assured me to be strong and then turned to my boyfriend at that time and asked him to always take care of me. We all just kind of sat there frozen in time, eyebrows raised and mouths hanging open in disbelief of what was happening. I was sixteen and this was not at all cool by any means. I wanted to crawl under the table and die. No matter how much he had secretly touched my heart so deeply, I wasn't about to show it.

Those chats were the only emotional heart to hearts I've ever had with my dad. They were extremely influential for me. His verbal apologies and physical actions showed me he meant he was sorry. It was apparent that he so desperately and sincerely wanted my forgiveness. I could sense he knew he didn't deserve my apology. I don't think he really believed me the first time, why else would he have asked me again?

The first time he asked me to forgive him I knew my answer but still avoided his question. Eventually my heart poured out and I told my that dad I forgave him. I didn't just tell him I believed it, I knew that was the key to setting myself free. He knelt down on one knee beside me in our living room and cried in appreciation and thankfulness. We both knew that I forgave him to set myself free, to live free. Forgiving someone does not approve of their actions in anyway. By doing so you free yourself, give comfort to another and please God at the same time. A highly honorable and valuable practice.

At a young age I learned the true meaning of forgiveness and mercy at a very high price. If it were up to me I would have considered all was fixed at that moment, but I guess my dad thought otherwise and couldn't live with himself. I figured we could get through it somehow. I had thoughts like we all hope for, that there just may have been a chance to have the type of family I always wanted.

Four or five years after my dad died I felt an urge inside of me to finally get out how I felt about my dad committing Suicide. I needed to release my thoughts and tried my hand at writing a poem. I didn't realize it would be worth anyone else's read at the time, that is until fifteen years later for the heck of it I submitted it to an online poetry company. I actually did it just for the fun of it.

To my surprise a few months later my poem won 'Editors Choice Award'. The company sent me a request for permission to use it for further poetry product publications. Not sure of the legitimacy behind it all but it sounded so sincere and I was flattered by that. I did not send back a reply as that was not my intention. I wrote the poem solely to release how I felt deep in my heart. My poem was a personal good bye to my dad, it validated the fact I was ready to be free from his invisible clutches. Every couple years or so I pull the poem out of my closet and read it. It keeps my dad close where I want him. Then I put it away and sigh, feeling good about letting go.

Try writing out your thoughts and feelings into a story of your choice. If that doesn't work for you then you can jot down point form notes, create an ode to yourself or a collage of words spread over the sheet of paper going in all directions. All of these are great releases for your mind and soul.

I encourage you to use these powerful forms of expression and experience the weight that will be lifted off your shoulders.

This poem is very personal to me and I share it with you in hopes to inspire you to do the same. Here is my poem:

"Family Suicide"
"Dad, though I try not to hide
these tears of pain I hold inside,
when you left me years ago
you left a forever remaining hole.
Your last words to me
"Be strong my dear"…
I have lived by throughout
each and every year.
When I think back to when
we were together,
"Be strong my dear", should be
the last thing I'd remember…
I did need you, I'm spending my time
thinking about you.
I have no place to visit,
I do have a place to hold…
I hold you in my heart, my mind and soul.
Until the day we may reunite… *Goodnight*!"

You are truly forgiven. Your daughter
always ~ Janet Kingsley

EXERCISE SHEET: Use separate sheets of paper or a journal style book. It helps to record the applicable chapter names along with the relevant page numbers from this book on each of your writings for easy reference later.

Record your story: How you relate, situations, agendas, notes, thoughts & anything else related to this chapter. Use paragraph writing, point form or whatever you're comfortable with. Think back & take a deep breath! Now take some time to read over what you wrote.

_____

_____

_____

_____

_____

_____

_____

_____

_____

_____

_____

_____

_____

_____

_____

_____

_____

_____

_____

_____

_____

_____

_____

E.R.A.S.E.D. = Easy Real Action Spiritual Exercises Deliver:
Erase the chains of abuse that bind you using EASY made, REAL life, ACTION steps with SPIRITUAL outlook & hands on EXERCISES that DELIVER!

"Happiness can be found, even in the darkest of times, if one only remembers to turn on the light."

- J.K. Rowling

DISCUSSING PERSONAL MATTERS WITH OTHERS
Time to let it out!

Do you have something to say but you're not really sure how to say it? In that case maybe you just don't know what approach to take to get the ball rolling. I understand, I too have struggled with that. The most valuable piece of advice given to me was to learn that the best thing I could do for myself was to get it out! Release and let go of any pain, guilt and anguish that you feel so that it can no longer contaminate your mind or your soul.

A fairly easy approach I took which helped enable me to talk about my past with others was to wait and listen for a topic that I could relate to be brought up in a conversation around me. What caught my attention was when some people I knew were chatting about child molestation by an adult in the family, they were giving their opinion about what they heard or had seen on the news. I am not sure where it came from but I jumped on it right away hearing myself blurt out, "That happened to me too!"

If you are lingering around people or sitting in wait to hear something pop up that your listening for that may take awhile. I was lucky I was given that trigger in their conversation back then. It does happen when the timing is right. If you want to have more of a chance to see some results sooner you will need to be more provoking. By doing this you can bluntly bring up any topic you want that you feel comfortable enough to share.

Something may come about when you are having coffee with someone, working out at the gym, in school with friends and teachers or even in the lunchroom at work. Heck you could be so bold as to be sitting in a park or another public area with a bunch of strangers around, this may even start a new friendship for you that you weren't expecting to have happen. Take the chance and politely jump into their conversation whenever opportunity arises.

Where and who you do this with is all up to you. A blunt approach may be out of your comfort zone, so consider your surroundings. The more at ease you are with the people and the setting around you, the more successful you will be. I'm not saying you have to take this blatant approach but if you ever feel the urge to say something about yourself and your life story, don't hesitate. I am offering some solutions that work. Some people are extremely comfortable with delivering and receiving communication in this style, while others not so much.

If you choose to be daring you may want to start your topic off with, "Oh guess what, I heard (such and such) on the news…?" or another way could be along the lines of, "…someone was saying that (such and such) happened, what do you think or feel about that?" From that point on you should be able to tell if the person is interested in a serious discussion or if they just want to fire off an opinion or two. You can be the judge and take it from there. Talking it out is something you need to do. Keep in mind that there is no shame involved in helping yourself. You may just be helping someone else open up too, you never know. God does work in mysterious ways.

The alternative to this is to take a more passive inquisitive approach. Use soft probing questions to achieve your goal. You have some personal information you want to share so it is natural to be concerned with the outcome of what you dish out. I try to usually think ahead and plan for the outcome. When I speak of my past personal life stories and being as sensitive in nature as they are, I like to be prepared in my mind in advance. I never know what response I will receive or what action I may provoke. Some people get it while others won't understand.

You need to seek only those who are positive and caring to help pull you through. I admit I still sometimes seek empathy [not sympathy], understanding and advice. Being a survivor does not mean I have stopped the need for continuing to improve and strengthen my spirit.

Probing people took a lot of practice for me. You want to find people that will give you what you desire so you need to be clear with yourself of all the outcomes you wish to achieve. Write them down. It was a bit of a process for me and it is done over time and not in a recruiting setting where people are lined up to be questioned or looked over. Patience is a virtue, <u>your results will</u>

come.

The first few people you choose to poke for information may or may not be the right people, therefore you first need to find out where they stand on an issue or where they come from in their life. If their background is different than yours then they may not have any of the information you are looking for. You may like to make a point of probing a certain amount of people each week that is feasible to your daily schedule. It may be time consuming but it's also a necessary. It is an effective way to get through your first steps and at the same time get to know others a little better too. The faster you heal the better for you.

I like to probe people to see if there is a personal connection. Sometimes you can bring out the chemistry You need support when you reveal your privacy for the first time and for all the future times to come. Spend time finding those right individuals, stay focused and they may just come to you.

This is a healing process not a healing quick fix. It took me months to years to finally feel comfortable enough as I do now to randomly reveal any of my stories to just anyone. I still do it to strike up a conversation to see what the other person has to say, sometimes I'm just curious. Periodically I will be inquisitive of another person because I've sensed something about them or heard something they may have said that triggers me into telling them a bit about my past. Occasionally I will find them opening up as well most times about something very interesting and even better, something I can relate to.

Sometimes people open their floodgates unexpectedly so be prepared! You never know when you will learn something new as well. If I find that I am not receiving the answers that I actually set out looking for, I then use my gut instincts to decide if I will tell them anything else further. I take everybody's information and comments into consideration, I then decide if any of it may be of use to me at that time or at some point later on. I used to keep paper notes now I just keep mental ones.

After taking action I with lots of practice over the years have pretty much mastered it, you will be able to as well. I go on a feeling with others now and get excited about it. However, I do remember feeling shame and anxiety and having shaky sweaty palms before asking relevant questions. There were times when I already knew the person well enough to know if they would be more than happy to hear about my life and times when I didn't.

Not to intentionally be rude but quite often while someone was talking to me I was focused mainly on rehearsing my probing questions in my head. I was doing my best to pick out potentially related key words or phrases that I was seeking. Sizing people up for important information I needed on top of analyzing their body language was definitely a multitasking effort.

Once you do this a few times with someone, like everything else it becomes easier. You may already naturally be doing it in your life and not realizing it. People carry out this juggling act as a personal defense mechanism when they encounter someone new to them. My goal is to attract people that are on the same page as me. I have progressed in my stages to the point I want to discover people that can help me and where I can help them in some way at the same time.

Okay, that's enough explanation let's get down to it! Once you find someone or figure out who you are comfortable with here are some example questions to help you get started. One great way to begin talking with someone who you don't know much about is to open the doorways into their past, if they let you. From there you can establish a collection of mental or written notes of who was interesting enough for you to possibly look into further and match up. Eventually you will be able to screen them by asking deeper more upfront questions.

IDEAS FOR SOFT PROBING QUESTIONS:

• "So tell me about where you grew up?"

• "Did you have both parents/guardians growing up?" *You may be able to tell by their reaction if that is a sensitive topic for them or not. If so, probe further.*

• "Would you say you had a good childhood?" or "I did not have a very good childhood, did you?" *This will put out there that you want them to further ask questions of you. You can change the word childhood to marriage or relationship, whatever you choose.*

• "Were your parents strict too? Mine sure were."

• "Were you ever involved in a '*bad*' relationship similar to mine?"

These questions were designed in relation to my own past experiences of course. You can use them or make up ones of your own that are more suitable for you matching your life's story. Record into your journal some of your own customized questions or use the exercise sheet at the end of this topic. Use your own wording that you are comfortable with. Practice reading them out loud so it will become second nature to you. When you are ready to use them they will be fresh in your mind.

Once you have asked your probing questions and received your answers you can then decide if you are willing to go any further. If you choose to probe further you will need to remember some keys words from the other person's answers to fit them into your next questions. Essentially you are paraphrasing. In the next set of questions start off by saying, "So you're telling me…" or "I'm hearing that you…"

I have created a list of screening questions you may choose to use. Use them as guides into creating your own choice of words to fit your story.

MORE INDEPTH SCREENING QUESTIONS:

• "Did you grow up in a neighborhood without other Kids around?" *You may use this depending on if that kind of situation applies to you or not.*

• "What kind of things or activities did you do with your parents/guardians?" *This will help you find out their relationship between them and if it is in relation to anything in your past.*

• "If you could change a couple things about your childhood, what might those be?" *Finding common opinions or likes and dislikes helps bring people closer. Empathy can ignite that hidden spark you are looking for.*

• "What kinds of punishments did you get as a kid?" *This is another way to compare and see if you have any particulars in common.*

Don't forget you can change any of these questions to reflect your own story. These reflect mine. If you find they reflect yours then we have a lot in common don't we?

• "What kind of role do you feel you've played in your relationships?" *Let them know the part you feel you played in your relationships. i.e. did you antagonize? Were you passive & non aggressive etc and so forth?*

You will find that most people will elaborate on their answers especially if they like to talk. That is ideal for you. At this point I want to add that I do not consider my friends and associates to be my subjects although it does sound that way. I do not mean for it to come across that way at all. They all play a valuable and key role into our healing process whether it is known to them or not. In finding the right people they will help you learn and enable you to let out your thoughts, feelings and stories. For you to be successful you will need to be open enough to allow them to ask questions of you as well and dig deeper if they choose to. That may be hard for you I understand but please try after all that is really your whole purpose.

There are many other alternatives I'd like to suggest to you in the case where you don't have relations with anyone nearby or not at all. Pick up the phone, send an email or a letter even go out to an establishment for coffee or sit in a park on a bench. There are many places you can go to come in contact with others who may be unaccompanied themselves. First of all don't think you can't approach a stranger you can, in fact a friend of mine is quite comfortable doing this regularly. I am still working on it. You can wait and see if they will approach you first but that may take a while and could waste a lot of your time.

Use your senses by putting your 'feelers' out there. You may encounter someone that seems sad or lonely in which you could be that one person that they need to brighten their day. Who knows? You won't know until you do some scoping. Approaching someone that appears to be sad is fairly easy. You may try, "Hi is everything okay?" Just be prepared for what you may open up! If they say everything is ok, what is wrong with asking them if they would like to talk? You may be drawn to a happy go lucky person where you can simply say, "Hi" and start with small talk about the current weather situation. Fortunately there are many different ways that even the shyest of them all can use to overcome meeting someone. All it takes is seeking out that right individual that you can consider to be your 'sharing' friend to start on the road to getting bottled up feelings and stories out of you.

Reading this handbook or another book in a park, restaurant or beach may attract someone to you. They may have read it too or their curiosity of it may strike up a conversation with you. The law of attraction basically says you will attract what your thoughts are. So with little effort if you put yourself out there you could eventually attract people around you with very similar pasts and stories as yourself. I did and many others have too. Along your road you may want to meet more sharing friends but you will need to start with that first one. Keep sifting out people using your pre-planned questions and you will arrive at your destination.

I know for myself I have encountered others on numerous occasions with similar backgrounds with no effort at all, why is that? I find it positively stimulating but at the same time it also saddens me to see how many people there are out there that have endured similar pasts. I enjoy talking with them and getting out what we both need to get out of us together. I know people with very similar backgrounds as mine that mysteriously showed up in my life for different reasons. If it weren't for small talk, probing questions and being receptive to their being I would not have those great mutual healing friendships as I do now with them. I am very grateful, I will never forget all the years I wasted not talking.

As I carry on with my life I continue to meet more people of all different ages that I can relate to and share my stories with. Now I have this handbook to reach even more people, it's wonderful! People have popped out of the woodwork at just the right times to help me with this. It is such a pleasure to know them. I especially enjoy it when I see their face light up and sigh with relief that they too finally found someone they can share with.

It is very important for you to tell people your story. Telling them about all your hurt, pain and sufferings will in turn help you learn and receive advice. It will get better. You will get used to talking about yourself. You will receive comforting empathy and caring that you surely deserve. For the sake of your well being don't hesitate just go for it because you will find that once you do, new doors will open for you. Keep your eyes open and look for opportunities. New people entered my life when I least expected it and it will happen for you too. I believe everything in our lives do happen for a reason but we have to allow it to. Don't resist! Let this be the new you.

From time to time when you're in the company of other people and you notice a television program, commercial advertisement or even a radio announcement that you can identify with, don't be afraid to speak up about something from your own experiences. You could try starting with something along the lines of, "That happened to me also!" or what about, "I went through that too!" Maybe something like, "I remember that happening to me, I hated going through that!" These are all good openers to peak your companies interest and attract some questions.

It was hard for me to open up and offer information to just anyone, but for your sake and peace of mind do your best to do it. You will be another step closer to where you want to be. Do you agree? I enjoy my personal intimate chats with people that I share a common background with, it feels good. We help each other with tips, suggestions and advice while sharing our feelings. Always take in advice; you could surprise yourself at how much you don't know. Advice is a free learning too that you can take with you as you travel using your roadmap on your journey to personal mental well being. What are you waiting for? Get to the coffee shop and start searching!

Speaking of the coffee shop, just the other night my boyfriend and I went out for a nice dinner at a local restaurant. Our hostess was a very personable and likeable woman whom felt we were the right couple to use as a sounding board. Before we even ordered our meals we were inundated with a personal family tragedy of loss our hostess recently experienced. This all came about from just one thing my boyfriend said to her in regards to her taking a smoke break.

A waitress asked our hostess if she wanted her to make a place for her at our table as well, insinuating she was having such a lengthy chat with us. I overheard our hostess explain to the waitress that one thing triggered her to spill all to us.

Our hostess told us about a close family member passing away very recently and all his struggles with lung cancer right to the end and how it affected her and other members of her family. She gave us her thoughts and beliefs on keeping the dying person alive longer saying that she feels it strictly satisfies the needs of the living. Feeling the same way as she did I told her I too lost someone not too long ago to cancer and that I was also in the midst of hanging onto hope and prayer for another friend going through the same thing. It was a good conversation which we all enjoyed very much and I'm glad she spoke up.

The point is she was a perfect stranger who had something to get out and jumped on the opportunity instead of letting it pass her by. Taking into consideration the surrounding setting at that moment, I know the right time came for her to talk to us. I could also tell she wasn't the type of person to go around to every restaurant patron and tell all. She herself said at the end of our visit that she needed that very much and thanked us. When we were leaving the restaurant I went up and gave her a hug which surprised her and by her verbal response to it, "I think I love you!" I knew she needed that too.

This incident has once again validated for me the purpose of this book that GETTING IT OUT is one of the most important healing steps that anyone can do, anytime and anywhere. We both thanked her for making an everlasting impression on us.

EXERCISE SHEET: Use separate sheets of paper or a journal style book. It helps to record the applicable chapter names along with the relevant page numbers from this book on each of your writings for easy reference later.

Record your story: How you relate, situations, agendas, notes, thoughts & anything else related to this chapter. Use paragraph writing, point form or whatever you're comfortable with. Think back & take a deep breath! Now take some time to read over what you wrote.

_____

_____

_____

_____

_____

_____

_____

_____

_____

_____

_____

_____

_____

_____

_____

_____

_____

_____

_____

_____

_____

E.R.A.S.E.D. = Easy Real Action Spiritual Exercises Deliver:
Erase the chains of abuse that bind you using EASY made, REAL life, ACTION steps with SPIRITUAL outlook & hands on EXERCISES that DELIVER!

"Everyday God gives us a moment to change everything that makes us unhappy."

- Paulo Coelho

Chapter Four – Research it, Find a Solution

WHEN ENOUGH IS ENOUGH!
When we know we deserve better - let the research begin!

Everyone has a breaking point, what's yours? I did not have a clue what mine was for the longest time as I was able to endure long periods of unhappiness and torment. I was also not able to see any opportunities or alternatives as my mind was closed to them. Not being able to think or see outside the box was such a terrible thing, it blocked me from seeing anything in a positive light.

I was in my own world for many years just dealing with life and the way I was. I couldn't see any other way because I saw no need for improvement in myself. It is quite common for people who have grown up in abusive situations to say they didn't know any different. I know where they are coming from.

When a child says they didn't know any different that is for the most part understandably true. However, when we get older there are some people including myself who continue to fall prey to that excuse because many of us get blinded by our circumstances we are in. When our situations alter to where we may be enlightened to another way or even presented with an opportunity for growth, we unintentionally and sometimes intentionally end up ignoring it.

I guess we learn to not feel deserving of anything better in our life. The want to change may all of a sudden be there but we end up mentally refusing to take our blinders off. With our blinders on we are not able to notice opportunities of change let alone do anything with them.

Forgive me for repeating myself again but resistance is human nature. Of course we would all like everything in our lives to go smoothly all of the time and for the most part I believe it can. If we don't take action or change our view on things when we are given the chance to, how can we learn anything about ourselves or others. If you do not learn how can you grow?

Are you serious about wanting change in your life? If you are then know that when you believe you can learn a better way to be, that is when you will begin making improvements in your life.

I was mentally beaten down because of other peoples crap! There came a time when I reached my breaking point and found myself saying, "That's it! Enough is enough, I want change!" I am so thankful today that I learned to listen to my inner gut feelings. I don't always listen to them though but I try. Have you been in a predicament where you have felt off because you look around and see that something doesn't seem right or feel right? I'm sure you have. Have you ever turned around and realized what wasn't feeling right - was you? I have.

For years something kept trying to alert me to change things in my life by putting positive voices in my head. These voices were just as scary as hearing the negative ones I was used to. I didn't listen though I just kept ignoring all the signs! I had troubled and uneasy feelings going on inside of me all of the time. It was bumpy road. Deep down I knew that I was meant to shift into something better for myself but that would have meant taking a leap into the unknown.

Those uncomfortable strange feelings just kept eating at my conscience. The more they did the more I resisted and by doing so I wasn't allowing life to take its natural course. I'm glad I gave into them, others I know are not so lucky. People resist any type of opportunity for change at any cost. Now that I have learned otherwise it bothers me to see people fight it.

We all strive to make our lives easier and smoother running. Sometimes when the signs are obvious and right in front of us in plain sight, we still won't hesitate to spend a ton more energy going through unreal amounts of agony to go against the grain rather than if we just went for it. I have learned to go with the flow most of the time and by doing so I am set free from always feeling like I'm struggling.

When I started allowing things to take their natural course, I now find it hard to see things with a negative outlook. Things that bothered me before don't seem as significant as they once did. You can also train yourself to see the good in everything and everyone if you want to and it can transform your life.

Do you believe you deserve better for yourself? If you don't then you have some uncovering to do. This is the time to take action and read into your feelings and focus on those nudges and voices. I suggest you don't spend too much time on them as it is much easier to just take a risk and go with it even if you are feeling extremely uncomfortable. Once you give in to your inner guidance mechanisms you will find it becomes easier to notice every little beneficial opportunity that arises in your life. You will look at the world differently.

It all starts with taking action and you know that nobody else is going to do it for you. Stop brushing things off because you talk yourself out of them by analyzing every dire outcome. Try finding one good outcome and go with it. This new outlook will make the difference between reaching true happiness and inner peace or not.

You never know, you could very well be set free from many things holding you back in life that at this time you don't even realize they are doing that. I am going to give you an example but first off I'd like to make it clear that I am speaking from my own personal experience, own preference and no one else's. Keep in mind we are all shifted from different things in different ways for different reasons.

The first time I felt a strong nudge from my inner guidance tool was way back to when I was nineteen years old. I had smoked marijuana all throughout my teen years and really saw no need to stop as it took me away from my horrible realities. Until one day it happened, it seemed as if everything around me fell silent and time was frozen for me and no one else. My friends were still moving but I couldn't hear them talking. I felt lifted away from my circle of friends who were passing around a joint. It was pretty freaky!

At that point I hadn't partaken in it so I knew what I was feeling had nothing to do with the drug itself. The scene felt foreign to me. I remember even feeling a bit frightened wondering what the heck was going on! I looked around in my group at everyone, they were still having fun passing around the joint. I felt as if I was an outsider watching a movie. This actually scared me, it was very strange.

That same scenario happened a few times where I was left feeling like I didn't belong any longer. It's hard to describe with words really. I felt different than the others around me and at the time in my life that didn't feel like a good thing at all. Everyone wants to fit in right. I was confused as to why this was happening to me and of course I tried ignoring it. There came a point when over a short period of time I couldn't ignore it anymore, I was being drawn away from my friends and I was being pushed into a new path of life, the one designed for me. It was an awesome feeling when I finally figured that out.

We are all unique beings with our own unique paths, feeling different than everyone is a good thing! My eyes were opened to the fact that I didn't need to force myself to fit in any longer. I was growing! The resistance was that I had a hard time letting go of something familiar and comfortable to me. You may not fit into that particular activity or group even though you may think you want to, nevertheless you will fit in somewhere and be quite pleased if you go with the flow and stop resisting. I know it's a hard thing to do however going through the motions does help ease it for us.

Those moments changed my life for it was then that I knew enough was enough. It was time to do something more positive with my life, something other than just hanging around doing the same thing over with people that really had no other ambitions themselves at that time. God was telling me that I was better than that to be spending my time so non-productively as I was doing. I believe he wanted me to see that I would be much more fulfilled following another path. Guess what, he was right!

After awhile through no effort of my own I had lost complete interest in that type of social activity all together. Well it was sometimes a social activity but most of the time it was an all day routine to keep me sane. It tired me out and to be honest it made me lazy with no motivation to even go get a job. I had the same day repeat itself over and over with no end in sight, how exciting. I knew inside of me that there was a better life for me out there and I knew that I wasn't going to discover it the way I was going. That lifestyle was clashing with me it wasn't my thing.

I look back and see the peer pressure I had to endure, that

was tough. My friends disbelief, lack of support along with their taunting and pushiness made it difficult but I stuck to my guns and was successful. It was no longer for me and I didn't need it to cope with life any longer. I now look back at that time in my life and can only assume that my friends reacted that way because they felt threatened by it. People are generally terrified of change. We can train our brain to accept and adapt to change eventually but usually that happens after we get defensive struggling to comprehend it.

In many situations I have witnessed responses and behaviors people have toward others in group situations where people are doing drugs or drinking heavily. Without realizing it they made it obvious to me that they don't like people leaving their pack. Their comments and gestures showed me as a third party [from across the room] that they feared it may force them to take a look at themselves and that change may come after them too.

Looking at this that way while I was quitting made it easier to separate myself and actually quit. When I reached the point of success and my friends realized that my change didn't affect them, they finally congratulated me. They seemed impressed after all that? Life is funny.

I have experienced other times in my life where everything would fall silent and come to a halt. I usually just go with it now because I believe everything happens for a reason. I am also aware that if I choose to ignore it I MAY LOSE OUT. Not only will I be wasting my own precious time, I may have to wait a long time before another window of the same opportunity comes my way again.

Please pay attention to your feelings and your senses. There are many ways to get around something and more than just one way of doing things. I suggest keeping your mind open and just accept change as a part of the course of life. If you find yourself stuck in a dead end situation, allow yourself to think outside the box. Opening your mind takes your senses to a new heightened level and will only end up benefiting you now as it will in the long run. Too many people believe what they hear and then settle with their current situations. Be different it is okay to stand out.

Keep both your ears and eyes open for signs and symbolic messages as maybe your gut does know there is a higher being at work. If you allow that higher being to help you along, you will be guided along. Learn new ways by asking questions of others. You may be able to adapt to them yourself and make use of their knowledge and abilities to help you grow.

So, how can you grow by observing other people doing things differently than would? Let's just say you notice someone else's lifestyle being that it is different than your own or maybe there is something about their behavior or actions that appeals to you, in both cases you could ask questions out of pure curiosity. Ask the other person how they do that or how they learned to do it, give compliments by letting them know that you would like to do that too or be like that as well.

It may seem odd to be that forward with someone especially when you don't know them but what's the worst that can happen? Perhaps you may learn something new. So, what can you do if you're brushed off or if you receive a negative response? In that case you move onto asking the next person that intrigues you, that's all. You will find someone else.

IN THIS STEP I ask you to take the information that you discover along your way and store it away in your memory banks or better yet record it in your journal! How can you forget it if it is written down? You will then have gathered a group of ideas that you can sift through when you need, they may help you find a solution to your current circumstance. You will then be able to alter it.

TO DO THIS STEP write down in your journal or on the following exercise sheet what it is you feel inside. What do you feel you need to learn more about to be able to change? Write a short or long list, that's up to you. Every step counts to being one step further ahead. Choose today to start listening and watching for people, things, events and visuals around you that you can hone in on. Get digging for that information!

It's time to realize enough is enough! Especially if you know inside you feel that way and the voices in your head are telling you so. Rise above your abuse by letting your walls down. It's time to take a stance, let go to grow!

EXERCISE SHEET: Use separate sheets of paper or a journal style book. It helps to record the applicable chapter names along with the relevant page numbers from this book on each of your writings for easy reference later.

Record your story: How you relate, situations, agendas, notes, thoughts & anything else related to this chapter. Use paragraph writing, point form or whatever you're comfortable with. Think back & take a deep breath! Now take some time to read over what you wrote.

_____

_____

_____

_____

_____

_____

_____

_____

_____

_____

_____

_____

_____

_____

_____

_____

_____

_____

_____

_____

_____

_____

E.R.A.S.E.D. = Easy Real Action Spiritual Exercises Deliver:
Erase the chains of abuse that bind you using EASY made, REAL life, ACTION steps with SPIRITUAL outlook & hands on EXERCISES that DELIVER!

"Go Confidently

in the direction

of your dreams"

- Henry David Thoreau

MY RESEARCHING STAGE BEGAN HERE
Deciding when the time is right…

There came a time when I finally had enough of feeling 'bad'. I was tired of always living negatively for so long. I could no longer resist or control the feelings I was getting. These were like rushes of desire that kept coming at me in attempt to try and force me to change. It was all about timing and being perceptive, it felt right to change my ways. From within me I just somehow knew that there was something better waiting out there for me, the scary thing was that I didn't know just what.

At anytime do you recall feeling this way? I am sure you have and probably not on just one occasion. How are you suppose to know when it is right to make changes in your life? This can be difficult to determine especially when our past experiences have altered our character, shaded our values and even darkened our spirit. Sometimes the changes that are required can be drastic ones and when knowing this we will tend to ignore them. We dread the possibility that it may make us a completely different person altogether and the person you have come to know won't exist anymore. That alone was terrifying for me!

Our minds have a way in making us think we have to become somebody totally new when we make changes when in actuality we will still be the same person. If you choose to make changes in your life you will be doing things a bit differently and conducting yourself in a different manner that's all. Your priorities will change but for the better. You will *not* be lost like your mind may have you fearing, you <u>will</u> be found.

The good news is you have gotten this far in life as to pick up this book for yourself which is one step into change that <u>you</u> have initiated. This is where you need to decide when change is right for you. How do you decide that? Well, if you are anything like me you have spent your whole life being one way and now you are settled comfortably in. If your mind and your gut are both sending messages to you from time to time, it is time.

Prepare for your big day because it's coming! You're not expected to change immediately; you need to soak it up first. You will continue to be nudged until you are ready, well if you don't wait too long that is. You may need to still experience other things before an ultimate change can occur so don't fret. When you feel the pressure to change use the information I gave you in the last topic to start on your researching process. Being human gives you the need to be ready in advance. I'm with you on that. Change your fear into excitement!

Do not ignore the messages you are being sent, they are being directed to you for a reason. If you choose to ignore them, you may continue living a life of unhappiness. For your own sake decide that the right time for change is now then start working on seeking out your resources.

If you are hesitant on changing certain things in your life try investigating those things you know you want to change first. Talk to people, ask questions, seek information on the internet and read books. Put your energy into finding something to give you that push into changing and changing now. I am trying my best to cover every angle I see that may be needed. I am hoping you find inspiration in this book through me and my life. You've gone through enough you don't need to wait for peace and joy any longer.

If you are suffering abuse of any kind you need to do what you can to put a stop to it now! Break free, learn to be you and adapt to your changes. Being the new you will be easier than you think. I must remind you that if you believe there is a higher being at work then you will know you will have help along the way and most importantly you won't feel alone. You will need it, you will want it, just trust it.

Researching new ways for myself began when I use to lie in my bed and seriously wonder what it would be like to have lived a life of freedom. A life with no abuse and to be able to stride with confidence. I dwelled on that often. Today this truth makes sense to me, what you wish for you will dream and what you dream will happen if you focus on doing it often. The key is to believe it, feel it and know that you deserve it.

I decided it was right for me to change when I finally felt that I had enough knowledge of the unknown. The unknown being the person I would become which was a very worrisome thought for me as I know it is for most people. Once I felt I had asked enough questions, read enough books and watched enough self-help television shows, I then took the time and wrote down all the things I wanted to have happen differently in my life. I read those religiously until I felt comfortable enough to change. I hope this helps ease your stress.

IN THIS STEP I ask that you to write in your journal again or on the following exercise sheet any time you may recall 'receiving a message'. Think hard. Maybe at the time you were unreceptive and just brushed it off? You may not have been aware that it was even a message at all. Take some time now and really focus on any times in your life where you felt your gut or the voices in your head may have been nudging you to do something differently. It's not too late to reactivate a nudge!

You may want to record how you were conducting your life at that time. Include any times you can call to mind that stand out where you just didn't feel right in a particular situation. Title tho top of your page: My change instincts or something along those lines.

"If you don't like something change it; if you can't change it, change the way you think about it."
-Mary Engelbreit

To save some bewilderment I'd like to give you an idea of where you are headed with your journal and exercise sheet information. In the wrap up of this handbook and near the end of your journey with me, you will be asked to collect all your written pages of notes and stories in a particular way. This will give you clear-cut access to it all when you need it.

GOD DURING MY ROAD TO RECOVERY?
With & without him

I grew up in a home where both of my parents had negative experiences within the religions of their families when they were younger. It was the latter part of the forties and fifties when they were children themselves. Mom complained about having a very strict Roman Catholic upbringing while my dad griped about being raised in a family with Anglican beliefs. My parents did not hold back from telling us kids how they felt forced into these religions. I guess it was quite common for people to feel that way back then which makes sense because when we are children our choices are restricted so feeling that way can be expected. They were completely turned off from conforming to either religion. They brought their strong negative beliefs into our household which I guess is understandable, isn't it?

I remember my mom telling me stories of enduring physical abuse in the Roman Catholic school she attended and from what I learned of my dad's childhood he did not like being controlled by the church's ways. My parents ended up breaking free from their religions when they grew up and entered adulthood. They moved across Canada, got married then had us kids. They raised us in the dark about any religion or aspect of, we were raised complete atheist. I had no knowledge of God, Jesus or any religious idol figure.

When I heard things at school or at a friend's house that had to do with religion or God I would take my questions home to my parents. It didn't matter who I would turn to, I would only receive one sided and opinionated answers. I know their responses were derived from their own negative personal experiences and I understand that. I do remember dad getting angry when I would bring that topic up because he had told me a few times over the years that we were not allowed to talk about that sort of thing in our house.

I didn't really learn anything. Back in elementary school it upset my parents so much when in grade four they found out that my teacher was making us kids recite the Lord's Prayer before starting class. I rarely repeated it as my dad ordered me not too. I had no idea who the Lord was so that was okay with me. I was curious but it wasn't a topic I brought up a lot for I knew what to expect if I did.

I remember it went as far as dad getting overly upset about the fact that I had to go into the basement of a church to get my annual shot. This church was directly across from our schoolyard. The teachers would take a class at a time over when it was their turn to receive medical shots. There were no walk in clinics in those days that I'm aware of, so from what I know it didn't seem to bother mom much. Dad on the other hand would go on and on about how horrible it was to make kids go in that awful place when we were not religious. At the time I was naïve when it came to anything to do with any sort of religion or spirituality being controversial so I didn't know why he would get so upset about it.

In my opinion I feel that regardless of what we experienced in religion or with anything else in life for that matter, those are our own memories and not that of our children. As parents it is our job to educate our kids and let them decide for themselves what they want to learn more about. This being in a perfect world I might add.

So to answer the above question, "Where was God during my road to recovery?" At that time in my life when I was enduring my life's troubles and struggling like mad to heal I would have responded, "I have no idea, what God?" Nowadays, I can joyfully answer the same question with a more knowledgeable answer. "God was always there with mo, I just didn't know it because I was too overwhelmed with stuff to see it." It wasn't until I was in my late thirties when I was led down that path.

I was introduced to God and during my discovery journey I found out he was with me all along and waiting for me to find him! He was waiting to guide me but needed me to take some initiative in my own life first for this to happen. That alone made me feel so very much cared for, like wow he was waiting for me.

Everything I came across in my learning's gave me the desire to believe. It still blew me away that I of all people had God waiting for me. I didn't want to question that too much as I happily accepted the fact I was special after all.

My point of all of this is not to get too involved with discussions on any religious beliefs or non beliefs but to share that part of my life with you. I would like to encourage you to educate yourself on God or in spirituality if you haven't already been involved for an uplifting perspective to add to your life. If you have ever been or are now being led at all in that direction where a part of you is curious, pay close attention to the signs of opportunity around you and educate yourself.

Do you have bad experiences like my parents did with religion or maybe some unanswered questions? Why not give it another chance, try digging deeper within yourself and just remember to keep an open mind. You never know what direction you may be led in and what you may find. It is good to have something to believe in.

As I grew older and away from the parenting grip I fought any conversations in regards to religion in every way. I was trained well. In July 2005 I think I gave up when I realized fighting takes a lot of energy! With the help of good friends I began educating myself as much as I could. When I felt all my questions were answered to my satisfaction I figured what harm can be done. I chose to believe. Shortly after a light bulb lit up for me and something just clicked! I felt an undeniable fire inside me that I will never forget.

From that day forward my outlook on life has been completely transformed. Even if I wanted to stop believing I can't because all the inner peace and joy I do feel is of God and is so pleasurable and fulfilling. For myself I know it's real and that is good enough for me.

Well that there is a bit about my personal beliefs and choice. I am not a preacher and I don't mean to preach. My purpose is definitely not to strike up any sort of controversy but more to put out there another option for a source of healing for those whom may be unaware. This of course will depend on what your own needs and personal beliefs are as well as where you are at in life in regards to overcoming the affects of any type of abuse put onto you by others. Whatever your decision is I am behind you to help support you, don't forget too that I would love to hear about your healing journey.

"There are three stages in the work of God:

Impossible, Difficult, Done."

-James Hudson Taylor

EXERCISE SHEET: Use separate sheets of paper or a journal style book. It helps to record the applicable chapter names along with the relevant page numbers from this book on each of your writings for easy reference later.

Record <u>your</u> story: How you relate, situations, agendas, notes, thoughts & anything else related to this chapter. Use paragraph writing, point form or whatever you're comfortable with. Think back & take a deep breath! Now take some time to read over what you wrote.

_____

_____

_____

_____

_____

_____

_____

_____

_____

_____

_____

_____

_____

_____

_____

_____

_____

_____

_____

_____

_____

_____

E.R.A.S.E.D. = <u>E</u>asy <u>R</u>eal <u>A</u>ction <u>S</u>piritual <u>E</u>xercises <u>D</u>eliver:
Erase the chains of abuse that bind you using EASY made, REAL life, ACTION steps with SPIRITUAL outlook & hands on EXERCISES that DELIVER!

TIPS ON MAKING FRIENDS WHEN WE NEED THEM
Are there times when you feel you don't have any?

Have you ever felt alone without a friend in the world? I have and it's a terrible feeling. It's a feeling of such deep sadness that unless you've been there yourself it would be hard to imagine. I'm guessing that everyone has felt that way at some time or another in their life.

What gets me though is the people I know including myself that have felt this way have never really been alone. People choose to think and feel they are friendless when they are not. War stricken and third world country children left behind by their parents deaths [and in some cases where they have no siblings either], yes they are alone and friendless. Most people in North America and in other parts of the world, not so much.

In fact we have quite a few friends in our lives but certain social restrictions and beliefs some of us carry keep us at a distance and in denial of that. For instance, I know for myself I judge others on what they will think about me if I were to approach them with something before I even do it. I sometimes will concoct different scenarios in my head with various ways the other person may respond to me, then by the time I'm finished doing all that I end up giving up on the whole idea.

Unfortunately we can continue doing this until it is pointed out to us. Same goes with when we are involved in our own sadness or dwelling on something, sometimes we need someone else to point it out for us.

So many times we fail to notice that the majority of people around us are not cold hearted individuals who don't care, but rather people who do care but don't know how to show it openly. Sometimes our own initiatives can bring these people a chance to show their true self in a loving and helping manner.

If you are feeling alone you may be able to change that. With some serious thought I bet you could come up with a list of a few people you do know. Your list may include persons you have met or been introduced to at some point where you felt at ease and a connection with them in some way. When I wrote out my list I found that my eyes slowly started to open up which helped me to look at things differently.

It is a good idea to **STOP** right now, and before reading on use your journal or the next exercise sheet and <u>write down the names of five people</u>. Write down people you may know locally or long distance. Your list can include family members that *you may think* are too busy for you. Over the years I've had wonderful talks about anything and everything with the man and lady at my local convenience store. They are a friendly couple who are always interested in what their customers are up to. I found them to be quite interesting people themselves hearing a few of their great life experiences that they shared with me.

You may consider writing down a clerk at your local corner store, a teacher, coach, coworker, waiter or waitress. Your list should consist of people where you know deep down if the need were to arise they would accept a heart to heart with you. Maybe they will just lend you an empathic compassionate ear for even a short time. I know the moments that someone is willing to give me of their own time when I am feeling down truly count and are appreciated.

I remember wallowing in loneliness and thoughts of having no friends until the point I pretty much made myself sick. I do remember hearing or reading somewhere along the line that everybody has a friend and it's just a matter of opening our eyes. Some social media groups on the internet are good with helping people stay connected.

I know it's a huge step but the next time you feel 'friendless' or alone for an extended period of time, please try to pull yourself out of that state and contact the people on your list. I wasted a lot of time feeling alone and hurting until I chose to do this. Whether you go down to the store, the restaurant or make a local or long distance call you will benefit from doing it and heal a lot faster. As for any family members you feel wouldn't have the time of day for you because of long gaps in association for one, you don't know until you call. Sometimes we get trapped in assumptions.

Cold calling or cold visiting someone is a difficult thing to do because we fear what the other persons response may be. You can ease the pain of it by simply saying 'hi' then asking them if they have a few moments for you. Let them know you need someone to talk to, "Do you have a few moments, I really need someone to talk to?" You may be surprised by the reaction you will get. If someone approached you in that manner that you didn't know all that well or hadn't heard from in a long while, how would you respond?

If you have put careful consideration into the people you have selected for your list you should be okay. If you are into social media, networking or texting you are luckier than you think. I'm sure if you screened your list of people down that avenue that you would find there are others who are waiting for someone like you to contact them. Connect with people by starting your own blog online, you may find out that you could be doing them a favor too without realizing it.

Take control of you, get out there and make a friend. You can do this on the internet sites where they hook up adult locals with common interests the same as you. You may want to arrange a trip where singles to meet other singles. Churches hold functions where it is made quite easy to meet people during fellowship. Other options are to sit in a coffee shop, in a food fair or on a bench in a busy mall. If you're a young person some communities have teen gathering places for sports and hold functions like teen dances. There are lots of choices for you out there go look, there is no reason to feel alone.

There are many reasons why people become drawn to each other. Something as simple as what we are wearing, reading or eating may attract someone to you and that someone could very well turn out to be the friend you are looking for. I have made a few friendships from taking courses and evening classes and the best part is you already know one thing you have in common. Another tip is to smile, it will attract attention!

These are my suggestions. Take some time now to record these on the sheet provided or in your journal in an easy to read point form. When you are feeling alone and in need of a friend you can simply locate your list and select one, two or even three of the ways to brighten your day up.

When I went through that time in my life I found it fun to take myself out for Greek food at a nice restaurant, wait for the waitress to ask me how I was? I would take that opportunity to be honest and upfront. Some servers for obvious reasons don't have time for that but this lady did. You may encounter that too. It was well worth the few moments that she was willing to listen to my crying heart or my venting fury. It was more therapeutic than staying home alone in my wallowing dismay.

There are so many people out there you haven't met yet with

huge hearts that want to and will help you without even being asked. You need to source them out. Depending on how much you are willing to let out, they will come to you. Read between the lines and actively listen to other people. Jump on it if you feel they are an open and accepting person but try not to overstep your boundaries with bombarding them with too much personal information at once.

You will come across people who are interested in helping you in some way which could make you feel awkward, I know that receiving can be a very difficult thing. It was and sometimes still is for me, it takes practice. It took me years to learn to receive. For me it was a tough thing, it made me feel less independent. I learned the hard way by having a dear and generous friend yell "Just accept it for God sake!" at me. This ranged from buying my drinks, movie passes to helping me with repairs and projects around the house.

I managed this by swallowing my pride and learning how to accept others help. Just don't overstep your boundaries. I learned that by saying yes more often it has helped enhance my world in so many different ways! On occasion my stomach still knots up depending on the type of help that I'm being offered in which I find I have to catch myself from saying no and give in. Thankfully!

We are not all designed the same giving everyone something different to offer. It doesn't necessarily mean that we are not able on our own abilities, it can be that we are graciously allowing the other person fulfill their need to give.

EXERCISE SHEET: Use separate sheets of paper or a journal style book. It helps to record the applicable chapter names along with the relevant page numbers from this book on each of your writings for easy reference later.

Record your story: How you relate, situations, agendas, notes, thoughts & anything else related to this chapter. Use paragraph writing, point form or whatever you're comfortable with. Think back & take a deep breath! Now take some time to read over what you wrote.

_____

_____

_____

_____

_____

_____

_____

_____

_____

_____

_____

_____

_____

_____

_____

_____

_____

_____

_____

_____

E.R.A.S.E.D. = Easy Real Action Spiritual Exercises Deliver:
Erase the chains of abuse that bind you using EASY made, REAL life, ACTION steps with SPIRITUAL outlook & hands on EXERCISES that DELIVER!

Chapter Five– Take Action & Apply it!

CONGRATS, YOU'RE HALF WAY THERE!
Hanging in there while keeping an eye on your prize

Way to go you made it! You are sticking it out and you are half way through the stages. Go through your schedule and slot in some time for your action steps. Too many times we forget about ourselves. You need to focus on you right now. If you choose you can buy a calendar or make your own to organize your agenda.

You can focus on yourself by doing things for you in many ways, all of which releases your good energy. Focusing on you can be anything from treating yourself to something nice or even reading a couple self-help books. You will make this all about you by reading your agenda that you created along with your exercise sheets or journal, make it a practice and do your best to stick to it.

Your agenda will help to keep you on track with all the action steps outlined in your handbook. You can write it all out on one sheet or in a book style. At the top of the first few pages list all the delightful things that you will do each day to pamper yourself. Following that make a list by creating calendar type reminders of what you are to be doing. You may also want to include when or at what point you will need to refer to your exercise sheets or journal according to the instructions or time frames in your handbook. I had fun doing this step when I needed to.

Put the agenda that you produce some place where you can easily refer to it daily. You may find it easy to locate on your night stand, wall or mirror. You need to visually see it to be reminded that there is time blocked in to do something for yourself. The activities may change from time to time depending on your progress and how you decide to approach it.

Be accountable to yourself to take action! Whether that is following the same steps that helped me or even revisiting chapters that you found of help to yourself. Change in you will occur when you apply the effort. Doing this is your first step in taking action.

Your second step in taking action is allowing someone or

something to hold us accountable. This handbook is very private and personal in nature so it will be you and a piece of paper holding yourself accountable. To help you to stick to it, write out a list of your commitments as in the example shown in the next few paragraphs. Your commitments should reflect the action you will take to complete your handbook and how.

Write these commitments in where you find fitting. Use your agenda/calendar that you created in the first step. You want to make sure you sign these action steps so you can visually see your own personal contract you made to yourself. Make a couple extra copies on loose leaf paper. What I found that worked for me is folding one up and keeping it on my person at all times so it is easily accessible. It's a great help if it's a bright colored piece of paper that would stand out from the rest that you will find easier to spot.

Another copy of your commitment is best kept out somewhere where you will easily be able to see it daily. I find moving it to a different spot every couple of weeks helpful. It helps our mind notice it much more often. If placed in the same location all time it will blend in and become a piece of the furniture. When we move things from one spot to another our eyes notice the change for we see something 'different' and out of place.

The idea is simply to remind yourself of its importance to you. Since we tend to get sidetracked easily this will help to remind you of the viable important role it plays in your life. You may like to model my example I'm about to give you or make one similar to it that you come up with yourself. It's your choice.

"I need and want to overcome any abuse I have suffered or currently am suffering. I want to and will live a life of well being where I feel free to do so. I will not be burdened in any way or chained down by my past situations. My past is my past and my today begins my tomorrow."

To do this:

▶ I WILL thoroughly read this book on an ongoing basis throughout my journey into mental well being.

►I WILL complete all the exercise sheets provided.

►I WILL follow each step outlined by practicing them frequently.

► I WILL consult and utilize the helpful information in the resource section in the back of this book.

► I WILL make a conscience effort to take notice of these prompt sheets that I have made for myself by placing them in various yet accessible locations every couple weeks.

X (_Your Name/Signature & Date_)

(Record the date & the stage you are at using the headings of the related chapter/s where you feel you have reached in your journey. For example, "Taking control & talking about it".)

Let me tell you that hanging in there while keeping your eye on your prize is not to be taken lightly. People usually need a reason to do things. Your prize is your reason that you had for picking up this book in the first place, improving your well being and freeing yourself is your ultimate goal. Let go of any and all horrible crutches of abuse you may have endured to release all the extremely restraining and emotionally draining ties that came along with it. There is light at the end of the tunnel for you, I found it and I know you will too.

It's really a matter of how much you are willing to put up with or tolerate in your life. My anger from it started to affect my everyday life. The affects from my abuse were taking over and controlling me and the last thing I want is to be controlled. I've had enough of that. I guess I got fed up and decided to fight back. I found that the only way I could be free to be me again was to take action. I felt I didn't have a choice. I cannot express enough the importance of taking action. Nothing will ever get done if action isn't taken and you are the only one who can decide that.

Further into this chapter I will share with you some tips on how to get yourself started on taking action but for now in this next topic I am going to divulge another story of mine. This is one that

I still find challenging today. You may or may not have the exact issue in your life and that's okay, perhaps you have something similar that you need to get out and share. The purpose of this next exercise is to help you practice letting out the things like abuse and other burdens you hold within yourself. Allow them to come out of you so you can manage them more easily. It will become easier for you to deal with them. As for myself I am comfortable telling you pretty much anything and that is mainly how I continue to be in control of my healing.

After you read the next topic you will be prompted once again to remember and acknowledge something you feel you're holding inside of you. This could be abuse you are being subject to now or an abuse that you feel chains you down in your life. If holding it in affects your personal freedom in any way from being able to live however you wish, you need to get it out of you. Dig deep and remember you are the only one that will know about it, see it or hear it until the time you choose otherwise.

"Nobody can make you feel inferior without your consent."
-Eleanor Roosevelt

CO-DEPENDANCY/SPOUSAL ABUSE/BEING A SPOUSE OF A SUBSTANCE ADDICTED PARTNER
Take on their pain not their burden. Do you stop being you?

This one is a tough one for me to talk about because I feel it took away another greater part of my life. I understand that some stuff just has to happen so I try to see it as that. It is especially hard to look at things this way when we are tangled in a web of somebody else's addiction where we love and care about that person. Already being in the middle of a relationship with them when drugs or alcohol take over is difficult because you watch your partner change from sober to somebody you don't even recognize.

At the time I entered a relationship like that I was still being chained down by my own past. On the outside I didn't show how it really was on the inside. On the inside I was feeling very much like I did as a child and a young teen. I was insecure, negative, self-doubting, and distrustful. I was far from being self sufficient, even though I tried hard to be independent. Being involved in a relationship gone wrong didn't really much help me either as it intensified all of the above for me. I felt utterly trapped.

I was working and I was childless, so you would think it would have been easy for me to set myself free having no direct ties to him. Unfortunately the chains of abuse I carried tied me down from really being me. I allowed myself to suffer and let the affects of abuse take its course. I felt helpless but I also know now I didn't put any effort into trying to change.

I really wanted to change my situation more than anything but I was too scared to. I had no confidence in what that would bring. I did have support from a close friend who made suggestions of what I could do by pointing out to me things she felt I was doing wrong. Even though I could hear her I found it hard to follow her advice because I didn't have faith in myself which made it hard to relate to and envision what she was saying.

I wanted those changes but couldn't see myself changing. You need to visualize it and believe. I wish I had that knowledge then. I had not reached the point in my life where I was serious about getting on a path to healing myself. I felt weighed down. I was in my early adulthood years trying to work on other pains I carried around as I shared in earlier chapters.

Truthfully, I was scared to death to think about not being with him and at the same time I feared being with him. "What kind of mess did I get myself into?" I kept wondering. The longer I stayed the weaker I became. Turns out I didn't get myself into any kind of mess as I thought. I was not mentally healthy enough to deal with the situation properly and my well being wasn't being taken care of. If I had liked myself or better yet loved myself I wouldn't have been in that type of relationship in the first place. I know I would have looked at everything much differently. I do believe we draw negative as well as positive things to ourselves.

In fact if I did choose to stay in that relationship and if I did at that time love myself, I may have been able to have empathized with him. I may have seen his cocaine addiction as a severe problem that he needs help and support with. Instead I took it as a personal attack on me for forcing my life plans to change against my will. Through my hurt heart and tear filled eyes along with my own unhealthy self being, I felt I was in competition with his drug addiction.

I tried to fight to get back what was mine by trying to control his addiction myself. I took on his burden and carried it on top of the ones I already had. In doing that I let it ruin different areas of my life in and around the relationship as well. I started to change for the worse at work and within my friendships. His addiction was transforming who I was. It added a whole new element to my life that needed healing too, as if I didn't have enough of that already.

I was in an extremely toxic relationship that became quite disastrous very quickly. It spiraled out of control. This was more than just the drug addiction, his addiction just added fuel to the fire. I learned from our past hang ups and insecurities that we both went unhealthily into the relationship with needing our own individual self healing and even without having his addiction added to it we were still a bomb just waiting to explode.

It is really no different than blending two conflicting chemicals together, what kind of a reaction does that produce? How can two people love, support and lead each other through life without knowing their true selves? These toxic relationships that I and my friends and many others have been a part of are also very magnetic. When two people are involved in a relationship like this it can be very difficult to break away from because they both feed off each other's negative forces.

I found out the hard way that there are no boundaries when it comes to personal safety, lying, cheating, stealing and violence when in addiction. As the non drug addicted spouse I endured many lonely nights waiting for him to come home in which a lot of the times he didn't. I lived with him but wouldn't see him for a couple days at a time. I stayed up sick and worried. I repeatedly found drugs and paraphernalia hidden in and around our home, every time I went looking I found something without fail.

I don't even know why I bothered other than to torture myself with the hurtful disappointment that came with it all the time. Lies rule over any promises made. Sadly, promises don't hold water in these types of relationships even though they are made rather frequently. I thought if I could control him I could manage the situation. I honestly felt I was helping him. All I wanted was to change him into the ideal healthy, honest, loving and trustable spouse that I wanted and knew he could be. What's wrong with that? Nothing except that his drug addiction continued to urge him into resisting change. Unlike what I wanted he did not feel the desire to change from within. He had no plans to change and I was enabling him.

He would make repeated promises to me and I believed somewhere in his heart he sincerely meant them even though he broke every one. I also knew that at those moments when he would promise to change his ways, that it was only to appease me and shut me up for awhile. During one of the short lived times where he became clean for awhile, he admitted to me that he figured one day maybe I would give up the fight in hopes he could continue on with his ways.

He honestly never thought I'd leave him, he thought I was just threatening him all the time but in fact I was warning him trying my hardest to prevent what I knew was inevitable. In his eyes he just assumed I would learn to deal with it and was hoping I just wouldn't notice anymore. As ridiculous as that sounds, it's true.

I fell for all the times he promised to change based on certain circumstances or upcoming events. He promised he would make these changes before we moved in together, before we would get married and before we had a baby and so on. The more I clung onto the hope the more my heart was crushed in disappointment. Whatever it was that came up he just kept on grasping at straws each time being under the duress of being confronted on the spot.

I could not get out of my head the memory of what he was like before cocaine took over. I tried doing everything that was within my power to change him back to the way he was before the drug addiction. Our relationship was too destructive, there was nothing that I could do myself to accomplish that goal. I added poison to the relationship as much as he did by reacting in such a way that I did to his every action. We were doomed and not meant to be.

Looking back on it now I know that I attracted that relationship in my life. I thought it was meant to be when really it was there for a chance for me to look at myself. I was not in a position to look outside the box I was living in. I was not in a position where I was able to consider his well being at all. I waited and endured years of torment in hopes he would change. I can actually say that I am glad he didn't change while he was with me. All the wonderful things that I treasure in my life now including my healthier well being, may not be.

Hanging onto my fantasy life did not work for me. All it did was prolong all the physical fights, neglect and mental abuse. He was going to change when he wanted to change at that was when the time was right for him, not me. He ended up in a new relationship where he received support and has been clean now for several years.

In a way I am glad all of that happened to me, I learned from it. Dissolving memories can be challenging but eventually they do fade and that is what I clung my hope to. Making every effort to look at my experience from an outsider's point of view is what helped me to understand alot about myself. It helped me heal, I woke up so to speak

I thank God for my friend who put a stop to my insanity by pointing out to me that I was changing and letting his addiction rule my life when I wasn't the one on drugs. Many times she went over this with me pointing out the pros and cons and how the cons outweighed all the pros. Finally one bright day sunny came when I pulled out my bravery card from within and put my foot down ending the relationship for good.

Learning to see beyond my emotion and anger into what was really happening and why was nearly impossible to do. It is very easy to be blinded by our current circumstances. We can drown ourselves in it when we are in the middle of that kind of situation. A friend of mine also had many experiences in a relationship with her partner who was addicted to hard core drugs. She shares with us one of her coping methods she used to be able to deal with her situation. She found this method to be very effective. Here is her personal solution to what helped her heal in her own words.

"It sounds funny but one of the tools I often used was to view my 'bad' experiences as if they happened in a movie. After a fight or similar situation between my spouse and I had occurred I would replay it in my head as if it was on television. By replacing my husband and myself with unknown characters then playing out the scene in my mind, I often noticed that my reaction to what I saw happening on my 'mental' screen was very different to what had occurred in reality."

My friend gave her reasons for doing this, "Not viewing myself in these videos removed the personal and emotional attachment allowing me to look at my experiences from an outsiders view. It made it much easier for me to identify other alternative reactions that I could have taken. It also proved to me that our imaginations can truly work to our benefit if we let it. I found this method to be effective because it allowed me to see other possible outcomes of what should have or should not have been said or done."

She informed me of her successes with it. "Without a doubt this was certainly an amazing way to analyze my own behaviors without having the embarrassment of somebody really filming me!" She has a great point! "Doing this time after time helped me justify my own actions, it brought me to standing my own ground being defensive about it. Taking it upon myself to play out the scenarios in my head like a movie saved me from feeling hurt, sad and even angry. Not being directly involved helped me to see where I could have done something differently myself." My friend strongly feels that doing this saved her from allowing her husband's actions along with the toxicity of the marriage from taking her life away forever.

Well there you have it, another wonderful self coping method! I agree that doing this can be very beneficial just as long as one doesn't get too carried away with it to the point of having difficulty deciphering fiction from their reality. My friend has shown us the importance of what it means to take initiative ourselves and how it does benefit us. We can successfully create positive avenues other than the ones we've been travelling for the sake of our own well being.

Another significant thing to look at is the betrayal we feel. It's hard when we did everything we could to make the relationship work by trying our best to get our spouse off drugs to only be pushed away. I know myself how heartbreaking it is to watch as they prance into another relationship and end up making all those changes that we longed for with somebody else. It's like a huge smack in the face I know but believing God's work is done helped me come to terms with this being okay. They may have been our spouse at one time but they are still a person on a path of their own designed with specific things for them to learn from as well.

Sometimes it can be hard for us to accept being the ex and feeling that wasn't by choice because we were forced into it. It's okay to feel that way, we were the ones that endured the brunt of the addiction and put ourselves out there on a limb. We also risked things in our lives like our jobs and our own friendships for that person. Some of us have spent years trying to educate and support that person in our own way from our hearts. I understand that. I felt that way for a long time but we can only control what we can control.

There were many reasons that I felt like I got the short end of the stick and that is very disappointing and heartbreaking. On the other hand though, I personally felt a sense of relief especially when I finally let go of the bitter feelings that I was hanging onto. I experienced contentment and happiness with the change that did happen, even if it was while he was with someone else.

It absolutely made me feel like I failed or that something was wrong with me. So not true. I will always remember that I was the one who got the ball rolling. The job of a seed planter is surely a powerful and important one! Without anyone there to plant some guidance seeds first, the people in these types of relationships may never be led to cleaning up their act at all.

Looking back now I can clearly see that I rid myself of one of the major links in the abuse chain that held me down for so long and that was bitterness. From the day that I recognized this it started me out on a much better path, I began laying stepping stones to walk my new adventure.

Each story is different but they hold the same pain. It is normal to feel the emotional affects of your past negative experiences even if you have well overcome the situation with those people and have moved on. Even though we are survivor's and have succeeded to put it out of our minds for a very long time through an entire healing process of our own, the second we are made to remember what hell we were put through still gets us just as emotional as we did when the events were actually happening. That's okay and it's healthy. Sometimes we have events in our lives that are so prominent in our minds that last a life time for a reason.

I almost enjoy thinking about certain happenings from my past knowing that it will make me upset and cry. It keeps me real. It keeps me on my toes. I look at those moments of reflection like doing a personal self check up, a mental tool to keep me on track. I rely on those moments to help keep my life intact and moving forward. Some of those past occurrences involved people we loved. So even though it was abuse that we remember them by it is good to remember them. They were the ones who helped in an odd way to make us stronger.

I remember my dad and I smile. I remember the good things about my dad like going on family picnics, to the beach, the mall with him and how he spoiled us at Christmas time. This warms my heart and takes away from all the sexual and mental abuse. I'm definitely not saying it justified it or made the abuse okay whatsoever but remembering and still being able to feel all those emotions whether good or bad does help me to touch base with my heart.

These self checks help me look at my current situations to ensure that I haven't fallen back into any old ways in any area of my life. Being programmed into somebody I was not year after year has me catching myself from falling into familiar behavioral patterns every so often.

While writing this book I asked another good friend of mine whose story I was familiar with if she would be willing to share it, she didn't hesitate. After she gave it to me she told me how bad she shook while she was writing it, those memories were brought back to her ever so vividly and that she didn't care much for. It was good for her to 'get it out' and I appreciate her input. We may want to forget it happened but it will always be held somewhere in our minds with no guarantees of when or how we will feel when we remember.

I take control of my memories now by giving them a more positive and purposeful use. Realize it's never too late to get out of a dangerous and unhealthy situation and to move toward healing and bettering yourself. There will always be somebody out there who is willing to help. In hopes to help another in her own words here is my courageous friend's direct and powerful story.

"I recall when I was first married probably eighteen years old at the time, my spouse and I were fighting about something. I can't remember what it was about as we had many fights. He kept poking me in my shoulder hard enough to move my body. When he was doing this I knew I should have gotten out of his way but I was too stubborn. I believed in the beginning of our relationship he would never hit me, sadly I was wrong. I found out the hard way that the more I pushed back the harder his poking would get. He eventually picked me up and tried to throw me in the bathtub, luckily a friend of ours was on his way over for a visit when he heard my screams and came in and stopped him. After all that, I forgave him. "

Being a familiar story for me recalling my own past, my breathing stopped sharp when I came to the last line in her writings above, "I forgave him." Simply put but far from simple. I know for myself that was one of the leads into the vicious cycle I couldn't get out of. To forgive doesn't mean to keep allowing it to happen to us as I did. I forgave...it happened again, I forgave...it happened again...and so on. It's difficult to know what is best for us when we can't see what is coming in our future if we decided to make changes to our situation. Learning to have faith helps. My heart broke in sadness and in anger reading her letter. She continued on reflecting on her past with this story:

"Another time when he was abusive toward me was while we were holding a party, he chose to drink hard liquor which for him meant `liquid mean`. While drunk he figured I was speaking to his brother too much so he hit me. His brother's sexual preference is not women so he really shouldn't have posed a threat. I tried to run from him but he chased me. When he caught up with me he picked me up and threw me into my eight month old baby's crib while she was asleep in it. Grabbing me again he brought me into our bedroom and choked me until three of our friends came to my rescue. After they finally got him off of me my friends ended up taking me away and over to my mom's house for the night.

Before I went back, his parents told me that he was setting up a noose in our basement for me. Being angry with them I asked if they thought I should go back as I figured at the time it would be better for him to kill me than kill himself. I was wanting a way out of my misery. Again, after all that I went back to him. His parents promised to assist me in getting him help but they never did. The battle raged on. My final straw was when he threatened to hit my eighteen month old baby at the time for playing with the TV. I left that day and never looked back. He never saw his kids again and he claimed in court that if he had to see me every two weeks he would kill me."

Everyone has their breaking points and she was lucky she realized hers before it was too late for her and her child. We all have our coping methods, for her it was smoking pot and being surrounded by lots of family and friends. I can`t recommend the latter for personal and professional reasons even though as a teen that was how I dealt with my father committing suicide.

Counseling, meditation and alot of self analysis are also a few obvious and not so obvious coping methods. Experiencing these for myself as well as listening to others and their experiences with each of them, together we have found these ways to be quite successful. Getting a handle on things allowed us to move on from the anger, it helped us control our reactions which opened more doorways into making necessary changes for ourselves.

We all do what we must do. It can be a long road of daily effort refraining from frequently falling back into old behaviors. When they do start creeping their way back in, learning to recognize it is key for the happiness and joy you will feel. You will have some power and understanding over yourself and you will be able to open many doors that will allow you to access your path of betterment.

"It's just the dawn before the morning & the hurt before the healing."
-Josh Wilson

BREAKING FREE - IT'S TIME FOR ME!
Learning to be strong on our own can be a great thing!

For the most part no one can really hurt us emotionally unless we let them and in saying that how can we appreciate love if we haven't felt hurt? By making sense of your own pain it will help you realize that you're stronger than you give yourself credit for. I mean really, take a look at what you can withstand. You're a rock inside and you probably don't even realize that it is not easy for anyone to suffer abuse and if you have, you've made it through.

Looking back on what I have endured sometimes amazes me that I was able to get through any of it. So many tears shed and too many fears and worries felt. I lost self worth, my dignity was stolen from me, and I was ashamed of being me. I was the one walking around feeling like a loser when in fact my abuser was the loser.

Abuse gives some people a sense of power and control and of course they don't consider all the years it takes for the other person to get their life back. After a lot of hard work, time and bravery it can be done. I had to use all of my will to get back everything I lost while remaining open to others advice. I love talking with people. Talking is the best medicine for you to get the bad stuff out of you.

Getting the courage to be alone without a partner was tough. I didn't think I was worthy or deserving of any type of healthy independence. I eventually stopped my self-destructive ways and broke free. Once I did that I learned and accepted that I was worthy of a healthy, loving, educated and free life to live as much as anyone else. I learned to have fun and enjoy my existence.

All the signs were there pointing me in the direction to leave that relationship and the next couple for that matter for good. It was easy for me to get stuck in the vicious cycle of going back and forth to the same person because it was all I knew, it was dangerous yet comfortable. Are you confused, or can you relate?

I know it doesn't make sense unless you have been in that place yourself. It became addicting and habit forming for me where I would continue the relationship as if nothing was wrong. I continued to mentally beat myself up feeling weak and worthless all over again. I felt undeserving of any positive outcomes and settled with what I had come to know.

I clung to abusive relationships where we fed off each other's negativity. Eventually it got to the point where I allowed their physically abusive ways toward me sober or not to twist me into violent retaliations all too often. I was so angry and so frustrated I saw no other way to express it. I had the notion that the key to my mental survival was to be vindictive, when I looked at myself in the mirror I would wonder who I was. I never felt right, I didn't feel at all like me.

I attempted to run an abusive threatening boyfriend over in my car when he tried to stop me from driving away. I have keyed and kicked in their vehicles as well as them themselves in what I thought was self defense all the time. I would not normally do these things when angry under different circumstances. There is really no excuse for my behavior but this is all I have. I hated myself for the longest time because I allowed myself to go down to their level and become no better than they were.

I added more feelings of disappointment than I already had of myself by allowing these abusive guys to win. Nonetheless, there were times when I didn't have any other choice but to fight back in self defense. One horrible incident I went through was when I was brutally strangled around the neck to the point I was unable to get one iota of a gasp of air in.

This guy had me pinned at the throat in the driver seat of my car! I was panicking thinking I was going to die. It got past the point where I couldn't hold my breath any longer, I was terrified! Then all of a sudden no matter what I did I could not breathe, my struggling slowed down and I actually felt myself relax and give up. I'm guessing he snapped back into reality realizing I wasn't breathing because that is when he finally let go.

As if he didn't do enough he then spat in my face as he got off of me. I felt like dirt. I couldn't breathe right away it took a bit. I remember choking on air in pain, my whole body was trembling and shaking so much that I couldn't control it. The passenger door slammed shut as he left my car. I sat there in shock for a very long time.

That wasn't the end of that night. Still shaking and in tears I was in distress of what had just happened to me, after I gathered myself together I managed to get out of my car. With my eyes wide open while looking over my shoulder I made my way across the parking lot and into the grocery store pretending nothing ever happened. I didn't go directly to the police because I had a hard time with getting somebody I cared about arrested, so I did what I could to avoid it. In all honesty I knew it was a pretty foolish way to think.

I felt safe once I was inside the store but then all of a sudden out of nowhere there he was! I don't know if he was already in the store or if he followed me in after waiting and watching from somewhere outside. Within a minute I was poked and shoved from behind as I was walking toward the isles past the front customer service counter. He was trying to provoke me by threatening me. He ran out the store doors when I yelled out for someone to call 911! The clerk behind the counter didn't say anything but it appeared she grabbed the phone to call the police.

I hung around in the store for a bit longer in a daze, upset and not sure what to do. The police were taking too long so I decided to leave before they got there. I needed to go home to where my baby was being watched by my mom as I feared this guy may end up at my house. As I left the store I did notice that one of the grocery clerks had kept an eye on me as I headed to my car.

This guy didn't stop! As I was driving home he flew up behind me and tried to rear end me! It felt as if I were living a in a horror movie. Being extremely frightened and angry I slammed on my breaks, jumped out of my small grey car and headed directly toward him. There were bystanders walking on the sidewalk nearby so I felt safe in doing so. These people appeared to keep watch as he and I had a short altercation in the middle of the road, while I was yelling at him he drove away and disappeared.

I figured he was finally backing off but when I arrived home I drove into the carport to find him pulling up in behind me. As my mom opened the door I signaled her to call the police and she did. I guess he figured that out and took off. The police ended up making the arrest at his place and detained him for that evening.

I allowed the same type of abuse to continue into the next relationship which was just as dangerous if not more. My next relationship actually worsened after it was over. The stalking and threatening ruined my life for well over a year, this new found torment brought more threats and more violence into my life.

After our relationship ended this man brought weapons into the picture. Making his rounds around the neighborhood letting everyone know he was going to kill me, it didn't matter who just any man that was seen with me regardless of who they were. I didn't get it, we were done weren't we? Some people just don't accept that.

I feel for all women who have been stalked, you literally fear for your life. It is even worse when you fear not only for yours but your child's life as well. This particular ex boyfriend had the police after him and he wasn't even in the same province as I was anymore. He continued to call me and tell me he was going to marry me and on the alternating calls he repeatedly told me that I was going to have his baby whether I wanted to or not! Can you say nuts or what? I would quickly hang up on most of the calls and give him a piece of my mind on the others. Nothing worked he just kept calling and calling.

He did his damndest to ruin my job for me by spending many nights calling me at work nonstop hour after hour. He knew that I had no choice but to answer the phone as I was alone and worked in customer service. It was difficult to work. Unfortunately we didn't have call display, it would have come in handy. Having him thrown in jail a couple times prior to this, he learned nothing.

This guy went as far as mailing me letters threatening to fly back to where I was living and always demanding to be with me. I brushed them off but it wasn't long before his threats became real. Just like it happens in the movies I was at work one day when I received flowers from a local florist, they had been sent to me from him wishing me a happy anniversary. The creepy thing was that there wasn't one day of that week or in that particular month that had any significance to any event that involved him or I together.

I freaked out right away and froze in my chair while sitting at my desk. My coworkers got the same feelings they said as I did and threw the flowers out. It struck me strange as to how he had the flowers delivered, I knew he didn't have any credit cards so I called the local florist right away. The lady on the phone stopped my heart from beating when she described the man that came in that morning to purchase them! I almost dropped the phone! I waited behind for awhile before leaving work that day and when I did I repeatedly looked over my shoulder. I even considered that maybe he had other business to take care of out here in B.C. but I thought the chance of that would be nil.

I was wrong he flew out from across the other end of Canada for me and only me. The next morning while on my way to work after dropping my daughter off at daycare I was stopped in traffic, idling there I looked up from changing the music on my stereo and saw him running directly at my car! He came out of nowhere, I panicked and quickly locked my doors! I saw him mouth the words, "I love you" before he disappeared. I was shaking so bad I couldn't dial my cell phone, I frantically looked in my mirrors and couldn't see him anywhere, I was terrified and in full blown panic thinking he was ducked down around my car!

Thank God the traffic finally moved. Shaking and crying I got out of there! I managed to call a coworker to let her know what happened and to ask her to watch for me. I drove to work which was located a couple cities away because I felt safe in the secured office unit.

In my state of terror, embarrassed to say but once again I didn't call the police right away. Another issue I had to overcome by learning the hard way was the fact I struggled with not wanting to overreact. Being lectured by the police I eventually learned. It seems like common sense I guess until you have walked in those shoes.

The police were eventually called and after a cat and mouse chase [the game that he found so amusing to play with the authorities], he was eventually arrested again and incarcerated for a few months. The police in both of the cities where I worked and where I lived were very supportive of me. They educated me on stalking cases and informed me of the best personal safety actions I could take for myself. One helpful tip is to tell as many people as you can that you are being stalked and give the details. The more people that know the more eyes of protection you have for yourself out there.

He stayed physically away from me after that but kept on breeching his probation boundaries. Often he would cross the forbidden lines and end up in drinking establishments near my home. I would hear rumors through neighbors and friends that he wanted to kill me. This tormented me especially when he went around spreading the word that he was packing a gun! He was confronted and arrested again by the police near my home for having possession of a knife from what I heard.

In talking with the police they told me I had valid reasons to fear for my life. They were really concerned with him which frightened me even more. I found out through them that in his past he had been charged with assault using weapons on others prior to my meeting him. He also has had a couple restraining orders previously ordering him to stay away from ex girlfriends. He was one of those people where you would look into his eyes and see his evil spirit in cold darkness in place of a soul.

I endured many days and nights throughout a year and a half where it turned my stomach to walk from my front door to my car which was less than ten feet away. I remember freezing in fear at the sound of leaves falling from the trees to the ground and branches snapping in the wind on the other side of my tightly shut, locked down windows and doors. I constantly lived in fear. Holding my breath I could feel my body tighten as my adrenaline rushed through me when I had to stop for red lights in traffic. It took a lot of courage to step out of my vehicle to go into a store or other places of business even in the daytime.

One of my most nightmarish times happened while I was sleeping. I was suddenly startled awake with my heart pounding and my breath panting! I don't think my heart has ever thumped like that before, it actually hurt. At first I had no idea what woke me up as I didn't recall dreaming? I felt a strong evil presence around me in the room. I rolled backward in the direction of the window to look behind me and there he was! My stalker sat two feet away from me on my gym equipment just staring at me.

He sat there glaring at me with the creepiest smirk on his face, his elbows on his knees and his chin resting in the palms of his hands. In an alarming frenzy I flew right out of bed and up hard against the wood closet door! I remember screaming something profane at him in the form of a question as to what he was doing there. I clung to the closet door frozen in shock and fear, I felt utterly weirded right out. Nervously I intensely watched him very closely.

He kept very calm which made me feel like I was overreacting! "I was just watching you sleep sweetheart, what's wrong?" he coolly asked me in a soft and gentle voice. Yelling at him I asked him how he got in, he said he crawled in through an unlocked window. He chuckled as I watched him calmly leave my room. When I heard him leave the house I contacted the police and secured the laundry room window, a nearby friend comforted me until they arrived.

There were many days and nights that I spent walking around wide eyed, shaking and checking over my shoulder constantly. This took over my life as well as my daughter's life. I am thankful she was a toddler at the time which saved her from many disturbing memories. Often times no matter where I was day or night I would break down crying out of overwhelming fear.

The crunching of a leaf as an innocent person would walk steps near me or the sound or sight of any vehicle pulling over anywhere near me as I walked down the street would send me into sheer panic! I experienced extreme anxiety when people would pass me in a mall while I shopped. That was enough to make my fight or flight senses kick in full force. Just like he did in traffic that day in broad daylight, I expected him at any given moment to pop out suddenly from the midst of a crowd.

I was so tense all the time and always on the verge of tears. My heart would beat faster and my stomach would knot up all in the flash of a moment that it took to became conscious of his possible presence. He had me thinking and feeling I was literally going insane. The constant terror that lived in my head and the feelings I experienced were really nothing that can be expressed with words, it just didn't stop.

For anyone who has experienced such fear as I have from being stalked and threatened I know where you're coming from. If you or someone you know are now being stalked, harassed or threatened by another, surround yourself with as many people as you can and if possible do not go out alone. Tell as many people as you are able about your situation including store clerks where you frequent, neighbors and schools if you have children. You need to protect yourself as much as you can. It is a very lonely and scary place to be in that situation, you want to get as many people as you can to watch out for you.

You only have two eyes, remember that. I can tell you that it will help you mentally build an invisible coat of armor. It increases your confidence so you can be in a better position to stand tall and get through that frightening time in your life. If the police say there is nothing they can do until your stalker makes physical contact with you, make it a point to frequently bring your case to their attention. It may be their job but unfortunately as I found out I had to keep them on their toes. The more you bring it to their attention the more chance you will have being visually recognized in public and possibly having the officers in your area being more actively alert to your abusers whereabouts.

I had a hell of a time trying to get over the creepiness and endangerment of being stalked. For me, the mental abuse was harder to overcome than the physical abuse was. No bones were broken in my situations and my bruises healed but the mental trauma of it all can sure go on for a lifetime if you let it. He had me fearing my own shadow, for all I know he was probably no where around me.

If you can help it do your best not to let your mind wonder and take over by creating things happening in your head like I did. I envisioned him popping out of every dark corner while he was probably on the other side of town. Do you know what I mean? Sometimes you can't help it but try to stay in control. Always be alert and prepared, get a cell phone if you don't already have one.

It was a long time coming but with lots of advice and support from friends, family and coworkers I managed to gather all the courage I could. I feel that I've always learned the hard way in life. I am a trusting and forgiving person by nature, I am an Aries! If you recall I have spent most of my life due to past experiences feeling insecure and unworthy of a good relationship. I know that everything I have survived had to happen in my life for me to finally see the light and change. I knew this was not the type of relationship I wanted to be involved in any longer. I recognized my abusive relationships as being repeats of each other. They were never going anywhere but down. I stuck to my guns and broke free.

I followed all the personal security precautions that the police, victim services and probation officers said to do. Instead of dwelling on what happened to me, I chose to focus on what I wanted for me in my life. I found that thinking this way helped my mind deal with what happened to me. It helped to make the trauma of all my abusive relationships seem not as significant in my life anymore which helped me to grow stronger. My freedom from it became easier and a lot safer to achieve.

Well, finally I ended a series of going from one relationship to another that started way back into my teen years. No relationship meant being alone and that is the road I travelled. I had to learn to be single, sleep alone and enjoy my time with me. That's right me. I knew it would be a long time before I entered into any type of long term relationship again, so I figured I better just accept it and make the best of it.

I started doing small and simple things for myself that made me feel happy and comforted. Other than being able to spend more time with my daughter I got to know my pets a bit better too. I treated myself to bubble baths, a good movie and some of my favorite foods. I have also done my best to make it a habit to hang out with good positive people.

I focused so much on what I wanted to have happen in my life, it happened. Peace, joy and to know myself better was what I wanted. Seek and you shall find I'm told. I began loving myself and my own company. It took a couple years but it was worth the anguish. Now I can say it is a great thing!

I had reached the point of feeling stronger and free from the chains of abuse I suffered through being relentless. Through all the ups and downs that I went through struggling to learn how to be alone I finally transformed myself into a much more confident, self reliant and independent person. Without a doubt it did take several years before I felt ready to enter into a new relationship. I actually learned to enjoy being alone. I now love my *'me'* time when I get it, I have spent the few years trying to integrate that into my relationship that I am now in. It's been fun and with his support it all works out.

I walked into this relationship this time a lot wiser being more experienced. Knowing who I am and having clearer ideas of my expectations of what I want very much helps me stay true to myself. My partner has similar experiences as I do and the same outlook on life therefore we make a great team. Naturally we have our ups and downs and our relationship was pretty rocky for the first while but we both have agreed to learn from our past mistakes and it works. Unlike anything I have ever experienced previously we are both in cooperation of building a strong, loving and understanding togetherness. I know that if I did not take my time alone as an opportunity to learn and find myself again, this relationship would not exist.

None of us live in a perfect world. Not everything that we want to see change will actually change, but that is no reason not to try. Nothing is impossible if you want it bad enough. For me I know that a part of the reason I had a hard time changing was the fact my pride would get in the way. Without much realization of it at the time I held pride high up on my list. I didn't want to admit to needing help, let alone own up to not being independent enough to deal with things on my own.

My past experiences, thoughts and feelings about things may have brought me to those relationships but along the way I was being taught a lesson in humility. I know this now. When we allow our pride to rule us how can we experience humility? Humility is a good thing, it wakes us up and brings wisdom to us giving us courage to change. A person who chooses to hang on to the anger and disappointment from another person is surely doomed for unhappiness in their life. Unfortunately people will always disappoint you and let you down, they are just people and no one is perfect.

Pride causes great stubbornness, let go of it as it will get you nowhere. I've learned that being stubborn can cause us to stop asking for help. We all need help from time to time. It can make us too proud to 'give in' or 'make the first move' when we don't see eye to eye with another person. Being stubborn simply does not help us accomplish what we want to have happen, it invites more negativity to remain in our lives. How important is it for you to reach your hearts goal? Don't waste time missing out on some of life's great opportunities. Set yourself free.

Where it involves another person such as in a parental, spousal relationship or even between friends it doesn't matter, be the wiser and stronger one and set the example. Some people need to have their mistakes subtly pointed out to them. You may just be that one chosen to show the other person that pride is the main factor blocking any positive progression in your relationship with them. It's so worth it even when only one person makes a change for the better. If you make a change yourself it can help the other person involved give into their own stubbornness and they too will be able to maintain longer and healthier relationships because of you. If they don't give in you can keep trying or let go of it and allow nature take its course. Believing that everything happens for a reason helps to understand and accept it all that much easier.

If you truly and honestly seek real change <u>you</u> can make it happen! Yes <u>you</u> can. You are the one who holds the power within to do so. By seeing what is wrong in the relationship you are already more knowledgeable than the other person who does not share this same wisdom. That right there is enough reason for you to make the first move. With any hope the other person may realize their faults through recognizing your efforts. They may learn from you, it does happen. Either way, I believe you will eventually be in a better place.

Step up, take action and change your life! If people and things around us can improve so can you. At this point in the book I hope you are feeling more empowered, just remember your spirit grows stronger with every day that goes by.

HOW TO DO SOMETHING NOW & NOT TOMORROW
Tips on taking action!

How many times have you put something off until tomorrow knowing full well you could have done it that day? I used to be famous for procrastinating. I had a hard time bringing myself to do something when I knew it was going to be difficult or if it would take a long time to do. When I had a long list of things to do I procrastinated by not doing anything at all which only caused me to feel extremely overwhelmed! A lot of people can identify with that I'm sure.

It was fortunate that I landed a job with a high volume, fast paced and ever changing company or I would never have learned the importance of being proactive. Spending more time 'doing' and less time 'thinking' is key. That particular job position did not allow any room for procrastination unless I was willing to suffer the consequences. Well I had no interest in ending up with a 'to do' list three times longer than the one I started with, no more than I wanted to be given a low rating on my performance appraisal which in turn meant a lower wage increase if any. I felt I had no choice but to learn how to just get things done.

So to keep up with the pace of things it required that I learned how to get things done right and done on time. My theory worked to my benefit for almost twenty years there and helps me run my home life too. All it takes is to be proactive. Sounds like a lot of work, it's not. Being proactive means you are always one step ahead of the game and when you can get yourself into the swing of it you will find out that it is a really great feeling! Less work piles up on you and if you can manage yourself properly, you will see that all your tasks will easily flow simultaneously. You may have to keep on moving but tackle it before it tackles you!

It took me years of practice but if I did not change the way I was thinking I would never have learned how to get things done and get them done now. I have turned myself into a 'doer' and an 'accomplisher' by changing the way I think about things. Knowing the mind is very powerful I take advantage of that. You also have to have a healthy mind too. Off the topic you can consult a doctor or get online information about how to properly care for your brain. You will be surprised at how much easier things are to handle if you take care of your brain. After all your brain is your main internal computer in charge of your every move.

What gets me up and going off my butt every time is that I know if I don't start now I will be doing this project or task over a longer period in time. It will seem like there is no end! I learned the hard way by having projects and other things that I had to do pile up so much that a paper list wasn't sufficient enough to keep track. I had to do something about it as I was tired of feeling unnecessary stress. Changing the way I thought and changing the voices in my head helped.

I guess you can say I also got tired of being inundated with tasks and projects lingering around. Have you been there? It's enough to drive you crazy isn't it? So to help you get a started on the right track I'll offer my suggestion. These helped me get my butt into gear each day. To follow these you need to commit to them and hold yourself accountable. Be persistent and eventually being proactive will become second nature for you.

My #1 RITUAL:

Each morning before getting out of bed come up with just 2 things that can be done to further along the progress of already started projects and tasks, maybe consider starting something new that you may have been putting off. *(If working on existing projects or tasks start on the ones that hold the most priority and work your way down. Don't be concerned with what will take longer and what won't, just get 'doing'. I wouldn't recommend having more than two or three 'things to do' on the go at the same time. Control yourself as it is easy to get carried away.)*

My #2 RITUAL:

Once out of bed pour your cup of coffee or tea; write out the 2 things you came up with at the top of a piece of paper in large or bold letters. Create your daily agenda or to do list. (*The top 2 things you wrote down in bold lettering is your priority for the day, they must be done. You need to do something **every** day that brings you closer to your goal. Write down any other tasks for the day in smaller writing and not so bold. You want your main project or task to stand out*). PLACE YOUR AGENDA/TO DO LIST IN A PLACE WHERE IT WILL EASILY BE SEEN SEVERAL TIMES A DAY. (*Beside the kitchen sink, fridge, table are all good visible spots.*)

Don't allow yourself to get overwhelmed!

It's a good idea to write down a list of all the things you want to accomplish. Hide this list under your daily list or put it away somewhere, you only want to see what you need to focus on daily. If you are looking at your entire to do list everyday and checking off what needs to be done, you will be inviting in the stress and chances are procrastination will kick in. I love the feeling of accomplishment and what better way to feel it more frequently is to use short daily lists derived from the master one. For me this is the way to do it, it's kind of like tricking your brain.

If you start to feel overwhelmed take a deep breath and a <u>SHORT</u> break!

Hold yourself accountable again!

You can try playing a game with yourself. I find making a game of my 'to do list' helps to make it more fun and it's more likely that I will get going on tackling my list. Here are **2** suggestions you may choose to follow that will help you hold yourself accountable. If you can come up with a way that you know will work, even better!

If you find you missed one or both of the goals at the top of your list during the course of a day for no good reason, add one more from your master list. You will have 3 things the next morning at the top of your page to work toward accomplishing, then you best be getting started on checking off one of them right away. This is one option that may help you get going. You can try this or something along those lines if you feel this may put you further behind.

Doing this has always worked for me. I had no need to continue adding them one by one. Once you have 3 at the top of your page do not add more, you will become overwhelmed. If you feel this will not work for you then create something to discipline yourself that you know will work. Maybe come up with an incentive rather than a discipline. Buy yourself a treat every time you mark something off as completed!

> **You can also choose to write another promise note and sign it. Leave it in a visible place. It's okay that you may require a few promise notes. Don't give up, hang in there! It will be worth your while.**

These same rituals will help you to organize your notes from the topics, suggestions and steps in this handbook that you have marked off or highlighted for yourself to do. These will help you stay on track. You will be proactive. You will also see that YOU are important by seeing what you need to do for yourself in bold letters at the top of your daily lists. You will get things done that you need to do to reach your goal of personal freedom!

EXERCISE SHEET: Use separate sheets of paper or a journal style book. It helps to record the applicable chapter names along with the relevant page numbers from this book on each of your writings for easy reference later.

Record your story: How you relate, situations, agendas, notes, thoughts & anything else related to this chapter. Use paragraph writing, point form or whatever you're comfortable with. Think back & take a deep breath! Now take some time to read over what you wrote.

_____

_____
_____
_____
_____
_____
_____
_____
_____
_____
_____
_____
_____
_____
_____
_____
_____
_____
_____
_____
_____
_____
_____

E.R.A.S.E.D. = Easy Real Action Spiritual Exercises Deliver:
Erase the chains of abuse that bind you using EASY made, REAL life, ACTION steps with SPIRITUAL outlook & hands on EXERCISES that DELIVER!

"Every time you don't follow your inner guidance, you feel a loss of energy, loss of power, a sense of spiritual deadness."
-Shakti Gawain

Chapter Six – Be Determined

WHAT DRIVES YOU, CAN GUIDE YOU!
Focusing on YOU!

Look deep inside to find out what makes you tick. What are your motivators? What makes you get up each morning and keep going? Why do you do the things you do every day? Get down to the basics of it. Dig deep at the roots to find really what gets you out of bed each and every morning.

If you're a parent what drives you to be that good parent? If you are working what is driving you to keep working and doing a good job? Is it just the money or is there more to it? Is it passion that drives you or do you make the best of everything you do? You may want to consider how you feel. Do you feel forced to get out of bed or do you look forward to getting out of bed? Knowing the answers to these questions can make a difference in our day.

<u>Finding your personal motivators</u> is a very important step in this handbook. It is a good idea to have a couple personal goals that you can fall back on during your journey to healing and bettering your well being. When times get tough you will be equipped with some great ammunition against whatever is tossed your way.

Personal motivators are just that, highly personal. These motivators need not be shared with anyone else but you. Even if you can come up with one motivator as simple as why you picked up this book or what your goal was or is, then you have a good start on filling your ammunition belt. Life is definitely not easy for anyone so let's go through it armed and ready! Your motivators are hidden deep down inside so it will require you to put some effort into pulling them out. Some people find that easier to do than others. I know I didn't realize what my personal motivators were until I had the opportunity this year to pull them out and actually see them on paper. I guess subconsciously I knew but never had them in front of me in such detail. When I did this my life all of a sudden made sense to me. If you are persistent with this exercise your determination will allow you to clear up a lot of things in your life as well.

Your actions have motivations, your motivations have goals, and your goals have reason. What keeps you on track? I was pleased to find out why I work extremely hard as I do to the point of over doing it in my dedication and loyalty. Not only am I passion driven but I also create an extremely stressful fight toward perfection. This is great where my daughter is concerned but I realize now I go overboard and knowing this about myself helps me keep it under control.

I put a lot of thought into the questions above and came up with a few good reasons for myself. I learned that the things I do are for God, my daughter and to make myself feel good. Sounds plain and simple but it gives my day meaning. Next I'll share with you a couple of my special reminder motivators that I use for guidance when I need to pull through a rough time to keep me going. I hope you are getting the hang of the writing and reading process in this book. I would suspect it's becoming easier for you. This step requires that you take similar action as you did in the previous steps that you have already conquered.

Two motivators in life I use daily to guide me and to keep me focused are:

- *"I will make every effort possible into setting the best example in life I can for my child no matter what. I will do what it takes for her to be led into adulthood using my hands on real life knowledge. I will continue to use my examples in hopes that I can help prevent her from making any needless mistakes, so she can enjoy a good quality of life."*

- *"When I see unhappiness I feel a need to help other people. I want to help them experience a better quality of life for themselves. I will try to plant the seed for them. I will try to educate them and provide information from my real life examples as a guide for them to follow if they choose to do so."*

I hope I cleared up my meaning behind all of this for you to see how I came up with this information.

<u>BEGIN THIS STEP</u> by taking a good look at your strengths, character and style to be able to observe your own individuality. At times there are choices we make influenced by our behaviors toward them that make us question ourselves. There is nothing wrong with that because learning something new about oneself is just another opportunity to grow. Seriously put some thought into this exercise and please don't rush through it if you can help it.

EXERCISE SHEET: Use separate sheets of paper or a journal style book. It helps to record the applicable chapter names along with the relevant page numbers from this book on each of your writings for easy reference later.

Record your story: How you relate, situations, agendas, notes, thoughts & anything else related to this chapter. Use paragraph writing, point form or whatever you're comfortable with. Think back & take a deep breath! Now take some time to read over what you wrote.

_____

_____

_____

_____

_____

_____

_____

_____

_____

_____

_____

_____

_____

_____

_____

_____

_____

_____

_____

_____

_____

_____

_____

_____

E.R.A.S.E.D. = Easy Real Action Spiritual Exercises Deliver:
Erase the chains of abuse that bind you using EASY made, REAL life, ACTION steps with SPIRITUAL outlook & hands on EXERCISES that DELIVER!

WANTING TO FIT IN & JUST BE ME
Finding YOU again is possible!

Yes it is possible to find yourself again! The real you is in there somewhere buried beneath all of life's doings but you may have no idea how to dig the real you out. Let me start by saying that there is no easy method or magical wand that will make this happen for you, it can be a lifelong process and may take many helping hands including your own to accomplish this. One cannot be helped unless one wants to be helped. Agree? So when you reach your point of wanting to be found, greet assistance from all helping hands that may come your way.

Sometimes people let pride get in the way then they end up missing out on very pertinent things in their lives. I am guilty of this also. In my past I did find it a lot easier and less shameful to not accept help in any manner. I figured that people wanted to help me because they thought there was something wrong with me and felt I was incompetent. As sad as that is, it was my reality. There was nothing wrong with me, just something wrong with the way I allowed my pride and insecurities to get in the way of my well being. When people offer advice or lend a hand I find that it's in our best interest to take it and not turn it away. Everything happens for a reason and it starts here.

It takes courage to ask for and accept help so don't feel alone on that. My recommendation for you which works great for me is to tighten your butt cheeks, take a deep breath and go for it! As silly as it may be or as funny as it may sound tightening my butt cheeks gives my brain something else to focus on. The voices in my head have something else to talk about while I'm pushing the YES word out of my mouth when someone offers to help me out.

While holding your head high, try this butt tightening method out when you're feeling nervous or angry then see how you feel. I found it to be just as effective when asking a librarian where a book on a sensitive topic such as abuse is. It could also come in handy when calling around to find out where a local group session may be held on private topics like codependency, substance abuse or family crisis and many more. Tightening your butt cheeks won't kill brain cells, holding your breath will as I've done may times out of shame and embarrassment. I like to look at this method as an exercise that'll get our cheeks in shape!

When it comes to going to group sessions or therapy of any type it's okay you're not the only one. There is nothing to be ashamed about. Put your pride in the closet and realize these groups were formed for a reason. There are many people in need of help attending them. Local group sessions can be an in-depth way of finding yourself where you will have the opportunity to listen and relate to others. Private therapy is two sided, just you and your therapist. Both these types are highly recommended. Depending on the severity and the nature of what it is you have suffered, that will be what determines which type of therapy is appropriate for you.

Other therapeutic ways that I found helpful into finding myself were taking walks alone. Walk around the block, around a park or a lake. Go to a designated hiking trail and just walk, walk, walk. While you are walking you are getting the blood flowing to your brain. Fresh air to your brain cells and exercise to your body both make the atmosphere for thinking advantageous. You will be able to think clearer. Don't forget to take your journal or a notepad with you so you can record anything you may want to revisit that pops in your mind.

At times I used to feel like I was someone else and not really me at all. Have you felt that way? I'm sure you have. Talk about an unpleasant and confusing feeling. Throughout my life and abuse experiences I took on a cover up role of cleaning my house like a maniac to keep busy. It worked for the time being. I didn't have to think about my life or think about any areas that needed improving. I understand now that we all have areas we can improve on no matter how perfect we see ourselves.

Growing up I really never felt like I fit in with the other kids. I always felt like an outsider when it came to what I wore for clothing. My dad was a strict used clothing shopper [That is fine and I did it myself when my daughter was younger, but geez at least buy your children used clothing that is somewhat in the same league as the current fad].

The items I wanted for myself when I was younger were not priced much higher if at all than the ones my dad would insist on choosing for me which was his choice of style. I would have been more than willing to sacrifice a garment or two to get one of my liking. I guess he wanted us kids to stand out from others for whatever reason, maybe it was his way to control us further which did absolutely nothing in the way of boosting my self esteem.

Wearing those disturbingly ugly, very colorful and sometimes way too small clothing articles definitely contributed to enhancing my insecurities. The opinions from children should be taken into consideration within reason and so should their feelings! I try to sound out all my daughters opinions, suggestions and thoughts with her in hopes to give her a better understanding behind my reasons. I want her to learn for her own future decision making why certain choices are made. All it would have taken was a bit of eye opening and some effort on my dad's part with us kids but sadly he allowed his kick for control to play a large part.

At Christmas time my dad would go overboard to spoil us and shower us in gifts, giving us toys and games we actually wanted. His logic on this mixed with his choice of attire for us during the rest of the year did not and still does not make any sense to me. When I look at all the events in my life and then add these views into it, I feel as if something was at work forcing me or not allowing me to be myself in any aspect of my life. It seems to have come from every direction no matter how I look at it.

This brings me more to the point of expressing a need for change, you can bring this on yourself. Start digging at who you really are and who you want to become. Focus on it enough and it will happen. Little by little you will start to see things change, some small and others not so small. So what are you waiting for? Take this book and go for that walk, hike or read something spiritual on the beach alone. Do whatever you need to do to get in touch with yourself, the earth and your God to make things happen.

IS IT IMPORTANT TO HAVE GOD IN OUR LIVES?
Dare to believe!

Well that's for you to decide. Do you believe in God? Do you believe in a higher power? Do you believe in spirits or other higher beings? I know I do. I know too that everyone is entitled to their own beliefs and disbeliefs. I remember my life without God, it was quite trying living it on my own. Having God in my life now makes the rollercoaster ride a lot easier to keep going back up and over each hill that I need to face. This is why I say to you, dare to believe.

Clearly I can't push God on people for everyone has their own beliefs. I can on the other hand share my personal experiences regarding this by letting others know that having God in my life now does help me live easier with purpose. Let me ask you, do you really think you're in control? Having a spiritual guide in your life is no different than having a partner or personal trainer at the least. I sure wish I had that when I was younger. It was so tough doing it on my own. Well I had sisters of course but we didn't talk about that stuff.

It think it is important that we have something or someone to believe in to take some weight off our shoulders. Seriously look at what we have to carry in life, it's a lot! Just because things are right for me I know it doesn't mean they are right for all. At the same time though how can I not share this? I find life to be a lot simpler to deal with now than in my past where I would struggle without God. So now I share this in hopes a light bulb may get turned on for another.

It was a few years ago when my bulb mysteriously lit up for me bringing me closer to God, eventually I was led into actively having God in my life. I was brought to him by messages he sent through close friends even customers where I worked.

I don't know your story, for all I know you may already be a believer and if you're not that's cool too. However, just out of curiosity I must ask why that is? Why not believe in God? Have you done some sort of research, maybe listened to others advice or their opinions? Perhaps something negative happened to you which made you form an opinion and from that point on you have stuck with that? There can be many personal reasons and that's okay, I just want to point out that there is no harm in exploring again. You may come across something you haven't considered before or you may be lucky enough to receive signs or messages like I did by waiting it out, who knows?

It was the television that turned me around from being a non-believer into a believer. Sounds wacky I know, but it's true. I had no knowledge when it came to God or spirituality of any kind as I mentioned before. One morning out of the blue while watching television I kind of sensed a feeling or a nudge of some sort, this somehow led me into watching various Christian programs. While channel surfing I noticed that I kept coming across those types of shows, it wasn't too long though before I caught myself turning the channel back to those same 'silly' shows as I thought at the time.

I found a new interest. These shows were daily life related, some of which involved current events and other topics covered my experiences. I should say that I didn't realize it right away and that it did take a few shows before I started to wonder what the heck I was watching them for? However, I surprised myself when I found out how much I really enjoyed their point of view on life. It felt really strange so I hid this from others being embarrassed by it. I would quickly change the channel anytime someone entered the room while I was watching one of these shows. I didn't want to be questioned or to have them wondering if I was turning weird on them or something!

So there I was watching these half hour episodes occasionally without a second thought. Then wham! It hit me one day while sitting on the sofa, "What the heck am I doing? I hate this crap!" Seriously I thought I was losing it until I felt a tickle in my tummy that told me it was okay to watch these and learn as I go. These types of shows became a part of my morning along with my coffee before I would get ready for work.

Today I love watching these shows in bed after a long day. They are so inspirational for me and great wake up call. They touch my heart and my soul. I love listening to the views and stories of different people they have on as guests, it really opens up my mind. From that information I am able to form my own opinion and grow in that.

My experiences in God started to expand for me. One day a customer of mine walked into my place of work and for no apparent reason asked me point blank what kind of music I enjoyed. I thought that was a bit personal since I barely knew him, but I told him anyways to be polite. Nice man but he caught me off guard a bit when he went off on a tangent. He didn't appreciate it when I laughed when he asked me why I don't listen to Christian rock or Christian contemporary music. He seemed more concerned rather than offended.

He explained to me what great therapy it was for him. I personally thought he was kind of coo-coo at the time but despite that we ended up being short term friends. After I accepted his message he continued to educate me from his experiences until I was on the brink of accepting and believing in God, then he was gone. He moved away and left me hanging in wonderment and wishing that this would have happened to me many years before.

I know now that he accomplished what he set out to do. His mission was to plant a seed and he did just that. Because of the bazaar way our transaction started out and how our interaction in general went, it stuck with me for quite a while. A short while after my curiosity got the better of me, guess what I found myself doing? Yes, checking out that specific genre of music. Turns out I liked it! He was right in saying it works like therapy. Who would have guessed? I found that when I opened my ears and my mind I heard more than just praise and religion, I heard life messages and real life stories I could relate to.

By this time I was starting to clue into what was happening. Listening to Christian music and watching Christian shows could only lead into one thing right? Turns out I was being given bits and pieces at a time and before I knew it I was attending church. I know it was meant for me and meant to be at that time. That might not be the way it is for everyone. You never know where you may be led into. If I wasn't paying attention I could have possibly missed out on something crucial that brought me to this point in my journey.

Not necessarily speaking of religion or church, can you recall a time when there was something negative or something that you didn't like happening in your life where you managed to turn it around into just the opposite? Did you do this by thinking positive thoughts or did you manage to pick it apart to find something about it that you liked? If so, congratulations that's the way to do it!

If ever you felt that you may have missed out on any *signs* or *messages* during your life, try to patiently and consistently focus on mentally reliving those events that took place where you feel some signs or messages may once have occurred. You never know, over a period of time you may be given the opportunity again where these *signs* will revisit you. If it was meant to happen it will eventually happen again. Remember to always keep an eye open as it may happen slightly differently the second time around.

People have all sorts of different views and beliefs on various things and that's okay. Whatever helps someone to not travel this road alone is great. Give the wheel to someone or something else then do your best to let go of the control. Feeling free to ride the roller coaster of life while learning to enjoy it with all its ups and downs is amazing! If you are open to it you will see life from a different perspective in a whole new light!

I wasn't particularly open to giving my control up, the thought of that scared me. "What if I let go and something bad happens?" I dwelled on this question for quite some time as it certainly wasn't something that I was going to rush into. Heavens no! I took into consideration how I was conducting my life and realized how much control I really felt I needed to have. It was alot!

Someone asked me at one point why I felt I needed all that control? I had no answer other than to make sure everything runs smoothly. Have you heard that before? I then thought about that statement and how unrealistic it sounded coming from my own mouth. Turns out I ended up letting go of a lot more control than I ever thought I could. Not to say I have let go a hundred percent but I have made a great improvement compared to the way I was before. I am still working on it.

What a great feeling! Scary at first yes, but it didn't take long to get used to. It helps me to know that nothing too bad really happens when we do choose to let go as I thought it did and I have learned that anything that does happen not to our liking can be fixed or worked with.

"With God all things

are possible"

-Matthew 19:26

Chapter Seven – Learn from it!

CAN OUR ENEMIES BE OUR FRIENDS?
A look into an enlightening response

I love this quote by Aristotle, "The antidote for fifty enemies is one *friend*." You could challenge this by trying to turn those fifty enemies into fifty more friends but the chances of that happening is unrealistic. Even if you adapted to their ways or played their game by giving them whatever they wanted, chances are you still wouldn't be able to turn each one of them into your friend. If you did somehow manage to pull it off it would probably take more than just one of your lifetime's to accomplish it. So on the bright and more down-to-earth side converting frienemies can be done so keep your aim at two or three.

There have been times in my life where I have felt all I had were enemies, how about you? It's an awful feeling to think everyone hates you. Talk about negativity being powerful or what! Unless you are some type of a public figure whom has gone wrong then I guess you may be able to say that everyone hates you. If you think about it even those individuals have family members or a friend or two that in fact like them. For you I don't believe this would be the case. I know that it may not feel this way for you at times but if you look around hard enough you will always be able to find someone on your side. That is just the way it goes.

Have you heard of the term 'frienemie' or 'frienemy'? Strange word but it is a term that according to online encyclopedia information it has appeared in print as early as 1953. It is a term used to refer to either an enemy disguised as a friend, or to a partner who is simultaneously a <u>rival</u>. The term is also used to describe personal, geopolitical, and commercial relationships both among individuals and groups or institutions.

In talking with teens I found out that this term simply means to them friends that are kind of their enemies, and enemies who are sort of their friend too. They feel that they are a particular person or group of people have two sides to them. These people are the ones we refer to as being two-faced. This type of person leaves them feeling unclear as to where they stand with each other. I see those people as confused souls. These kids do like some things about their frienemies but the enemy part usually plays the stronger role. Such cases may be when they know their own peers don't like a person or a particular group of people that they in fact like themselves, which they feel it wouldn't be very cool to step up and say so. Some kids are different when it comes to that, hats off to them. If they are not one of those kids it can leave them feeling frustrated or even angry about it.

Sometimes people are just enemies. I think some people get a kick out of being an enemy for they just won't budge no matter what you do. I know firsthand it's hard to have someone in your life that chooses to remain a rival instead of making peace with you. Sometimes those people can't let go or even inform you of whatever it is that bothers them.

Not knowing where I am headed with this probably has your head spinning in bewilderment right now hey? I'm hoping not too much. Regardless of what the proper definition of frienemy is I hear a deeper explanation behind the word from people who use it in their daily lingo. I hear lack of communication. This lack of communication that I was eventually getting to is why I originally asked the question, "Can you benefit from having enemies?"

Ask yourself that question, do you think you could benefit from having enemies? This is a tough one for people to answer with a reply other than no they cannot. There definitely is a reason they are called enemies, in general they are against us and of a negative nature in which we shun upon them. We are taught to keep our enemies close at hand. We believe in keeping an eye on them and we feel we need to stay one step ahead of them before they have a chance to make their dreadful move on us. I agree to a point but I also believe that feeds your enemy negative energy at the same time, it gives them power that you may not want them to have.

For most circumstances I do agree that having enemies is a very negative experience and who really needs that in our life? I don't. From here take a look at the enemies in your life that you've had or have if any, and seriously try and answer the above question regarding if you feel you benefit from having an enemy. If you can think of or see a benefit from having them then that is turning a negative into a positive. This is pretty tricky and if you can accomplish this with a frienemy then you will have a better chance at flipping anything negative that is tossed your way into something more positive. Getting back to friends who are also enemies or visa-versa, wouldn't it seem that they would be a lot easier to work with rather than a straight forward enemy? Of course they would be, with a frienemy you're half way there! What do you think would come out of putting some thought into it and identifying what it is about them that make you attach the word frienemy in the first place to them? I think you may just be on your way to uncovering a whole new part of you. These particular individuals are half a friend already and friends are willing to help out another friend aren't they?

It may even be to your benefit to slightly adjust yourself and your ways accordingly to suit that individual? You don't need to change for that person completely but you can make adjustments that are not so extreme. It can be done fittingly especially if you found that you may be a contributing factor in why you call that person a frienemy? Doing this could make it easier on you in finding out what you need to change in yourself. So what about enemies? I Look at enemies like they are there for a reason, to point something out to us in our lives or something about us that needs changing.

It may sound like a lot of gibberish right now but if you think seriously about it you may find that seeking out a frienemy has a purpose. It may lead you into finding out that you could possibly forgive more than you do, maybe think and speak more positively or even judge others a bit less than you may be doing. There are many things that by converting yourself or convincing the other person to convert their ways will teach you and them alike.

Patience, empathy, selflessness and letting our stubbornness go are all valuable traits to learn. To be honest I know this list very well as I had to learn all the above and it's still in the works. It is hard to break old ways that's for sure but I continue trying. The list could seem endless as to what changes you may need at the moment but don't fret you may not need as many as I did. That alone should be good news! Always remember change can be scary which it's just a feeling of fear but sometimes change can be a very good thing, it may be just what you need!

<u>DIVE INTO THIS STEP</u> by jotting down a list of people you can come up with that you consider to be your frienemies. Record their names down the left side of the page. Create a column beside each person you come up with and list the reasons why you have given them that label. Here comes the hard part now, this could be your wakeup call! Take a look at your list of frienemies and try to see what part you may have played that contributed to this if any.

It's hard to see ourselves for who we really are, trust me I know. Sometimes the hardest thing to do is to decide to change even when you know it is the best course of action. Carefully considering this will bring you to seeing a new list in the third column you that you will create. Fill this column with what you feel is necessary to change in yourself. Sometimes what we don't like in others or the faults we find in other people can pretty much be what we need to change in ourselves.

Once you have completed this challenge you are invited to take it further if you dare. Go through your list one by one and find ways within yourself that could help turn your frienemies into more of a friend than an enemy. You just might be successful with a few. With the others you may found what I found out, once you pinpoint their reason for coming into your life in the first place sometimes those people just seem to simply fade away. That's a good thing for their job is done. We usually will end up learning something new about ourselves that you may not have known before and with that knowledge we can't go wrong.

EXERCISE SHEET: Use separate sheets of paper or a journal style book. It helps to record the applicable chapter names along with the relevant page numbers from this book on each of your writings for easy reference later.

Record your story: How you relate, situations, agendas, notes, thoughts & anything else related to this chapter. Use paragraph writing, point form or whatever you're comfortable with. Think back & take a deep breath! Now take some time to read over what you wrote.

_____

_____

_____

_____

_____

_____

_____

_____

_____

_____

_____

_____

_____

_____

_____

_____

_____

_____

_____

_____

_____

_____

E.R.A.S.E.D. = Easy Real Action Spiritual Exercises Deliver:
Erase the chains of abuse that bind you using EASY made, REAL life, ACTION steps with SPIRITUAL outlook & hands on EXERCISES that DELIVER!

BEING AN ADULT CHILD OF AN ALCOHOLIC
Talk about exasperating!

What is alcohol intended for? Some people have a drink to warm up on a chilly night or to help them relax. Often it serves to lighten the mood in a room where people are socializing, it can also enhance the flavors of food and when mixed with various ingredients it can be enjoyed as a tasty treat. That is all fine and dandy unless it adversely affects yourself or others around you.

Not every person uses alcohol for those reasons I have listed. For example, far too many people see it as a numbing agent to mask unwanted feelings or memories which works for only temporary relief. This can easily become very habitual. By the time a person realizes that they have gone too far with using alcohol for this purpose, it has already taken control over them for the most part.

Unintentionally on her part this is exactly what happened to my 'non-drinking' mom. It utterly controlled her for quite some time completely changing her lifestyle and her behavior. Over the years I watched her become a 'functioning' alcoholic. Despite her constant consumption of alcohol she is still self sufficient, works full time and gets out and about often on her own. So far so good.

Mom started her heavy drinking during a very heartrending and tragic time in her life. As a result of being submerged in so much darkness, I feel it only added more gloom to her already existing day to day misery. Her view of life became obscured giving her a dull outlook on most things. Alcohol brought out the worse in her by changing her personality and altering her character. It is really unfair how our brain works; we spoil it with something to make us feel good to help us cope with life's difficulties then it turns on us. Sometimes knowing what could happen to us isn't enough, nobody goes into it with the intentions of becoming addicted do they? No, they sure do not. Sadly too many people are taken by alcoholism.

Indeed there are several different reasons why a person becomes an alcoholic. As mentioned already a common one being when someone uses it as a crutch to get through day to day life, this can totally make stopping the habit seem almost near impossible. It can be quite the battle for anyone to sit back and watch someone we care about abuse alcohol, it's even more difficult when children are the onlookers. Kids end up having to deal with their parents problem with alcohol because they don't have a choice other than to take on that burden. Hardly fair.

Looking back to the eighties to when my father died, my sister and I along with some friends introduced mom into drinking alcohol. We did it in hopes to cheer her up but our intentions backfired, it turns out it became a full time habit for her. I ended up taking on some guilt as I felt I was to blame for contributing to her drinking problem, this affected me deep down for quite a long time. Those feelings have since faded and honestly, not really all that long ago.

It wasn't until I was quite a bit older when I understood that my mom was the adult who made the decision herself to partake in what we suggested to her, we were her kids not her parents. Regardless, knowing this truth I suppose it is normal to take on some guilt feeling responsible as long as those feelings are not allowed to take over our lives. I sometimes wonder if I was just lucky that it didn't turn out that way for me, or if it was because I learned how to train my brain to control my thoughts? Wanting to drink and party with the rest of the group I do admit to knowingly taking advantage of my mom's vulnerability. While mom was in a state of mourning I helped to coerce her into doing what the rest of us were all doing.

I am being as brutally straightforward about myself as I can, it is not easy to admit these types of things of course but we all make mistakes. Letting it out is part of one's healing process. Feeling ashamed of my thoughts back then in particular my poor behavior, I had a difficult time letting go of the guilt that I carried it but I had to. Most teenagers I have met are fairly well behaved, so consequently I cannot fully blame the fact that I was a teen at the time other than it is a common trait among that age group to be selfish. In saying that, I know the group of us definitely pushed the bar on that one. I eventually accepted what was done and forgave myself. Forgiving myself helped me learn to manage those disabling feelings that I had, doing this enabled me to cope without letting it rule over me.

When alcohol takes over it can ruin lives. I am sure the most frightening time of my mother's life was the moment my dad left the picture. Having very little life skills joined with her fear of independence she did not give herself the chance to learn how to be a mother all on her own. Not saying she is not at fault but drinking, partying and meeting new people did become her priority. Mom was caged up and controlled pretty much her entire life then all in a blink of an eye she was set free. When this overwhelming change for her occurred she allowed her wild side to surface!

Alcohol was the main contributor influencing all of moms decisions in regards to raising three daughters alone. From being deprived of a normal carefree childhood followed by having to endure a very restricted marriage, she definitely took hold of her freedom once it was triggered. Actually all hell broke loose, there was no stopping her! Walking in her shoes without looking through the eyes of her daughter I can totally understand how she allowed this to happen to her, however, I am her daughter and reality is what it is. With no consideration of our needs or our safety I felt she sacrificed us, her own children. I know this happens to many other people all too often as well, for my mom's sake only she is not alone on that. Unquestionably she was not herself at all.

Finally getting attention drawn to herself mom was as free as a bird. I along with others close to me endured her rambunctious bar days. During my teen years it was rather uncomfortable and even scary at times to be surrounded by adult strangers in our home constantly. The list of people ranged from a rowdy bar band to a few biker gang members that she liked to invite over for all nighters. Love my mom but at the time mothering was not her priority. I learned to fend for food and other necessities in life myself, at the time that was the norm for awhile.

Since this was so very long ago and mom and I have now rectified our overdue relationship, I don't feel telling all the fine details is necessary. Considering the stories are directed more toward her actions than the affect it had on me, I guess mom could write her own biography but I don't think that will happen. In my heart I know if the circumstances were different and my mom was able to control her drinking on her own, she would not have let things go as far as they did.

Mom is truly a great lady who changed her ways, she overcame it all on her own and that for sure counts! I dealt with my own troubled feelings from all of this by knowing that bad things in life do happen and quite often it's out of our control. This view helps me to enjoy and appreciate the preciousness of life and also keeps me from harmfully dwelling anytime I have a terrible experience..

I feel a natural responsibility for my mom and her well being even though I am her child and she is my parent. I am not sure why, maybe it's a control thing? Maybe I care too much, is that possible? It was important for the both of us that I stopped enabling her as it just made matters worse. Changing our living arrangements was for the best for all involved and was certainly agreed upon by both of us.

Switching it up again, a girlfriend of mine grew up with both of her parents fully dependant on alcohol. From a young age she was forced to be witness to and be involved in abuse where alcohol was usually the catalyst in it. It continued right up to the day her parents separated and divorced. Her father abandoned the family and as a child from that day forward she was left to helplessly watch her mother's lifelong demons free themselves.

Dealing with her mom's alcoholism was the most difficult for her because she wasn't old enough to know what was really happening let alone be able to handle any of it. They often tried talking about it, but through deep anger, fear and awkwardness they accomplished nothing. As an adult herself now she has moved on from her past maintaining a close relationship with her mom. When she learned how to appropriately distance herself she stopped allowing her mother's behavior to affect her own well being. On another happy note her mother is doing well and has turned a new leaf through counseling, family, friends, faith and prayer.

When I was younger both of my parents only drank alcohol to celebrate Christmas and New Years each year. They would have a couple drinks during their small social gatherings with the neighbors on one or two evenings. Having a then sober mother figure in our home was far different than having to watch the non sober mom I eventually grew to know from living a large part of my adult life with her.

I don't want to put out there that my mother is not sober day in and day out, although there are fewer sober times than not. She regularly drinks one beer after another with no breathers in between, continuing well into the very late hours of her nights.

Her drinking often starts in the morning on her days off and immediately after she gets home on the days that she works. She continuously claims she's not hurting anyone else or affecting them but she is wrong. I worry about her and her health.

I remember when my mom used to have dry out days, this was before her drinking gradually increased from four and five to seven days a week. Being her daughter, living with her and seeing this happen daily is what had me feeling obligated to inform her of the help that is available out there for her. Through my taunting and yet sometimes compassionate reminders I desperately tried different ways to get the message across to her. I wanted her to know that her constant drinking was indeed affecting the people who care about her. I approached her countless times with all sorts of information all to no avail. I truly had all intent of helping her but I don't think she saw it that way at all. My mom wasn't in a position to understand how much my heart broke with disappointment each time she shunned me.

Alcoholics have a way of making us feel like failures without even realizing they're doing it. We can overcome feeling this way by distancing our emotions from these people the best we can and recognize that their problem with alcohol is bigger than we are. We can contribute to help the people who we care about in many different ways but really we shouldn't forget that only they are able to free themselves.

At the age of twenty I moved out of my mom's home, after we lived separately for some years we moved back in together with the intent of financial convenience. Taking a closer look within myself I can see that there was a part of me possibly hoping to recover what I had lacked growing up. In a fairytale kind of way I guess I figured there may have been a chance to somehow get back all those years that I envisioned a relationship with my mom to be like.

Over the years my mom did confess to having a problem with alcohol, regrettably though her admissions were under duress. She forced them out during a couple episodes of our many fights and discussions that we had about her addiction. I am sure it was all to appease me at the time. Even though mom didn't admit it to herself, hearing her actually say she has a problem with alcohol filled my heart with such great relief. Sadly, it was only a brief moment of excitement and hope. Mom's admissions were short lived before the vicious cycle would start again, all of which proves that people will change when they feel they are ready to and not when we demand them to. Again, she is not alone on that.

Having a parent who is an alcoholic is very depressing because it is so disappointing. It is hard to accept. Are parents not the ones that are suppose to take care of us when we are growing up and not the other way around? Even now in my forties I still worry about my mom and her drinking, sometimes it's too much mentally for me to handle.

I have spent a lot of time fearing the worse happening to my mom. I tried to let her know that I felt this way by scaring her with health details, I thought it would be enough to get her to quit drinking if she knew that she was pickling her brain and turning it to mush. I stressed the facts to her that because of beer she is destroying her liver and pancreas causing her own slow death. No matter what I came up with none of it seemed to faze her. Well, at least she didn't show it. It is very frustrating to hear my own mother say that she doesn't care about her drinking nor how much she drinks when the truth is I know she does. She shows no concern for the financial aspect of it or even the potential negative outcome it may have on her health. That to me is bothersome. After years of nagging at her about it I finally gave up. There is really is no point to it if it just goes in one ear and out the other. Let the seed be planted.

Nearly spending my whole life unwilling and unable to physically or verbally express how I really feel about my mom was and still is complicated. This is mainly because our personal experiences with love and affection toward each other have never really been there. I worry because I do love and care about her of course but how I would come across to her was irritated and angry due to my bitterness toward her. She wears an alcoholics mask that is hard to break through. I know the mom underneath this cover does hear me, but at the same time I can't force her to listen to me let alone believe a word I say. The power that alcoholism can have over someone is unbelievably strong. The disease in every way is pure evil in my eyes. I can only imagine how mom feels and what really must go through her mind. Nobody wins.

I recognized that my lecturing, scolding, threatening, playing along, condoning and bribing only got me so far with my mom. It felt like a waste of my breath seeing that all it did was help me to cope and carry myself through each day. With better judgment I would have chosen another way for myself to handle it all as it really didn't do much in the way of help for her.

As I mentioned before I tried helping my mom in the ways I felt I knew how, for example I visited a couple local rehab facilities and collected brochures for her. When she was at work I had snuck a few of these pamphlets in her bedroom for her to find when she came home. She never mentioned them of course. I had brought it up once by asking her if she had read them assuming she got them, she said she had but when I tried to find out what she thought she didn't give me much more than a hum and a haw.

Offering to take her to meetings, letting her know that I would sit with her during therapy sessions to even simply lending her an ear didn't get me anywhere. I suggested different hobbies and new adventures in life that she may want to partake in but nothing really attracted her to wanting to budge from her position. I feel all my efforts were pretty well exhausted. I had to ask myself, how much is too much?

At one point I considered a family intervention but it's really not that easy to get everyone on the same page with it. Through discussions with another companion of mine that went through an intervention with her own mom for her alcohol addiction I found out that she felt it was ineffective in their family. This individual is not certain if all her family members were included or if that would have made any difference at all. She believes that an intervention forces the alcoholic to get treatment under duress of losing their family and feels it is against their own will and not necessarily in alignment with that persons intended life path.

This friend of mine strongly recommends that if it is decided an intervention is the way to go then the family needs to be prepared for any relapses. I agree. It wouldn't be right for the initiators of the intervention to quit after they were the ones that got the ball rolling would it? No, but it does happen. She stressed the importance of family members maintaining continued support for the individual in therapy. Being a part of an intervention can take a great deal of effort and consume a lot of time on each members part. Families need to take into consideration what they would be comfortable with and how involved they'd want to be. Then after carefully thinking out the process, it would be a good idea to ask themselves if they still feel an intervention would be effective or not.

On the other side of the coin I also know someone who had found her own family intervention to be quite successful! This intervention led this woman's mother on a whole new path where she was able to gain skills to face different challenges by using new approaches. Every family is different so the outcome varies of how successful each intervention would be. It also falls back on the person with the addiction depending on if they are ready or not. There are professionals out there that will help families out with interventions by educating and guiding them to even participating in it if that is what a family chooses to do.

One purpose of this handbook is for me to share 'how not to let others actions affect us negatively', being human myself I feel I too have fallen into that trap many times. The time came when my mom and I reached a point where we couldn't handle each other anymore. I needed to instigate change to clear the toxic air for my daughters sake and my own sanity as well. It was a distressing reality for me when I came to realize that the struggle with alcohol is really my mom's problem not my own. Enough was enough. There was too much heartache and many tears shed by both of us and we were all ready to welcome peace into our lives.

Whatever I was clinging to I had to let go of. I no longer had it in me to carry on condoning my mom's alcoholic behavior in her addiction. Now that my mom has moved out after fifteen long trying years together we are back to living separate lives once again. It seems we both won. I strongly believe we were meant to go through all that we did together.

Good things have come out of this move for us both, I now have somewhat of what I wished for many moons ago and she can finally be a mom. I am happy to say my mom initiates affection toward me in a carefree way now. She surprised me with an 'I love you' and continues to give hugs every once in awhile. We are both learning to keep it going! Our relationship has improved to a happier one now. Mom is content with her privacy that she has been getting and has taken up decorating as a hobby. For me there is no more stopping dead in my tracks, holding my breath or gritting my teeth every time I hear the frequent sound of beer cans crack open throughout the day and night. That noise almost put me over the edge of sanity, it definitely tested my ability not to allow someone else's problems affect me negatively.

I remember one of my counselors ten years back asking me why I live with my mom if it upsets me so much to watch her drink her life away? I plainly told him that I didn't want her to drink alone. He brought to light for me that in fact she was already drinking alone. I wish I would have understood what he meant by that back then, but we all have to undergo the flow of life.

More than ten years after mom's party days were over she succumbed to limiting her drinking to five days a week with a couple dry out days in between. This routine lasted for several years. As the time went on her drinking progressed and has worsened these last few years. I watched helplessly in sadness as those couple of dry out non alcohol lime pop days, turned into rum cooler days. I honestly can't recall the last time I witnessed her drinking anything other than strong beer and rum coolers at home.

My mom defends herself by saying she drinks water and tea five days a week at work, she expects me to believe that justifies it. It wasn't just watching her drink constantly that saddened and frustrated me but rather the bitter, negative, angry and unloving character that she turned into while drinking that did. An adult or not, growing up with this can without a doubt turn us into being bitter, angry and frustrated beings too.

Being the bystander we watch it all happen with hurt in our heart being we have absolutely no control over the alcohol. We put up with the addict trying to outsmart us and pull the wool over our eyes. It's appalling and I find it hard to brush off easily. What gets me is these people honestly think that they do a good job of it! I have been told by recovering alcoholics that when they were drinking he or she was fully aware of their behavior regarding this. I am not sure if this depends on how deep the addiction is or not. They also said they would go to any length not to get caught despite their consequences. I'm also told that no matter how guilty these people felt or what opposing thoughts they may have had, they could not stop bullshitting even if they wanted to. I guess it comes with the territory.

I recently learned through some statistical cases that I came across in an article I had read that adult children who have grown up with parents that are alcoholics, can turn out to be in most cases very controlling and are very much stressed. They had no control while growing up therefore they unknowingly try to gain it when they are older. I am sure this doesn't apply to everyone but it makes sense to me. Learning this gave me a sense of relief. It helps me to understand a few things about myself and makes trying to adjust my ways a bit easier.

Being a child or an adult child of an alcoholic parent puts us in constant battle with that parent who lies to us and to themselves. It can be a difficult struggle as a lot of addicts eventually end up believing their own lies to be the truth or some reality that they deem to have experienced. How do you fight that? I've tried, I can't. From my own experience and what I know through others is that we tend to allow the alcoholic to believe they are outsmarting us leading them into thinking they are winning. What help is that giving them?

I wouldn't say we intentionally do this other than I guess we do it out of feeling defenseless and weak against the strength of the alcohol. I have to admit it is easy to do, choosing the path of least resistance that is. My heart breaks for all of us involved. I believe it's all really in the hands of God. I know a few people who have been freed from the deep depths of alcoholism so I pray my mom is one of them one day too. She needs to find her own reason to change and hopefully that is before she is left with any medical and rationale problems where it may be too late.

As heartbreaking as it is to know that our alcoholic parents may have had a hard life growing up, there is still that part of me that says it shouldn't matter what my parents went through before they had me. In a perfect world it really shouldn't matter but to me it does.

I believe parents are responsible to set the best example for their children the best they can no matter what personal sacrifice it may cost them. The voice of love is very powerful, it is forgiving and empathetic. It reminds me to have a heart by saying even though my parents were the adults they are still people with real lives and valid feelings. It's hard but I try to keep everything balanced and remain level headed without getting too tangled in the confusion of my own thoughts and emotions. When I don't take control and get a handle on these mixed feelings they become overwhelming, when this happens I tend to let everything slide until I end up struggling to endure the crashing waves.

Basically, that is how my mother and I survived all those years together in the same house. It worked. Not saying she hasn't made adjustments and compromises of her own, for she too has rode a similar wave. The first few years weren't so bad but after some time mom was very frustrated and dissatisfied with our living arrangements. Other than being in her sixties and leading an 'older' lifestyle, I could tell it infuriated her that she wasn't able to smoothly pass her problem with alcohol past me being that I was around her all the time. I know she wished I would have just shut up about It but that's not how I fly. I saw the look in her eyes when I called her on something, she wanted me to accept it and I couldn't. Mom is not always one of those quiet drinkers either, she became vocally belligerent and in my face with nasty and annoying gestures.

Again, when people are challenged with change what do they do? They fight back. I understand and agree that people need to accept each other for who they are but it's tough because of my bitterness towards her drinking. I tried hard not to let my mom's drinking behavior affect me, yet somehow it managed to bring out the worse in me. Too often I stooped in retaliation then kicked myself each time I fell into that trap.

How many times have you heard that actions speak louder than words? They truly do. "I would give almost anything to have my sober mom back!" I often thought. I use the word 'anything' instead of 'everything' for this reason, I will not give up my happiness, my joy or my well being that I've worked so hard at taking back for myself. Like many others I too have come close to losing all these by making the mistake of allowing other people's choices and actions influence me. We must remember we were each given our own lives in which we are all very much entitled to living, it is important we don't sacrifice all of ourselves when helping others.

My mother made a huge change for the better for herself several years ago. She generally fights any kind of new way presented to her with every iota of her being. I don't think she even realizes today how big of a triumph it really was. This change may not have come about voluntarily but still she did change and she adjusted. In comparison to the eighteen years spent with my dad she has now learned to be a strong, independent, opinionated and self sufficient person. Moms opinions may ride on the negative side of views and not be very constructive at times but what matters is that she learned to vocalize them when she couldn't before. For her that is a vast accomplishment!

No matter what stage a person may be at in their life or on their journey, do you agree that we are all work in progress? I believe it can be very hampering to us to try and stop things that are destined to happen, good or bad. We all welcome the *good* without a problem don't we? Well, as strange as this may sound sometimes we need to welcome the bad as well to be able to learn, grow and let go!

A friend of mine who from a very young age grew up as a child of an alcoholic mother watching her mom drink twenty six ounce bottles of rye like water. It was normal in her home to find her mom passed out on the table or in the bathroom after a drinking episode. Shortly after my father had died I went through that with my own mother as well witnessing her chugging down hard alcohol in the same manner. My mom liked to stagger off drunk on her own, it was her way to get away from life I assume. Walking around the neighborhood with my sister along with some friends of ours we spent endless summer days and nights chasing her down after my dad had died. We often found her passed out in the local baseball park or laying on sidewalks nearby until we came along to help pick her up and lug her home.

In both situations our parents behavior in the way they handled alcohol caused alot of aggravating embarrassment for us being their kids. As a child it was awfully confusing, angering and hard to take. Children are not suppose to be responsible for taking care of their parents well being but sometimes they end up forced into it by having no choice. The same for any relationship involved usually the children of the alcoholic undergo more than the alcoholic themselves. We suffer the mental lashings and endure neglect watching our mentors, the one's we care about most in life, turn into people we don't even recognize. We are constantly pushed away and rejected when all we want to do is help.

Several years ago now I attended a substance abuse class

just to see if it could help me understand the addiction my spouse had at the time. The class instructor made a point of saying that if someone is really unsure if they are truly addicted to something and they want to find out, the best way would be to stop doing whatever that may be. If you have confronted someone in your life about an addiction that you feel they have, would you be up to asking that person if they would accept a challenge of stopping whatever that may be for one month? If they choose to they will then have their answer after a short period of time.

In the event your challenge is accepted it won't be long before the ugliness of addiction comes to the surface. Most commonly seen are cravings, shaking, sickness and or many other behaviors and emotions will be evident that would not normally be present or occur in their everyday life. Most of the people I know and have known where it is obvious that they have an addiction won't even take the initiative in the first place to stop for even a few days, a week let alone a month. I suppose fear and shame play a part in this or maybe the person hasn't reached a point where they feel it would be of importance to know this.

For the record I am not a professional by any means on substance abuse addiction, however, I am experienced on the front line of reality. In the past I have been at the hurtful and disappointing receiving end of several of my acquaintances addictions, it is not a fun place to be when anyone's friendship is taken advantage of. A couple of friends of mine have owned up to being heavy drug users who have been through rehab a few times with short lived success. Seeing and feeling their frustration really gets to me. Hearing friends say they give up on trying to 'get clean' because it's too hard is understandably true but at the same time very disheartening.

When people say they accept themselves to be addicts they lose all intentions of putting in the effort into trying to quit. When a person continues to put forth genuine effort into overcoming something, it gives them a higher chance of succeeding. That reason alone makes them a winner. Do you agree? Is it fair to say when somebody gives up trying that is the time when they can declare they have failed?

Often times I've heard responses like 'ya okay' when I try to encourage others. I like reminding these friends that they do matter and are important enough to never give up trying! They pretend not to hear me but I know they do. I hope for the best outcome for everyone. I feel sometimes that I am a seed planter by nature, if I tried to stop that I wouldn't be able to. That's my addiction.

I am not the goody two shoes that last paragraph has made me sound like, unfortunately I do know how hard quitting a substance can be. I quit smoking cigarettes after nineteen years of it as well as using drugs when I was younger. I reached a point where I knew smoking had control over my life and was not only adversely affecting me but my young daughter as well. They had total control over my everyday actions and behaviors. I quit when I knew I was ready not when someone told me to, although I appreciated all the seeds they planted in me along the way. Even though I didn't let on I did take their comments, suggestions and advice into consideration. Replaying their words over in my head helped me to sprout those seeds.

I know people who have successfully gone through the same. These people I am referring to quit full time drinking as well after many long years of over-consuming it. Keeping in mind that everyone is different, one of them has never looked back while the other person has had a couple struggles but being many years later that is still considered to be very successful. It seems from what I was told that they reached a point where they had enough. Once they discovered the reasons they were drinking so much in the first place for so long, it helped them to understand themselves better which made it easier for them to face their problem head on. The band-aid was no longer needed.

One of these people told me he stopped drinking alcohol when he became aware of his insecurities, he learned that using alcohol was his way of covering up how tightly he was clinging to them. He understood what was happening. His drinking caused him to do things that only ended up making him feel guilty which then led him to drinking more to cover up those feelings. He learned it was all unnecessary, that his insecurities were lies and that he allowed them to play such a big part in his life. He shook his head in disbelief when he told me how he could finally see how ridiculous it was that he let his drinking cover up his troubles for so long. A light bulb definitely was turned on for him! His depression vanished along with his need for alcohol as more and more optimistic and hopeful doorways started to open for him.

In a conversation with my mom about his story I asked her to look around then come up with a reason for consuming such large amounts of alcohol all the time. I suggested to her that she do a self check just to see if she really felt that there is still a part of her life that is too painful or even unmanageable for her that she needs to continue to self medicate. Pondering what I said mom appeared to be in deep thought. It was a relief to watch her as she looked around to take a quick assessment of her current situation. Even though she came back with no as her answer I feel she took a positive step toward hope!

Seeing this in her prompted me to point out to her how far she really has come. I listed off what and who she has in her life now and also told her that I personally feel that she has a pretty good life. With a nod of her head she surprised me by telling me that she somewhat agreed!

According to others I know I come across as invasive or pushy but I don't see myself that way at all, alternatively I might add that I do feel I am more of a pretty thorough seed planter! Yes, I am giving myself credit for saying that without snickering. Anyways, remember when I told you that I believe people are all work in progress? Well, I do know that also includes me.

In another heated conversation with my mom I went onto asking her to think deeply into what she feels started her drinking. Without wanting to announce anything she nudged her shoulders and nodded. This only means one thing, she knows the answer. During my final attempt to really bury my seeds in deep in that conversation I then brought to her attention how long it has been and how many years have passed since she started drinking for that reason. Although I only caught a glimpse of it I did see the light come on!

When I saw that spark in my mom I jumped at the chance to bring to her attention that she in fact has a job close to home that she loves with coworkers she enjoys working with. I reminded her that unlike many others she does have most of her family living very near to her which includes some of her many grandchildren. Furthermore, I jogged her memory by loudly announcing that dad died over twenty five years ago! She looked directly at me with her eyes wide and her mouth dropped open, meaning she was actually listening to me. It felt good to finally be able to praise her for learning to stand on her own two feet after all those years.

Being that it is such a great feat, she needed to hear it from someone else that it is definitely something to be very proud of! By the sneak peek of a smile she showed on her face I am pretty sure she agreed with me.

I think my mom is slowly coming around in seeing that her current life is in fact supportive and abundant compared to her past. She did take a huge step in admitting that she cannot change the past and agreed that she should let go. Now it's up to her if anything further progresses in a positive direction, I hope and pray it does. The seeds are now planted in her. It's completely up to her if she will choose to nurture them or let them shrivel up, wither away and turn to dust.

I am aware there may be deeper issues than I know of and that some of us take longer than others to get to the point of wanting to overcome. When a person chooses to overcome something they find to be a challenge as I found out for myself, nothing will stand in our way. No matter what happens or what feelings are endured we do succeed. It's hard watching anyone go through such self destructing torment knowing there is so much help out there for them. It is very frustrating. We just want them to be doing what they are meant to be doing and that is enjoying the most out of life and what it has to offer. On the other hand my mother of course disagrees because she does not see the world through a positive eye. Not every person reaches a point in their life where they feel the importance of needing to overcome something that we know they should, this also includes our parents.

So how can we help others when they tell us they don't need or want it? From my experience I have found it difficult to tell if the person really doesn't want help or whether they are crying out for help, in either case we get pushed away. Fear and denial are tough to break through so what can we do? Most of us are not psychiatrists although out of caring and empathizing for others some of us naturally try to be. We can put the effort into trying to make sense of another person's situation and still end up losing the battle in the end. Is it worth it? I feel it that it is.

When we feel excessively burdened by the another person's problem it is a good idea to back off for awhile giving the person with the addiction their space. If possible after some time has passed, gradually continue to sporadically send out reminders or hints that may lead them in the direction of freedom. I see this to be harmless, it shows that we care and at the same time helps keeps their options fresh in their mind.

It is with good intentions that we the 'seed planters' or in other terms 'change promoters' can become very pushy and annoying. I have learned that this can backfire and be highly ineffective if gone overboard with. I see the similarity in comparing this to when our children are in their teen years wanting their parents to back off. They try to come across as they mean it for good but really what they want is for us to give them their space without going too far away.

I believe this also applies to when we are dealing with a friend or family member with an addiction. They too don't want to hear it nor do they want us to help them but they also don't want us to completely go away either. Pretty much the same thing in my eyes. People need some reassurance that there is a door available for them to go through when they choose to open it. When does an addict really say what they mean? If they did they would be discovered when they're not ready to be! I imagine it makes them feel caught off guard. In saying that, passive gestures and suggestions do go far just maybe not how or when we like them to.

I lost a very close friend of mine just a few years back. There were a couple factors that contributed to his death one being many years of a high fat diet and not eating right. This along with his inherited heart condition combined with a smoking and alcohol addiction is what started him off with his first heart attack and stroke. His final heart attack took him from us. Doctors warned him many times especially after his second heart attack and stroke. They told him that it would only be a few months before the final one would kill him if he continued on his same path.

My carefree and stubborn friend continuously laughed off what the doctor told him when he was around other people pretending it didn't bother him. I know this is not really how he felt as he did confided in me more than once in regards to how scared he really was. He had good intent to quit in his head but didn't do much about it in the way of action physically. When he finally decided to give a new lifestyle a shot, it was too late. His heart couldn't take whatever stress it was put under at the time, it literally exploded.

That was the end of my dear friend and the end of my constant nagging at him to quit.

No matter what I said, gave or did for him he fought all my good intentions tooth and nail for years. He would brush me off using his very much missed sense of humor. I tried so hard to convince him to lead a better lifestyle for himself and his kids. He would laugh and say, "I know, I know but Janet it's much easier this way." He was honest about it. He didn't have it in him to put forth the effort. He openly admitted that several times to various people. I have to give him credit for having good intentions, he was the one who generally came to me for help when he figured his drinking was out of hand.

I would do my best to intervene even though I just ended up hearing excuse after excuse. I never gave up trying. When we used to go camping we would engage in conversations for hours on end regarding his addictions. He had no problem initiating them but couldn't find the strength within himself to take the action to do what he said he wanted to do.

I lost the battle with him, but I never gave up trying. He knew I cared, I'm glad I got to say good-bye. In his own way he showed it was comforting to him and if he would have just dug a bit deeper to pull out his courage, he may have been successful. I can move on knowing his addictions were strong and out of my control. I was more than happy to be the messenger of good intent in every way I could while he was here.

To put it boldly, if you choose to be a messenger at anytime in your life be careful not to let the other persons addiction suck the life out of you. Sometimes we can offer too much of ourselves because we have big hearts, keep in mind we are not always successful all of the time and there is nothing wrong with that. In my life there have been times where doing this has made me feel like a failure. Not saying you will too but if it ever did happen just remember to not take it personally, it's not you. Addiction is a powerful force of its own.

Different things work for different people. Some people are more receptive while others may not be or even may _choose_ not to be. Once again this applies to our parents. Sometimes the best tool we have is walking away. Some people respond well to that and some don't. It's a hard call. You are the only one who can decide if you will support and carry that person or leave them to their own accord. Dragging them down the road of rehabilitation against their will because that is what you want for them may not be as effective as setting boundaries and limitations on your involvement with them. Either way there is no guarantee. The light bulb needs to go on for them, they need to feel ready.

Waiting in hope until they decide to take action if they decide at all, can be very torturous to our well being. Be careful not to bury yourself under someone else's life trials. You may have a difficult time crawling out from underneath it all. It can be hard for us to recognize when we are enabling somebody. Sometimes this can just be buying or bringing the person a drink, a bottle or their drug of preference to even just being around them. Giving the person money or housing them and paying their bills is also enabling. What is the right thing to do? I guess this depends on the circumstances and how deep the addiction is. I have enabled friends myself by loaning them money for their drugs, letting them borrow my car, going to pick them up to holding their crack pipe so they could fill it! Dumb. After having my car taken for several hours longer than was asked all that quickly changed.

In regards to my mom I am guilty of enabling her to drink by giving her rides to the liquor store. It may not sound like a big deal but really it is. Every bit of help we give the person to make it easier for them is enabling. When mom goes in and buys her beer she would get a look of excitement on her face that I hated seeing. She followed a specific routine like a creature of habit. Thinking I couldn't see right through what she was trying to do, she figured I wouldn't notice her leaving in a mad rush at the same time on the exact same day of the week.

Mom did her best in trying to cover up how uncomfortable she felt by over talking to distract me or completely trying to avoid me altogether, feeling self-conscious each time she left the house to go to the beer and wine store. It was hard for her to sneak by as a lot of the times as I would be seated at the computer near the front door writing this book. It was uncomfortable for me as well because it would annoy and anger me each time. I used to get upset and get into huge confrontations with her regarding her drinking. It hurt to watch.

Year after year mom did what she could to deter any turbulence that was in her way. I could only imagine the possibilities that would arise for her if she instead spent all that energy on becoming sober. Totally unaware that all her facial and bodily expressions showed that she was focused on one thing only, this was to get to her destination to stock up on her fix. Upon moms return she would be so weighed down by beer and cooler boxes that she struggled to walk down the hallway hunched over. I could barely stomach watching it every day. Just like on her way out he would attempt to distract me again which clearly showed that she did not want to be 'picked on'. Nagging at her was pointless. What did I say about addicts trying to pull the wool over our eyes? I find the excuses that she would come up with extremely annoying! They try to make us feel like we are the 'stupid ones' who fall for it.

It has now been a year since my mom and I have made adjustments to our living arrangement. Mom is quite content in her apartment in her own space now. We all can feel her vibes of happiness from the freedom she has now. She is back to her friendly and caring self that she once was and is not being smothered in lectures or opinions and has no one to hide from. It appears her heavy drinking has slowed down as well now that she is able to deal with or not deal with her addiction on her own in her way.

We, as mother and daughter have improved our relationship and are much closer now that we are no longer living in that toxic environment. Our homes are free from the burden of negativity so much now that our cat even seems to notice! My daughter is happy to have sleepovers at grammas' place and finally we all are able to simply live our lives without completely severing our relationships.

These stories may have triggered a story of your own. If you identify with these in some way or another write your story down to help you release some bad energies from your soul once again. What you choose to do with what you write at this point is completely up to you. Please keep your options open along with any suggestions and explanations outlined throughout each exercise. It doesn't matter if you choose to tell another person your story or if you write it out and crumple it up, do what works best for you. Mail your story to heaven or to another place it doesn't matter, they are all very effective ways for you to work towards getting it out of your system. Taking action counts!

My heart is with you and I admire all the strength you had to get through that time in your life. I also pray for you to be given the courage to help you through whatever it is that you may need to overcome at anytime during your life.

EXERCISE SHEET: Use separate sheets of paper or a journal style book. It helps to record the applicable chapter names along with the relevant page numbers from this book on each of your writings for easy reference later.

Record your story: How you relate, situations, agendas, notes, thoughts & anything else related to this chapter. Use paragraph writing, point form or whatever you're comfortable with. Think back & take a deep breath! Now take some time to read over what you wrote.

_____

_____

_____

_____

_____

_____

_____

_____

_____

_____

_____

_____

_____

_____

_____

_____

_____

_____

_____

_____

_____

_____

_____

_____

_____

E.R.A.S.E.D. = Easy Real Action Spiritual Exercises Deliver:
Erase the chains of abuse that bind you using EASY made, REAL life, ACTION steps with SPIRITUAL outlook & hands on EXERCISES that DELIVER!

"If God brought you to it,

He will

get you through it"

-Author Unknown

WHAT'S MY PURPOSE?
Finding a reason

I need a reason to be here on earth. I need a reason to get up in the morning to be productive in my day or to leave my house to go to work. I also need a reason to keep learning and to continue moving forward. I need a reason to listen to others the same as I need a reason to give and forgive. I need a reason to follow my gut instincts.

The list is an endless one. There are many different things we do each day that we need to have reasons for doing them. There is nothing wrong with that. If we didn't have reasons for these the majority of people would simply be lumps on logs or potatoes on couches, that is if we got ourselves out of bed in the first place. If you are healthy and able it's pretty hard to be either of those all of the time. Having reasons to do something makes the task at hand much easier or more fulfilling and rewarding in one way or another. Do you agree? Yes, of course you do!

There were many nights when I was younger where I laid awake all night wondering why I should do anything at all. I guess I was in a kind of a depression period. I was not open to and not really capable at that time in my life to think clearly about things. I was weighed down by too many layers of debris that I had collected along my road to be able to see through any of it. I am thrilled to have gotten rid of all that weight for I see clearly now. Having hope is very powerful and now that my blinders are off I feel like I am as light as a feather! I am free to fly or float to and through whatever I wish. While I am floating along and happily flying I still need to have to have my reasons and my purpose.

Without knowing my purposes in life I was a drifter going with the flow of life and in any direction that it took me. I found that to be extremely stressful and mentally exhausting. It kept my spirit negative and gloomy. My purpose is customized for me as yours is for you. I immediately experienced a difference in how I felt which changed my behavior. It felt so good and still does! When you find your purpose it is not something that will just go away and it is difficult to ignore. You are stuck with it and that too is a wonderful thing!

Everyone can get inspired or enlightened in various ways and from different sources so it is unrealistic and difficult to say where and when you will find yours. When you do, you will know it because you will feel it in your heart. Some people I have come across are not interested in finding their purpose so they say. They want me to believe they don't care. I think that is because they feel it would be too hard or take too much effort into discovering it.

Personally I find that kind of sad because once found they can contribute a lot more as a person than they already do. I'm pretty sure they feel that way because they are unaware that they even have a purpose worth seeking or they don't know where to look to find one. It could also be that they feel undeserving of one? Those people are wrong.

Finding your purpose can possibly lead you into finding your element in life and vice versa. I know for myself once I found my purpose, everything I needed to fulfill that purpose came before me gradually with little effort on my part. It's my job to take notice of this and to either claim it or not. I finally realized that all the challenges I face, the ones I triumph over are the building blocks that lead up to what I feel is my main purpose. For me it all started with God. Now that I have found my purpose and my reason to be I have also found my passion. I feel my soul is almost perfectly matched to my living being in this element that surrounds me.

To some people this may sound quite boring but being a writer satisfies a lot of my hearts desires. It gratifies me so much that I feel flushed when blood rushes through me as my heart beats faster. The tickle I feel in my tummy gives me goose bumps each and every time I sit down to write. I enjoy the pleasure it gives me even during the times when I find the editing or the revising tasks to be somewhat tedious. There is no doubt that someone or something saw it in me when I couldn't, knowing this helps drive me forward.

I hope and pray you find your purpose if you are seeking one. Stay as open-minded and positive as you can and it will come to you via something you see, hear, do or dream. Pull out your passions and mix them with your beliefs. While in wait remember to not give up hope, believe it will happen.

Chapter Eight – Start to Heal

FINALLY, LIGHT AT THE END OF THE TUNNEL
Thanks to a secret I learned!

Have you ever heard of the law of attraction? If you have, do you believe in it? Do you believe that it is fast at work every single second of the day? I can't help but believe it is and I'll tell you why. I lived a life of negativity and all I attracted was more negativity! Being now that I live a life of inner peace and joy, I attract joyful and peaceful things in and around my life now. When I stopped being negative most of the negativity in my life vanished and is still on its way to disappearing.

We can be negative without even hearing ourselves. I believe it's a trained skill to learn how to flip it around. We might not even use words when we are being negative, it may be just thoughts in our head. Start analyzing your thoughts whenever they pop in your head. You will see what I'm referring to. There are too many thoughts that fly through our heads to inspect all of them, so just analyze the ones you can capture.

After taking note of a few thoughts write them down or say them aloud, don't be surprised if after analyzing just a few of those thoughts you come across a negative one. That's normal. When you do this try and replace the negative thought with a positive one. Keep doing this practice until you can get the hang of it. That's what I did every day, I found it gets easier and easier.

Pay close attention to your words. Once you speak negatively you can change that by saying something positive in regards to it right after. It can be tough the first time you travel that road. You may encounter times where you feel guilty for letting one or more negative thoughts slip right by you. It will get to the point where you become conscience of your thoughts so don't fret.

You will have lots of time to practice putting it into play. Eventually the second you become aware of a negative thought in your mind you will have trained yourself to automatically think of something more positive to replace it with. You will be able to flip it around before you have the chance to even say anything.

Your goal is to be flipping these around on autopilot. Once you find you can do this with little effort that is the time when you will start to see real change in your life appearing. It will appear as if it came out of nowhere, good and positive things will start to happen more often in your life. It will come your way so make sure you are on the ball, alert and ready so you can act on them one by one.

Using the law of attraction benefits you and is fun. You can create games that only you know you're playing. I won't get too deep into the law of attraction as that is a whole other topic in itself, still it would really be worth your time to look into it .

What you can do though is start today focusing on what you already have or want in your life. Do not focus on what you don't have and don't want to have happen. Pretty much concentrate on seeing a picture in your mind of what it is that you desire to have or to take place. See in your mind's eye the outcome of receiving what you want, then do your best to feel it. Feel those exciting feelings as if they were really happening to you. Stay in those good feelings. Don't be discouraged with disappointment, just be patient. Things happen when they are ready to happen, all you can do is believe. So what are you waiting for? Give it a go!

This very well could be one of the reasons why we end up coming across people in our lives similar to ourselves with comparable back grounds or past experiences. We mull over on stuff without even consciously doing so bringing those things to eventually materialize in our lives. Imagine what you could attract to yourself when you learn how to knock out the negative and train your mind to think only positive thoughts.

I encourage you to make this a part of your daily ritual. Be careful not to read too much into your negative thoughts when you come across them. Negativity has its way of disguising itself back in us if we are not careful. Try and catch it all! Write down your thoughts and if you see even one word in a sentence that is not positively reflected, FLIP IT!

EXERCISE SHEET: Use separate sheets of paper or a journal style book. It helps to record the applicable chapter names along with the relevant page numbers from this book on each of your writings for easy reference later.

Record <u>your</u> story: How you relate, situations, agendas, notes, thoughts & anything else related to this chapter. Use paragraph writing, point form or whatever you're comfortable with. Think back & take a deep breath! Now take some time to read over what you wrote.

_____

_____

_____

_____

_____

_____

_____

_____

_____

_____

_____

_____

_____

_____

_____

_____

_____

_____

_____

_____

_____

_____

_____

_____

E.R.A.S.E.D. = <u>E</u>asy <u>R</u>eal <u>A</u>ction <u>S</u>piritual <u>E</u>xercises <u>D</u>eliver:
Erase the chains of abuse that bind you using EASY made, REAL life, ACTION steps with SPIRITUAL outlook & hands on EXERCISES that DELIVER!

HELP IS OUT THERE WAITING FOR YOU TO
MAKE YOUR MOVE!
Where you can seek help

When in need of personal help who and where can you turn to? At times I understand that you may feel like there is nowhere to go and no one to help you. You may feel that way but it's not what is true. Sometimes we just need to have a little push start and be pointed in the right direction. When we have reached a point in our life where we realize we cannot continue on our own without suffering further damage to ourselves, we need to do something about it.

I can relate to knowing and feeling like we should go get help, yet at the same time I understand that it can be hard to pursue when our self being is not well and in distress. It seems that when hurtful and harmful things happen to us it tends to take up all our thinking space. We are then left in a murky cloud of fear and confusion which can disorient us. This gives us more reason to accept advice and helping hands from others when offered.

Do not feel alone I am with you on that. I have been there many times and if you are in that spot now close your eyes, inhale a deep breath and trust that everything will work out.

You have managed to seek advice from another just by reading this book. You are allowing me to share my feelings, thoughts and suggestions with you from my experiences. Remember, you are reading this for a reason right? It is no accident that you have this in your hands. It is one of the pieces and just one of the many outlets for you to get the help you seek. I feel a kind of closeness with my readers even though I have not met them. Knowing you are with me sharing my journey is a therapeutic blessing for me as it validates that I too am not alone.

When you allow me to share my stories and my successes with you about pulling myself through my ordeals it touches my heart. I know you are reading my stories out of personal interest and from a caring heart. What I find touching is to know that you want advice and are seeking the help through me. For me to be able to provide that for you is comforting. Just being able to show you that it is possible to overcome things in your life that you may not have thought you could is more than rewarding for me. Being free from the affects of abuse is a magnificent thing.

I truly want you to open your ears, eyes and mind to what is out there and available. The referrals I will suggest to you may or may not be new to you. Some may require more effort on your part than others will. Some resources available are a phone call away, some are only hopefully a short travel distance away while other resources are online and at your fingertips.

Since you've already been through enough I know it would be nice for the 'help' angels to land the most fitting sources of help right on your lap and they may, but you also need to do what you can yourself to pull out your will to do so and your drive to keep going from within. You can do it, get hunting!

I found that when I started asking others for their help many more opportunities came unto me without putting forth too much effort. *I just had to get the ball rolling.* Crazy, but to me it seemed almost as if help was out seeking me and that is what you want for you. One thing will lead to another. Getting to the point where things may miraculously happen for you will mean that you need to act on your desire for it to happen. Start with initiating the activities by finding your will and seek out what really drives you. Fuel your objective.

The right and perfect time for you to act is now. Once again try not to follow in my footsteps too closely as I had to learn the hard way through my mistake of not accepting help when it was right in front of me. My pride and independence got in the way. This story I have to tell has really nothing to do with any abuse at all but it is an example of when I turned away help. It was a situation where I was in desperate need of it but still turned it away. It was because of this incident that I learned to act now and say yes to help. If you turn away help in the direst time of your life you may end up suffering the penalty of missing out and being left behind. Here is an example of my foolishness. Thank God I lived through it to tell the story. I am glad in a way that it did happen otherwise it may have been many more years of saying no to great help.

While inside a bar enjoying the company of friends I was unaware that we were having the first snowfall of the year. It was coming down in thick white snowflakes pretty darn quick. When I walked out to the parking lot to find this unexpected snowstorm I had an anxiety attack. The parking lot was white and there were no lines on the road. Winter had decided to land a fairly solid blanket over the pavement in which I had no idea how to drive on.

I needed to get home which was high atop a hill, well up a mountain really. A friend informed me that it's really no big deal, just drive slowly until I reach the bottom of the exceptionally steep hill that I needed to go up to get home. From there I was instructed to step on the gas and not to stop until I reached the top. Okay, well that sounded pretty easy so I gave it a shot. What my friend forgot to tell this new snow driver is anything regarding braking! If it was mentioned I obviously I missed it.

I reached the bottom of the snow covered hill, the light was green and I stepped on it! Away I went driving right up the hill passing all the people in their cars with the hazard lights on. Being inexperienced I was confused as to why those people were having such difficulty? Up I went until I reached about the half way mark on the tremendous incline. Then wham a red light! I came around a bend and there it was. It was glowing like a big red cherry atop a mountain of white ice cream. It took me completely off guard as I was only focusing on booting it to the top!

Well guess what I did? You got it, I slammed on my brakes! To make a long terrifying story short I will cut through my heart attack and get right to the petrifying twirl that happened all the way back down the hill! Yes that is correct. I couldn't tell how many three hundred and sixty degree spins my car had made but there were a few, all ending in one big sideways slide.

When the car finally decided to stop I just sat quietly frozen in shock wondering if I had died. Once my focus came back I looked around at my surroundings and found myself stuck in the snow at the bottom of that hill. I was situated along side of those cars I had mentioned in the beginning, the ones that had their flashers on. Feeling completely dazed and confused at this point, my embarrassment somehow still managed to sneak itself out from underneath all my distress.

Looking up the hill again I saw that I was positioned behind some trees around a bend and that my car was blocking both lanes of downhill traffic. This sent me into a panic I had to get out of there! Shaking, I snapped out of my stunned and frightened phase and struggled hard for a couple hours to get back up the hill again. Finally, I managed to reach that same light again by bouncing off the curb in deep tire ruts all the way back up. This time the light was green but to my dismay I couldn't go through it as I had officially got my car stuck.

Trying every method I knew from watching others, failed. My gas was very low, I didn't have a cell phone and it was way past midnight. I didn't know what to do. I waited alone and freezing in my car. I could only keep the heat on for short periods of time because I was running low on gas.

I sat for quite some time frustrated and tired on an angle with the back end of my car up on the sidewalk. I told you this story had nothing to do with abuse but here is where I didn't make a good judgment call for myself. The hill was cold and abandoned. I hadn't seen any activity from cars or people until out of nowhere a black all terrain truck had pulled up beside me. I saw it as it slowly came down the hill.

If I wasn't embarrassed before, I was now. I felt like an idiot sitting there in the dark stuck in the snow. I was hoping they would just drive on by for they had many others they could rescue down at the bottom of the hill. The truck pulled up beside my window, then one of the two guys in it asked if I needed help and if I wanted a tow? "Like hello! Isn't that obvious I thought?"

Here goes. I lifted my head up and proudly looked his way and said, "No thank you, I'm waiting for somebody." He looked a bit cock eyed and asked me if I was sure. I responded that I was. What and where did that come from? How could I have been that dim-witted to allow those words to leave my mouth! And on that note I watched through my rear view mirror as they drove away! There was nothing I could do about it now. Down the hill they went to rescue other folks that were stuck in the snow.

It was almost another hour before I got the courage up to knock on someone's front door that late at night to ask to borrow their phone. I guess I should have done that right away but obviously I wasn't thinking clearly.

Eventually I found someone to agree to come get me. I was getting colder saving my gas and only using the heat here and there. During my wait which seemed to be forever, I was stressed out and worried that I would run out of gas and not be able to have any heat. Once my help had arrived I still ended up having to endure a very long cold and tiresome walk up the rest of the hill to reach their vehicle which was safely parked on flat ground!

Well I learned my lesson. That event happened almost twenty years ago and since then it hasn't been very often where I have said no to a helping hand that's for sure! I have put saying yes into practice when it also comes to suggestions or advice from others as much as I can. Help is help; it just comes in different forms.

You can reach out yourself for help resources. If you are not aware already, there are many different places you can search for information regarding the topic or type of help you require. Use the following exercise sheet or journal for your research during this process.

Record the names, phone numbers, addresses and page numbers as well as websites and all other pertinent information you find during your search. You will need to follow up on these once your first stage of research is complete.

Your second stage of research will be going through the information you have written down by looking up, going to and or calling those places. You will want to make sure it is what you are specifically looking for. You will know and feel if it is right for you.

When you find something suitable to your needs please without a second thought go for it! You will put yourself further ahead and right where you want to be. This will be the beginning of allowing any future resources for help to come to you. To help you get started here are my suggestions that I have found quite supportive along my road into recovering my own well being:

ONLINE In the search bar enter in key words to bring you to the main topic such as the ones on this list: Social Services - Abuse (or the type of abuse) - Help Programs – Healing - Well Being - Abuse survivors - Living through Loss - Stop Violence. Select any words that come to your mind from one of your life stories. Enter your city or community where you live to narrow down information closer to you. Scroll through and visit websites that appeal to you. Don't forget to bookmark them and write them down as two places to hold information is better than just one.

There you will encounter books, centers, groups and many other tools to help you. Dig further and enter more detailed key words to get the sites better suited and more convenient for you. This is a good way to get a visual look into the facility before attending in the case of a center or a meeting When finding a website that captures your interest look for a 'Contact us' tab or something similar to acquire the phone number, address or email information you will need.

ON THE PHONE Call the operator or directory available in your area: Ask them to direct you to what you are looking for. If you're not sure of the specifics let the operator know some details using the same key words in the above online process. I have had operators list off a few different options to various crisis lines as well. If you have access to an electronic phone listing service with a business directory they too may be able to provide a similar outcome response.

The front pages of a phone book often list several types of crisis lines and public group toll free phone numbers. These numbers give you immediate emergency assistance. When connecting with one of them let them know what type of help you are seeking and ask where they can refer you. In the back of the phone books that I have seen there are colored pages of government and municipality listings for various contacts and agencies. Look up your municipality for Social Services fitting to your needs. You may have to call a main number and again be directed.

IN PERSON Make an appointment or drop into: Remember when I discussed the importance of having alone time by taking a walk and allowing yourself to think? Well this is a great way to do so. Make an appointment with your *doctor* or a *clinic doctor* let them know of your circumstance once you are in the office. It is private and generally they will be able to help guide you. Ask for a recommendation and a referral. You can also go into a *Library or a Church*. Check out your *local Police Department or Community Police Station* and your cities *Social Service* office as well.

When a person is seriously determined to help themselves there are many options out there for them. These places too are a great source of information. Try the *Chamber of Commerce* in your area or even a *School*. I think it would be best if it were a *high school* including *adult continuing education* or a *college* as elementary and similar schools may not have that type of information posted. The list of possibilities is endless. Visit the lobby of a *Leisure Centre,* they typically have bulletin boards. You could find brochures and guides of upcoming seminars, workshops or classes on the topic you are seeking out. DON'T FORGET TO ASK THE COUNTER PERSONS QUESTIONS TOO! They may know some valuable information that is not posted.

OTHER RESOURCE CENTRES <u>These places can be very helpful to you</u>: Consider *Community transition houses* or *affiliated used clothing outlets* in your area. You can look them up through your directory service. They usually will be able to provide you with information or some type of guidance. They may be able to recommend their own or another nonprofit organization such as *food* and *housing community services*. These places can guide you to various places that help support people suffering various types of abuse.

Be assertive and know what you're looking for. I recently found out that some *government funded job clubs* have very useful information. The ones I have visited carry large phone book style reference materials of information. They don't just have books pertaining only to job hunting they also have directory books filled with many kinds of crisis situations. These books provide information of suitable nonprofit places of business and the services they provide to coincide with the appropriate crisis.

Good luck with your hunt! Don't forget to <u>bring this book or journal with you</u> so you can record information on the way. Try and <u>obtain copies</u> of all pages you do read. Bring the brochures home and write down any recommendations that are suggested by the people you talk to. Next, ACT ON IT NOW! Plan ahead by writing down on your calendar each place you are going to visit or call then simply DO IT!

EXERCISE SHEET: Use separate sheets of paper or a journal style book. It helps to record the applicable chapter names along with the relevant page numbers from this book on each of your writings for easy reference later.

Record your story: How you relate, situations, agendas, notes, thoughts & anything else related to this chapter. Use paragraph writing, point form or whatever you're comfortable with. Think back & take a deep breath! Now take some time to read over what you wrote.

_____

_____

_____

_____

_____

_____

_____

_____

_____

_____

_____

_____

_____

_____

_____

_____

_____

_____

_____

_____

_____

E.R.A.S.E.D. = Easy Real Action Spiritual Exercises Deliver:
Erase the chains of abuse that bind you using EASY made, REAL life, ACTION steps with SPIRITUAL outlook & hands on EXERCISES that DELIVER!

MAKING A NEW NORMAL
The new you!

As exciting new and refreshing this does sound, it can be very nerve racking for some people because it has the word change written all over it! Don't let it scare you, rather be thankful for it as it will help your transition go smoother. I am excited for you! With what you have learned you are now sitting in a much better spot than you were putting you in an ideal position for setting an example for others. Not everyone is willing to change even when they know they should. Having fear of it, not having the knowledge how to do it or even the emotional support when it's time to can prevent someone from changing things in their life.

There are many times in life where people are forced to make a new normal whether they want to or not. They suffer a lot of worry because they are scared that they are not prepared, sometimes we just need to learn to adjust as we go. Having babies, changing careers, moving away to places unfamiliar, personal hardships and loss of friends and family members all require us to shift our daily comfortable routines or what we refer to as normal living. You are voluntarily making changes to create a new normal for yourself and now you will have the tools and some emotional support to prepare you to do so.

You will be fine, after all how can you go wrong when you are changing yourself for the better. Also, keep in mind that you won't be the only one changing. Why do I say that? Well, when you make changes in yourself, things as well as people in close proximity to you will have to change in some way or another to allow for your adjustments to take place. Some of those changes may not be very noticeable and some will be. Be reassured you're not alone.

Everything new takes some time to get used to so it won't be long before you will become accustomed to your new skin. Some of us are more easily and readily adaptable than others. If you feel you have difficulty adopting new ways then gradually ease yourself into each step of this book and don't rush through it. If you come across any steps or suggestions that make you feel uncomfortable take your time with each one of them but make sure you don't put it off for too long.

Remember your bravery comes from within, you managed to get this far in life so feel confident that you are able to succeed with it. It is kind of like taking a leap of faith, sometimes we just have to trust. Hold your head high and just go for it. It is for the better and you know it, you have nothing to lose. Be honest with yourself.

If you come across some instruction in here that you know you are brushing off due to fear or stress because you feel it may be too much work, revisit that section often until your courage is strengthened. Listen to your gut. If it's telling you to do or try something new don't just keep turning pages to ignore it as that will not get you where you want to be. Keep your eye on the prize and it will be worth it.

When you do become this person with new techniques and enhanced skills you will enjoy more freedom that comes along with it. Feeling free to try new things and escaping whatever chains that are currently holding you back is an exhilarating feeling of great relief!

When trying new things particularly when it comes to our emotions and mental well being it can be very hard to do. I know for myself it doesn't always come naturally and most times feels incredibly awkward. When I do fall and I don't mean tripping, I overcome it by talking to myself using positive affirmations. Like anyone else I aim to succeed too but we are human, therefore it's okay to fall as long as we continue to get back up each time to keep trying until we defeat it.

Look forward to your new normal because everything will eventually fall into place for you and things will just happen. You will be shifting yourself, therefore everything around you must shift too. Everything happens for a reason and you are being prepared for something much bigger and better. The key is to let go of any resistance that you may feel. Just dive in and let it happen to be able to get a better focus on the big picture.

LEARN HOW TO LOVE YOURSELF EVERYDAY
Practical fun methods that work!

One of my close friends many years back pointed out to me how she felt that I did not like my own self. Sadly she was right. I know today she recognizes all the changes I've made into becoming the new me and I thank her. She had a lot to do with it for many different reasons, I really don't think she realizes that she alone mainly triggered it all to occur. She was the one who planted the seed in me which helped me grow as a person. Offering me her words of advice knowing I deserved a better life she ended up developing a whole new being!

I thank her from the bottom of my heart for pointing these things out to me. At that time I knew she felt her advice was going in one of my ears and out the other. Actually I recall thinking, "Yes, okay and whatever." Being young, insecure and unreceptive at the time I felt kind of picked on, I wasn't able to see that she was caring about my well being.

When I was conducting my life in such a negative manner and allowing turmoil to take over, it was far too easy for me to become defensive even though I knew I was wrong and she was right. She gave me advice that she had used herself to build her own self esteem. I envied the fact she always seemed to love herself so I took her info in as she was planting her seeds in me. I stored them away for a rainy day you might say.

Thankfully that rainy day came. I found myself talking in front of the mirror in the bathroom where we worked. Silly or not, do it and you'll get used to it I promise. There are countless things you can say to yourself. Deep inside you know that everything you choose to say to yourself is true. You may just not be consciously aware of it right now thus the more reason you need to keep reaffirming yourself.

I sometimes wake up in the morning and talk to myself positively. I occasionally walk or drive down the street doing the same thing. It's amusing if you get caught because you get to look at the peoples facial reactions, it cracks me up! I have been caught in the aisles of stores whispering things to myself quite a few times. My face does go red but I just walk away grinning. It is few and far between where somebody will approach you to let you know they think you are a nut bar or to ask you who you think you're talking to? So don't be concerned with that, talk away!

I found it challenging to remember to say these things to myself all of the time which made it difficult to get into the routine of it. I knew the importance of doing this and I felt it had to be done if I ever wanted to heal. So from there I started writing down as many affirmations as I could come up with. Once I had written down my affirmations I then cut out each one of them and put them in a cup beside my bed. Each morning I made a habit of enlightening myself by choosing one strip and reading out what it said a few times over. I wanted it to stick in my mind. It has now become second nature for me where I can randomly pull a positive personal affirmation from out of my head when I feel I need to.

The following exercise will help you get started on your way. Take some time to think about what affirmations would help you achieve what you want to create in your life. I outlined a few of them to give you a general idea of how easy they really are to come up with. Smile and enjoy!

<u>TRY THESE</u> the next time your feet hit the floor in the morning or when you're in front of a mirror or even when you are out and about. Say one to three of them each day out loud using emotion behind them. After some time you will learn to believe them and that's a good thing!

SAY THE FOLLOWING ALOUD:

"I love myself!"

"I am strong & resilient!"

"I am worthy of love!"

"I am open-minded!"

"I enjoy learning!"

"I am confident!"

"I welcome change!"

"I feel joy and peace!"

"I am thankful for everything I have in my life!"

"Everything I need and desire in life comes easily!"

How do you feel now?

Create new positive phrases that suit your own particular desire at the time. Add them to this list of phrases to help you through something you are trying to accomplish. For example you may say, "This really is easy for me to do!" or something along those lines. All positive affirmations are reprogramming you into HEALING yourself.

Chapter Nine – Inspire others using Your Experiences & Accomplishments

HOW ARE YOU FEELING?
Seeing your achievement

Now is the time to take a look at everything you have gone through up until this point in the book. How have you felt through each chapter? What emotions have you experienced? Do you feel differently than you did before you started this workbook? Has your perception or philosophy changed on any topics or on any of the points in the chapters that were made? Did you experience feeling any new feelings or were any of your existing feelings enhanced or suppressed throughout the book?

These are important questions to recognize as those feelings are real and are inside of you determining your next move. Have you looked at feelings that way before? I find that almost every decision I make is not just based on knowledge but feelings too. Sometimes this is a good thing and other times not so good. It may be beneficial for you to acknowledge your feelings and would be best to do this one at a time as they come. Recognize if they are compelling enough to act on or if they are based on a fear or a belief you were programmed to believe.

The term 'Paradigm' means one that serves as a pattern or model. An example of this definition would be a set of assumptions, concepts, values, and practices that constitutes a way of viewing reality.

To keep it simple it's a belief we have that we were taught or made to believe by what we have witnessed or by what we have been told by others. It can also come from an experience we have had which makes us judge all future similar experiences. These particular beliefs are not necessarily true. You may have been programmed to believe certain things that are in fact preventing you from making good choices, right choices and even freedom choices for yourself. Without knowing this it is possible that you are purposely not placing down your next stepping stones so you can live up to your 'Paradigm'.

I recently learned the term myself through one extraordinary informative woman that I had the pleasure of meeting. I learned this from her through a college course I was enrolled in. She helped me discover that I in fact have a few paradigms of my own. One example of a paradigm I have given up is, 'Money is the root of all evil.' Another one of mine was, 'With success come stress, worry, isolation and failure.' Neither of these are the true meaning of the words money or success. Stress can be managed effectively and if you let it and believe it, money can do a whole lot of good things in your life.

Focus on what good money can bring you instead of what bad it could bring you. Good and bad go together in anything we can't do much about that. However, we can decide how we are going to take in the bad and how we are going to handle it when it does happen. I choose to focus my thoughts on success, being more positive and not worrying about stress or the fear of the unknown. This helps me dwindle away my paradigms.

I believe focusing on and recognizing our feelings and beliefs is a good way of tracking how far we have come. I can tell that today I have come a long way from where I used to be. Seeing how I feel about things now is definitely not at all how I felt before. I not only can see but I can feel my transformation. Since I have changed my thought patterns and the way I do things, a lot of good seems to come my way. Of course there is bad in there too somewhere but I just don't notice it as much as I once did. Positivity and openness to new adventures is the key to a more joyful life.

IN THIS EXERCISE I ask that you to think back to how you were feeling before you read this book.

- Make a **1st** *column* to the left and write down each individual feeling or thought you had before you read this book.

- Make a **2nd** *column* and write down the reasons why you were feeling or thinking that way to coincide with each feeling in the left column.

- Make a **3rd** *column* and record each feeling or thought you were experiencing while you were going through each different chapter.

- Make a **_4th_** _column_ and record each feeling or thought you are having now toward whichever topics are in connected to your life.

- Make a **_5th_** _column_ and record the reason why you think you are feeling those feelings today.

- **Final Step**_: Read along the top from your first column all the way across to your fifth column. Go down to your second column and read across. Then do the same for each row._

If your **_1st_** _column_ was like mine when I did this it listed one negative thought and feeling after another.

My **_2nd_** _column_ gave me valid reasons why.

My **_3rd_** _column_ expressed all the fear, nervousness, hesitation & doubtfulness that I was clinging to.

My **_4th_** _column_ showed me that I was feeling more at ease and how much my curiosity, positivity as well as my motivation had increased.

Finally, my **_5th_** _column_ outlined clearly for me how beneficial it was for me to revisit all those motions and steps. It also showed how doing so contributed to helping everything in my life flow more consistently, less aggressively giving it more joy and meaning.

We are getting closer to the conclusion of this book where you will have the option to discuss with me what you have discovered about yourself. You may have uncovered some things that you were unaware of before. Go through this handbook and highlight anything of significance you would like to share. Your feedback may be used to further help others sometime in the future.

EXERCISE SHEET: Use separate sheets of paper or a journal style book. It helps to record the applicable chapter names along with the relevant page numbers from this book on each of your writings for easy reference later.

Record your story: How you relate, situations, agendas, notes, thoughts & anything else related to this chapter. Use paragraph writing, point form or whatever you're comfortable with. Think back & take a deep breath! Now take some time to read over what you wrote.

_____

_____

_____

_____

_____

_____

_____

_____

_____

_____

_____

_____

_____

_____

_____

_____

_____

_____

_____

_____

_____

_____

_____

E.R.A.S.E.D. = Easy Real Action Spiritual Exercises Deliver:
Erase the chains of abuse that bind you using EASY made, REAL life, ACTION steps with SPIRITUAL outlook & hands on EXERCISES that DELIVER!

'RE' WRITING & 'RE' READING
YOUR WORK
What the heck! Why would I do that?

Let's go ahead and do what I had you do a few chapters ago. Hold on, I know it's time consuming and you may be thinking it is a big waste of time to be doing all this endless writing but from firsthand experience it was very valuable for me. It is a lot of work yes but it is not a waste of time. Every move you make today is crucial to making any kind of difference in your life.

Wanting to break free from chains that hold us back from being wonderfully free requires that we do something about it. The psychologist I saw back in my teen years suggested that I write out in detail areas in my life that I still struggled with along with any changes I wanted to see happen. He asked me to write out several copies of these. The idea was similar to writing 'lines' as they called it back when I was in elementary school. This is where teachers had us kids write over twenty plus times what we will or will or will not do in order to understand it better, the idea was to have it stick permanently in our minds.

Talking with this doctor and being sixteen years old at the time I figured the old guy had no idea what he was talking about. As time moved on however, I matured and eventually gave his idea a shot. I am thankful I did as I found out that it worked for me. Rewriting does help give us the chance to add content that we may have overlooked the first few times. Be as thorough as you can to discover everything there is to identify about yourself and learn in life.

I did these exercises sitting in my pink painted bedroom on my pink comforter until late at night while listening to my clock radio music. I surrounded myself with crumpled white balls of paper as back then we did not have computers so all editing and revising was done manually. Some of my pages only had one or two sentences written on them, others were full and contained many penned revisions converting my chicken scratch into more of a legible read. It was a lot of tireless work but very much worth it to me in the end. This could be true for you too, you may even end up with enough material to write a book of your own!

If writing continuously is not your thing then rereading is a must. Rereading does the same thing in helping you remember but may take longer to memorize. I recommend rereading everything you have written since you started this handbook three times over. Make a point to revisit your exercise sheets and or journal once a week to keep it fresh in your mind. Nowadays you also have the choice to do your exercise worksheets on a laptop or home computer if you are really not into paper.

If you don't mind the writing aspect I have attached an exercise sheet of course. You will definitely need extra sheets of paper or your journal pages to rewrite everything you have written so far. You can throw out all older versions every time you revise to keep your mood fresh. And if this is completely not your thing feel free to type it all out on a computer.

HELP OTHERS!
Easy tips to assist you

The first easy tip I will suggest to you to help you get a start on helping other people is to start helping yourself. Take action and start your own changing process first. Your job in helping others is rather an easy one. By you making changes to what you think, the way you behave and how you choose to feel will show dramatically on the outside of you. You will start inspiring and helping others right away without even knowing that you are. Someone has to be the one to start setting the good example, so why not let that someone be you! Every little thing you do for yourself to improve your well being betters somebody else at the same time.

People you may talk to and share your thoughts with will know you've changed and so will others that you come in contact with. Other people will silently watch and see if you have actually changed. You may not be fully aware every time somebody is observing you as people in general do this all the time but most of them don't make it known. These people may be witnessing some changes in you that surprise them or make them unsure of what is happening to you. Don't get me wrong, it's always in a good way they would have this reaction because it's natural to feel threatened by change in some way or another. I can relate to this can you?

Here is a story for example. I had a dear friend whose outlook on life was extremely negative for years for the most part in every way. One day I noticed he started showing signs that he was changing as a person, he actually ended up making a drastic complete three hundred and sixty degree turn! He completely changed the way he thought and how he conducted himself. This new positive outlook person honestly shocked the heck out of me as much as it scared me! I could not believe what I was seeing. I was totally threatened by his new ways for it made it very clear to me that I was in need of change from my negative ways too.

The thought of that freaked me right out because I was thinking about the effort and work that I may have to do to get to that point. I also feared that I would have to become a whole new person, I worried that I may lose myself along the way. Well I was wrong! This is not the case at all, we can still be true to ourselves while getting rid of old baggage. When we accept and welcome change we are making room for new luggage! You will be planting seeds all around you in other people when you do this. When these people are ready to have them watered, they will sprout and grow allowing them to flourish in their own changes too.

You can also help other people by sharing your true life story of survival. You are here today, you are a survivor! People generally enjoy listening to others while they open up and share something personal that they too can relate too. While you're sharing your story you are helping them and at the same time when they listen they are helping you.

If you really want to make it a point to help out people who have suffered abuse you could do things like volunteer at a crisis center, group therapy sessions and by furthering your education as well by taking required courses to apply for work in this field.

You can never go wrong when it comes to helping out other people. Know that we are all just as important as each other is. So really no matter what you choose to do to help others you are making the best decision by helping yourself first!

Chapter Ten – Enjoy Your Freedom Today!

TAKE A DEEP BREATH YOU DESERVE IT!
Soaking up your accomplishments!

That's it! Breathe a deep breath in, then let it out slowly. Look at how far you have come! Did you once consider that you would accomplish what you have done so far when you opened the front cover of this book? Did you know what you were getting into? Remembering, reliving, thinking, writing, reading and putting action into practice is a lot of work. So is courage and doing things out of your comfort zone. If you followed the steps and read thoroughly through the handbook, exercise sheets and journal then you should be very proud of yourself! See and feel the accomplishment you have made for yourself. You definitely have made a huge effort on your part to make a difference in your well being, it takes action to get this far and you took it!

No one else did it for you. You are the one that took notes and highlighted everything of relevance and importance for your life. Now that you have made it this far it shows that you can apply yourself. You are determined and strong enough to make the necessary changes in your life. These changes will lead you on a new path from now on and open doorways to bring you more joy and happiness into your life. Be patient and keep focusing on it.

You have worked very hard to get to this point I know. I am not sure how long it has taken you as I leave the preparation and development up to you. You should now be at the point where you can stop and say, "Wow, I have done all this, what else can I do?" Only don't stop there keep going and redo what you've learned to do. The thoughts, suggestions and expressions in here are the first few stepping stones laid on your new path for you. Now it's up to you to find more stepping stones, keep laying them out in front of you to continue walking along your customized path.

You can create part two of this handbook. Physically act upon all the action steps from each chapter of this book where you feel you need to in order to keep moving forward. These steps are the ones that will have you going out and meeting new people, talking to family and friends as well as conducting research online or by phone. You will be encouraged to take some alone time for 'thought walks'. You will also be led to visit your surrounding business establishments such as resource centers or other public places for seminars or meetings. Even going out and enjoying a cup of your favorite beverage is also included on this list!

You remember all those right? I know you do. I also know that it sure sounds like a lot to cover especially if you feel you need to do most or all of them. Don't fret you have plenty of time! Do them gradually, consecutively and consistently and it will happen. One day you will be looking back on this handbook and on the activities you chose to involve yourself in, you will then be able to say, "Hey I remember all that, I did it!"

A GREAT SELF ESTEEM BOOSTER
No turning back

You're here! You are at the turning point in your life now where there is no turning back. This is a very good thing! Hopefully you have made the decision to change your current path and change your destiny. Everything that you have read, wrote and participated in through this journey with me has changed you in some way or another. You have furthered your knowledge and greatly widened your eyes. You awakened your inquisitiveness to a stage where turning back would be pointless and a real waste of your good efforts thus far.

What a great self esteem booster to know that you have it in you to stick to it and hang in there. Feeling good about yourself helps you look at yourself more positively doesn't it? It sure does. You can hang onto this wonderful feeling for as long as you want to by continuing to learn, change and grow. Be willing to let life come your way and unwrap like a gift. Tear away one layer at a time to reveal your present inside, there you will find the gift of being able to choose freedom and joy in any circumstance or environment that you may find yourself in. Keep refusing to let other people's problems become your burdens. Don't be chained down any longer by the negative effects of others doings unto you and avoid living in the past. Believe there is no other way and you will be just fine.

Look in the mirror now and say, "Hey I love myself, I am strong and I am brave!" Hey, hold on one minute I'm not finished so don't walk away from that mirror…look directly at yourself and say, "I am positive, I am grateful and I am worthy!" Take notice of how are you feeling now? Keep it going, "I am open, I am willing, I am able and I am glad to be me!" Now for the finale, "I love myself!" Come on I know you can say it, be proud and say it with a smile. I love the feeling it brings me after saying these things in the mirror and you know what else? My day goes so much better too. I started practicing this when I made the choice to believe that you can't expect to love someone fully or be fully loved by another until you love yourself first.

This is who you are, not just who you want to be. You are already this person inside but you need to do a bit of internal house cleaning that's all. Clean up the garbage that is piled on top to find YOU again. Most importantly keep moving forward every day, work on this book like an ongoing project. You can make it a part of your weekly routine, carry it with you and refer to it when you need to. If you start to ever feel like your 'falling off the wagon' so to speak, you can easily thumb through the table of contents to find what key points you need to revisit. If you circled, underlined or highlighted as I recommended throughout the book then you should be able to find your way easily.

WHO DO YOU REALLY WANT TO BECOME?
Be free to grow!

Why settle for a basic stock vehicle when you can have some luxury components for a bit more? Well, in the world of financing a bit more could mean a big chunk out of your wallet. In your world it means effort. I cannot stress that word enough. Yes effort. Everything in life takes effort. Put the effort in and eventually you will get a return on it. Getting a return on your investment is a very glorifying and satisfying feeling.

Despite the fact that we are not a stock vehicles we are still people with room for some added features! You can tweak and enhance your personality and character, shape it yourself into whom and what you want to be. I did. I had fun doing it too. I wrote down the type of person I wanted to become and I feel I have almost reached my goal. Keyword is almost. No one is perfect so I will always be working on myself as we all should.

When I looked at my sheet of paper I saw that it was telling me I wanted to be more forgiving, giving, loving, open, non-judgmental and explorative. I thought, "Ya right!" I did not think any of it was possible because I was very much the opposite of it all.

Many times throughout this handbook I have said quite blatantly that changing your thoughts and your moves can make a difference. At this time I am going to tell you that planning out those thoughts and preparing your moves ahead of time will make the difference in furthering your development.

When we plan these things out it is like planting a seed. You are sowing the seeds for the path you will need to walk along to reach these goals. You are starting out on this path with a written guide of where to go, keep it a practice in your life and it will eventually become second nature to you. When messages persistently come our way it is a good idea to take the time to notice their presence, understand and appreciate the value they bring in order for us not to dismiss them so easily.

When I knew what I wanted but didn't know how to get it or get there, I learned to pay more attention by keeping alert for signs and signals. For me they begin to hold meaning and therefore I couldn't ignore them. I may store the information in the back of my mind but I don't ignore them as I find they will just keep popping up again anyways until I do deal with them in some way.

If the sign was a message that intended to show me how to get on the path I needed to be on, it would come up again. For example, when something peculiar resurfaces itself I go with it and investigate further to the best of my ability that time around. This way I feel I have more reassurance that it is some sort of sign. One example is when all roads led me to go to church for the first time after fighting it for so many years. I feel because I did pay attention to those signs when they appeared through other people I was fortunate enough to be brought to a place where I received free counseling. I do believe we are guided by the souls of our loved ones who have passed on through God the best they can.

In church I received counseling on many topics indirectly yet directly through sermons. Your life's path may or may not involve church and that's okay, I wanted to use a strong example of a sign that I gave notice too. That sign that met me on my path turned out to be very beneficial in enhancing my character, my personality and how I live my life in general.

OUTLINE YOUR GOALS: This is where you may want to use your journal or sheet provided to make a list of what kind of person you want to see yourself as. Create a list of what you would like to add or improve on in your personality and character to make you more awesome than you already are. Remember, have fun with it!

EXERCISE SHEET: Use separate sheets of paper or a journal style book. It helps to record the applicable chapter names along with the relevant page numbers from this book on each of your writings for easy reference later.

Record <u>your</u> story: How you relate, situations, agendas, notes, thoughts & anything else related to this chapter. Use paragraph writing, point form or whatever you're comfortable with. Think back & take a deep breath! Now take some time to read over what you wrote.

_____
_____
_____
_____
_____
_____
_____
_____
_____
_____
_____
_____
_____
_____
_____
_____
_____
_____
_____
_____
_____
_____
_____
_____
_____

E.R.A.S.E.D. = <u>E</u>asy <u>R</u>eal <u>A</u>ction <u>S</u>piritual <u>E</u>xercises <u>D</u>eliver:
Erase the chains of abuse that bind you using EASY made, REAL life, ACTION steps with SPIRITUAL outlook & hands on EXERCISES that DELIVER!

THE UNIVERSE IS YOURS!
You are a gem on this planet!

Do you know that you are an amazingly extraordinary person? You really are! You are unique. There is not another you out there...well on this earth that is, a few have come close I'm sure but no match. If you are a twin or a triplet or even a quadruplet you are still your own person with your own personality and your own character. Your life experiences build your character and so do the choices you make in life. All of these make you very special. Do not allow anyone to convince you to think differently, no matter what they may tell you.

You have many different abilities that you are capable of. I'm sure you're not even aware of all of them, think about that. There are many different ideas and strategies that you have in the back of your mind that others do not have but you haven't had the right opportunity to express them.

We feel different gut feelings periodically through life about things, people or situations in your surroundings that others do not. They are specifically meant for you. You have these feelings installed in you for life, they don't go away. I think it is a pretty cool possession that is ready for you to act on and or utilize every one of them. Gain knowledge of how to be everything you can be by learning to love yourself and learning to take some risks. Its okay to dive into the deep end sometimes because you just never know what treasures you might come up with.

You were created for more, so please don't live your life less than what you were created for. You can have spiritual strength on your team to help you along in life at no cost other than believing. To believe is to have faith and to have faith is to believe but the most important strength comes from within when you have faith to believe in yourself. Your life will begin to open up wider and wider to make room for all the joy, peace, happiness, knowledge and the love that there is coming. If you seek it and allow it to happen with no excuses of any kind standing in the way, it will happen!

There are different species of certain kinds of fish, turtles and others for example that only grow to the size of their environment. You are neither a fish nor a turtle, so to live this way because of the fear of change or the unknown is living life at a lesser scale than you are capable of.

Our world is a big place with plenty of room for all to explore but there are some people that do prefer to live inside a familiar world all of their own. If they were to expand their horizons they would find much more out there for them. I was one of those people who wasn't at all much into exploring. I was comfortable staying where I was doing things that took little or no risk without much effort. That was until I realized how big the universe really is and how many years I may be given to take advantage of it. It's really never too late to start exploring opportunities in life; we just never know how long we have. Act now. Start figuring out what you really want and need to get you moving on to your next stage in life.

I am living my life more than I originally thought I was created for. I have achieved quite a bit in my life in just this past year. Strive to accomplish at least three more things in life that you may not think were possible by just going for it without fear; you may be surprised at yourself. I went back to school to complete my high school education, found new methods to enhance my relationship with my spouse and changed my scenery and living arrangements in my home life. With writing this book I have learned a whole new passion. I'd say that's quite a bit in twelve months, imagine what we all can achieve in five years with the right mindset!

Everything I have completed this past year excites me for the coming year! I can't help but think that if I completed all this in within a year's time, what will I be accomplishing next year and in the following years to come. Sometimes we are just diamonds in the rough, but every one of us is truly a gem on this earth.

Use this last exercise sheet to jot down your agenda for the next few days, weeks or months whatever works for you. Your own plan of action from the steps in this book joint with your notes should give you a clear picture of where you want to be.

Date your action plan. It would be a good idea to create a column to the right where you can record a date that you want to see each one completed by. It will act as a great follow up tool that will help you hold yourself accountable, this is to ensure you accomplish what you have set out to do.

EXERCISE SHEET: Use separate sheets of paper or a journal style book. It helps to record the applicable chapter names along with the relevant page numbers from this book on each of your writings for easy reference later.

Record your story: How you relate, situations, agendas, notes, thoughts & anything else related to this chapter. Use paragraph writing, point form or whatever you're comfortable with. Think back & take a deep breath! Now take some time to read over what you wrote.

_____

_____

_____

_____

_____

_____

_____

_____

_____

_____

_____

_____

_____

_____

_____

_____

_____

_____

_____

_____

_____

_____

_____

E.R.A.S.E.D. = Easy Real Action Spiritual Exercises Deliver:
Erase the chains of abuse that bind you using EASY made, REAL life, ACTION steps with SPIRITUAL outlook & hands on EXERCISES that DELIVER!

Conclusion...

It may have come to the end of this handbook, but it's definitely not your end. This marks the beginning of your new book of life. You now have the tools to write your own story as you choose while you journey forward. We have covered all the steps in each of the stages that helped me heal which can be used as your action plan. In taking a moment now let's recap those stages that I found advantageous in helping me to release the chains that once tied me down. They are as follows:

- Begin by **Remembering it,** take the steps into **Seeing it** & open yourself up to learn to **Talk it out.**

- **Take Control** of it and start **Researching it,** move onto **Finding a Solution.** **Apply it** by being **Determined.**

- See from outside the box and **Learn** from it. **Start Healing** so you can **Inspire Others** using your own experiences & accomplishments.

- Finally, **Enjoy Your Freedom** and your inner peace because *you deserve it* and it's *yours*!

Remember that your commitment on your part along with the guidance from my personal experiences will get you to where you need and want to be for yourself.

I encourage you to refer to my contact information as I welcome feedback from you. I would love to hear about your challenges, triumphs and victories. I truly wish you every bit of success as you travel positively head on into and along your new adventure. You are a survivor who is nothing short of a winner. You are worthy of personal success, freedom and inner peace! May you continue to be blessed in every which way your heart so desires.

The '*You will be heard*' option

How to Contact the Author:

Please feel free to share your personal stories, successes & comments to jkundermywing@gmail.com or mail to the Author (Include a self stamped/addressed envelope for all correspondence):

20674 114 Ave. Maple Ridge BC Canada V2X 1J8.

In addition, if you feel you resonated with this book & would like to have a FREE (*Value $125.00*) half hour chat or discussion session with Janet Kingsley please email your best contact number and a convenient day/time to jkundermywing@gmail.com to schedule this. (*Please include a brief description of what you would like to touch base on in your email request*). Thank you.

Please allow up to 3 to 4 weeks for a response

Remember…

"The Secret to happiness is Freedom & the Secret to Freedom is Courage."

- Thucydides Greek

*R*esources...

Continuing the Hope, Courage & Knowledge

INFORMATION TO HELP YOU AS YOU TRAVEL ON YOUR
HEALING JOURNEY...

Recommended Reads:

Purpose Driven Life ~ *Rick Warren*
The Secret ~ *Rhonda Byrne*
Law of Attraction ~ *Michael J. Losier*
The Shyness and Social Anxiety Workbook: Proven Techniques for Overcoming
Your Fears ~ *Martin M. Antony/Richard P. Swinson*
Battlefield of the Mind ~ *Joyce Meyers*
Battlefield of the Mind for Teens ~ *Joyce Meyers with Todd Hafer*
Battlefield of the Mind for Kids ~ *Joyce Meyers/Karen Moore*

Online Information:

www.dancinginthedarkness.com
Read rape and sexual abuse survivor stories & post your own

www.adultchildren.org/
Adult Children of Alcoholics-Official site for the support group of people who
grow up with an alcoholic parent

www.12steps.org/12stephelp/shortreads/codependency.htm
Recovery Codependency-by Shirley Morris, from "The Bruised Reeds"

www.experienceproject.com/groups/Have-Been-The-Spouse-Of-A-Drug-
Addict/161111
Being a spouse of a drug addict- A place where you can vent your story, read &
comment on others stories or get advice.

www.surviving-abuse.com/physically-abusive-relationship.html
Physically abuses relationships- Surviving abuse

www.mayoclinic.com › ... › Healthy Lifestyle › End of life › In-Depth
Suicide grief: Healing after a loved one's suicide

www.books4selfhelp.com/self-esteem-self-confidence.htm
Self esteem and self confidence self help books/the guide to self help books

www.livestrong.com/article/14699-improving-assertive-behavior/
Improving assertive behavior

www.ginigrey.com/wp/spiritual-insights/letting-go/
Insights & Inspirations

www.stopprocrastinatinginfo.com/procrastination-quotes.htm
List of inspirational procrastination quotes

www.emofree.com/
EFT Emotional Freedom Techniques – Tapping

www.tapping.com/
EFT Emotional Freedom Techniques – Tapping

www.successconsciousness.com/index_00000a.htm
Affirmations and positive words to improve your life

www.ehow.com/how_5181421_deal-feeling-alone.html
How to deal with feeling alone

www.abundancetapestry.com/how-to-love-yourself-in-17-ways/
How to love yourself in 17 ways, by Evelyn on March 20, 2008

www.mindtools.com/page6.html
Personal Goal setting-learn how to

www.positivityblog.com/index.php/2007/08/22/7-ways-to-break-out-of-your-comfort-zone-and-live-a-more-exciting-life/
7 Ways to get out of your Comfort Zone

kidshealth.org › Teens › Your Mind
Depression Shyness and more for parent/s, teens & kids

NOTES:

Made in the USA
Charleston, SC
07 October 2014